EVALUATIONS OF POLICE SUITABILITY AND FITNESS FOR DUTY

BEST PRACTICES IN FORENSIC MENTAL HEALTH ASSESSMENT

Series Editors

Thomas Grisso, Alan M. Goldstein, and Kirk Heilbrun

Series Advisory Board

Paul Appelbaum, Richard Bonnie, and John Monahan

Titles in the Series

Foundations of Forensic Mental Health Assessment, *Kirk Heilbrun,*
Thomas Grisso, and Alan M. Goldstein

Criminal Titles

Evaluation of Competence to Stand Trial, *Patricia A. Zapf and Ronald Roesch*
Evaluation of Criminal Responsibility, *Ira K. Packer*
Evaluation Capacity to Waive Miranda Rights, *Alan Goldstein and*
Naomi E. Sevin Goldstein
Evaluation of Sexually Violent Predators, *Philip H. Witt and Mary Alice Conroy*
Evaluation for Risk of Violence in Adults, *Kirk Heilbrun*
Jury Selection, *Margaret Bull Kovera and Brian L. Cutler*
Evaluation for Capital Sentencing, *Mark D. Cunningham*
Evaluating Eyewitness Identification, *Brian L. Cutler and Margaret Bull Kovera*

Civil Titles

Evaluation of Capacity to Consent to Treatment and Research, *Scott Y. H. Kim*
Evaluation for Guardianship, *Eric Y. Drogin and Curtis L. Barrett*
Evaluation for Personal Injury Claims, *Andrew W. Kane and Joel A. Dvoskin*
Evaluation for Civil Commitment, *Debra Pinals and Douglas Mossman*
Evaluation for Workplace Discrimination and Harassment,
Jane Goodman-Delahunty and William E. Foote
Evaluation of Workplace Disability, *Lisa Drago Piechowski*
Evaluations of Police Suitability and Fitness for Duty, *David M. Corey and*
Mark Zelig

Juvenile and Family Titles

Evaluation for Child Custody, *Geri S. W. Fuhrmann and Robert A. Zibbell*
Evaluation of Juveniles' Competence to Stand Trial, *Ivan Kruh and*
Thomas Grisso
Evaluation for Risk of Violence in Juveniles, *Robert Hoge and D. A. Andrews*
Evaluation of Parenting Capacity in Child Protection, *Karen S. Budd,*
Jennifer Clark, and Mary A. Connell

EVALUATIONS OF POLICE SUITABILITY AND FITNESS FOR DUTY

DAVID M. COREY

MARK ZELIG

OXFORD
UNIVERSITY PRESS

OXFORD
UNIVERSITY PRESS

Oxford University Press is a department of the University of Oxford. It furthers the University's objective of excellence in research, scholarship, and education by publishing worldwide. Oxford is a registered trade mark of Oxford University Press in the UK and certain other countries.

Published in the United States of America by Oxford University Press
198 Madison Avenue, New York, NY 10016, United States of America.

Library of Congress Cataloging-in-Publication Data
Names: Corey, David M., author. | Zelig, Mark, author.
Title: Evaluations of police suitability and fitness for duty /
David M. Corey, Mark Zelig.
Description: New York : Oxford University Press, 2020. |
Series: Best practices in forensic mental health assessment |
Includes bibliographical references and index. |
Identifiers: LCCN 2019047231 (print) | LCCN 2019047232 (ebook) |
ISBN 9780190873158 (paperback) | ISBN 9780190873172 (epub) |
ISBN 9780190873189 (online)
Subjects: LCSH: Police recruits—Psychological
testing. | Police psychology.
Classification: LCC HV7936.P75 C674 2020 (print) |
LCC HV7936.P75 (ebook) | DDC 363.201/9—dc23
LC record available at https://lccn.loc.gov/2019047231
LC ebook record available at https://lccn.loc.gov/2019047232

Contents

About Best Practices in Forensic Mental Health Assessment

The recent growth of the fields of forensic psychology and forensic psychiatry has created a need for this book series describing best practices in forensic mental health assessment (FMHA). Currently, forensic evaluations are conducted by mental health professionals for a variety of criminal, civil, and juvenile legal questions. The research foundation supporting these assessments has become broader and deeper in recent decades. Consensus has become clearer on the recognition of essential requirements for ethical and professional conduct. In the larger context of the current emphasis on "empirically supported" assessment and intervention in psychiatry and psychology, the specialization of FMHA has advanced sufficiently to justify a series devoted to best practices. Although this series focuses mainly on evaluations conducted by psychologists and psychiatrists, the fundamentals and principles offered also apply to evaluations conducted by clinical social workers, psychiatric nurses, and other mental health professionals.

This series describes "best practice" as empirically supported (when the relevant research is available), legally relevant, and consistent with applicable ethical and professional standards. Authors of the books in this series identify the approaches that seem best, while incorporating what is practical and acknowledging that best practice represents a goal to which the forensic clinician should aspire, rather than a standard that can always be met. The American Academy of Forensic Psychology assisted the editors in enlisting the consultation of board-certified forensic psychologists specialized in each topic area. Board-certified forensic psychiatrists were also consultants on many of the volumes. Their comments on the manuscripts helped to ensure that the methods described in these volumes represent a generally accepted view of best practice.

The series authors were selected for their specific expertise in a particular area. At the broadest level, however, certain general principles apply to all types of forensic evaluations. Rather than repeat those fundamental principles in every volume, the series offers them in the first volume, *Foundations of Forensic Mental Health Assessment*. Reading the first book, followed by a specific topical book, will provide the reader both the general principles that the specific topic shares with all forensic evaluations and those that are particular to the specific assessment question.

The specific topics of the 20 books were selected by the series editors as the most important and oft-considered areas of forensic assessment conducted by mental health professionals and behavioral scientists. Each of the 20 topical books is organized according to a common template. The authors address the applicable legal context, forensic mental health concepts, and empirical foundations and limits in the "Foundation" part of the book. They then describe preparation for the evaluation, data collection, data interpretation, and report writing and testimony in the "Application" part of the book. This creates a fairly uniform approach to considering these areas across different topics. All authors in this series have attempted to be as concise as possible in addressing best practice in their area. In addition, topical volumes feature elements to make them user friendly in actual practice. These elements include boxes that highlight especially important information, relevant case law, best-practice guidelines, and cautions against common pitfalls.

We hope the series will be useful for different groups of individuals. Practicing forensic clinicians will find succinct, current information relevant to their practice. Those who are in training to specialize in FMHA (whether in formal training or in the process of respecialization) should find helpful the combination of broadly applicable considerations presented in the first volume together with the more specific aspects of other volumes in the series. Those who teach and supervise trainees can offer these volumes as a guide for practices to which the trainee can aspire. Researchers and scholars interested in FMHA best practice may find researchable ideas, particularly on topics that have received insufficient research attention to date. Judges and attorneys with questions about FMHA best practice will find these books relevant and concise. Clinical and forensic administrators who run agencies, court clinics, and hospitals in which litigants are assessed may also use some of the books in this series to establish expectancies for evaluations performed by professionals in their agencies.

We also anticipate that the 20 specific books in this series will serve as reference works that help courts and attorneys evaluate the quality of forensic mental health professionals' evaluations. A word of caution is in order, however. These volumes focus on best practice, not what is minimally acceptable legally or ethically. Courts involved in malpractice litigation, or ethics committees or licensure boards considering complaints, should not expect that materials describing best practice easily or necessarily translate into the minimally acceptable professional conduct that is typically at issue in such proceedings.

The present book, which is the first published in this series following a several-year hiatus, provides coverage of two important aspects of evaluations of police officers: the suitability of applicants, and the fitness of incumbents. Each is challenging in itself; the combination is even more so. However, David Corey and Mark Zelig were able to identify common ground as well as distinctiveness characterizing these evaluations, justifying their inclusion together in a single volume. We expect that it will be extraordinarily helpful to those involved in evaluations and decisions regarding either or both issues.

Kirk Heilbrun
Alan M. Goldstein
Thomas Grisso

Acknowledgments

As a boy, my summers were often spent with my aunt, uncle, and cousins in west Texas helping to tend their crops. On one of those summer days, Uncle Tom led me to an ocean-like field of cotton and demonstrated how to use the hoe's spade to uproot nutrient-hoarding weeds without damaging the maturing cotton plants. Then, placing the hoe in my small hands, he said he'd return at the end of the day to bring me back to the farmhouse, where Aunt Marguerite would have laid out a lavish meal of ranch-raised beef, locally grown potatoes and greens, and homemade chocolate cake. I so looked forward to that eventual comfort. But at the time, I cried. Seemingly illimitable rows of cotton wove into the horizon, and I chokingly confessed to my uncle that I would never be able to weed this entire field by dinner time. He squatted to my level and, in his slow twang, he assured me, "David, that's not the job I gave you. Your job is to hoe the one cotton plant in front of you, and when you've done that, move to the next one."

Over my 40-year career as a forensic and police psychologist, I estimate that I've conducted more than 35,000 evaluations of police and other applicants, candidates, and incumbents, and each one was uniquely personal and high-stakes, both for the examinee and me. In performing these evaluations, I've kept Uncle Tom's admonition in mind: The other evaluations scheduled for later in the day and throughout the week don't matter. Only the person in front of me requires my attention. This childhood lesson enabled me to be present with the persons I had the privilege of evaluating, and this book is in large part a product of what they taught me, individually and collectively.

Beyond my gratitude to these men and women, and to the remarkable public safety careers so many of them have gone on to perform, I acknowledge the following individuals: Yossef Ben-Porath, whose friendship and research collaboration over a decade has been singularly rewarding, and the other members of my peer review group over more than a dozen years (Michael Cuttler, Gary Fischler, Herb Gupton, Mike Roberts, Jim Tracy, Phil Trompetter, and Rick Wihera), whose contributions to our field are legendary and humbling; our series editors (Kirk Heilbrun, Tom Grisso, and Alan Goldstein); our developmental editor, Kate Scheinman; our senior editor at Oxford University Press, Sarah Harrington, and our production editor, Fabian Shalini; my coauthor, Mark Zelig, whose devotion to excellence is unparalleled; Beverly Kaemmer, Associate Director Emerita, University of Minnesota Press, whose lessons in style and parsimony I hope have not gone unheeded in this text;

my colleague, friend, and associate, Casey Stewart; and the many police administrators and officers, attorneys, and human resource personnel with whom I've had the pleasure of working. Finally, to my family—with special nods to Uncle Tom for his prescient wisdom and to my brother, Scott, for having fought the good fight: You are my answer to "Why?"

DMC
Lake Oswego, Oregon
January 2020

I have received few honors matching a phone call from Dave Corey inviting me to coauthor this book with him. That phone call marked the beginning of a 2-year effort that has been one of the most gratifying experiences of my professional career. As I reflect on this honor, I realize how fortunate I am to have been in the right place, at the right time, and around the right people.

My journey began by having a family, parents, and supervisors who supported my efforts to become a doctoral-level psychologist while serving as a full-time law enforcement officer. I had the fortune of befriending several detectives who allowed this rookie patrol officer to shadow them as they worked on a string of unsolved murders in Northern Utah, with crime scenes that bore evidence of unequivocal psychological overtones. I would later appreciate that they were pursuing one of the world's most infamous serial killers. The place that psychology has in police work became obvious, even though that was a time when very few professionals identified themselves as police psychologists.

When the opportunity arose to attend a doctoral program at the University of Alabama, Chief Willoughby did not hesitate to grant a leave of absence, with the understanding, of course, that I would return so that he could have a doctoral-level police officer in his ranks. Within days of my arrival in Tuscaloosa, my advisor, Dr. Stan Brodsky, cleared the path so that I could work with Dr. Allen Shealy, a psychologist at the University of Alabama School of Medicine. Allen was one of the first psychologists to use psychological tests to improve the applicant pools for various police departments in Alabama. Allen not only shared his data so that I could author a dissertation on the relationship between Minnesota Multiphasic Personality Inventory scores and police performance, but he also allowed me to accompany him to the FBI Academy in Quantico for several week-long conferences, where I met a handful of people—some of whom are now regarded as pioneers in the field of police psychology.

I completed an internship under the supervision of Dr. Tom Schenkenberg at the Salt Lake City Department of Veterans Affairs Medical Center, who tailored the experience to accommodate my full-time duties at the police department. Tom also provided an inspiring model of professionalism, along with imparting an appreciation for neuropsychology that I have integrated into my research and practice in police and forensic psychology.

I have considerable gratitude for working alongside many of the nation's finest police officers—some of whom are also the best psychologists I have encountered, despite their lack of a formal academic degree. I will never forget Sgt. Ronald Heaps. And, since 2007, my professional development has been aided by my colleague in Anchorage, Alaska, Dr. David Sperbeck, who included me in his lifelong efforts to elevate the professions of forensic and police psychology in North America's last frontier.

I also appreciate and value the efforts of Ms. Heather Angus, whose proofreading and critiques of earlier drafts improved the final product.

I hope my contributions to this volume permit an opportunity to give back to a profession that has given so much to me.

MZ
Anchorage, Alaska and Salt Lake City, Utah
January 2020

Introduction and Key Terms

Police officers[1] may be the most closely scrutinized professionals in the free world. Given the potentially catastrophic consequences caused by corrupt, biased, impulsive, or otherwise unsuitable police officers, this scrutiny may be a necessary safeguard. A federal appellate court observed that "police officers are members of quasi-military organizations, called upon for duty at all times, armed at almost all times, and exercising the most awesome and dangerous power that a democratic state possesses with respect to its residents—the power to use lawful force to arrest and detain them" (*Policemen's Benevolent Association of New Jersey v. Township of Washington*, 1988, p. 91). The court concluded that it is this uniquely "awesome power" that establishes "the need in a democratic society for public confidence, respect and approbation" of its police officers (p. 91). That confidence often is earned; it sometimes is not.

In many jurisdictions, body-worn and dashboard cameras record virtually every police–citizen encounter, and bystanders everywhere supplement these recordings by use of their own ubiquitous cell-phone cameras. Official recordings showing police officers performing their jobs with professionalism and conformance to the law seldom are seen on cable news or social media, but they can facilitate quick resolution of lawsuits alleging police misconduct. When they reveal officers abusing their authority, the scenes are often viewed virally on millions of smartphones and video screens across the globe.

US federal law establishes a cause of action for any person deprived of rights secured by the Constitution or US laws by a person "acting under color of state law" (42 U.S.C. § 1983). In response to these claims, huge sums are paid out each year on settlements and awards for police misconduct suits, collectively exceeding a billion dollars in the cities of Boston, Chicago, Cleveland, Dallas, Denver, Los Angeles, and New York alone between 2002 and 2015 (Wing, 2015). Even if a police officer or recruit does not create liability for the employer, a hiring mistake can be costly. For example, a recent study (Brooks, 2018) found that hiring and training a single Alaska state trooper can cost as much as $200,000.

Against this backdrop of scrutiny, accountability, and cost, few would question the importance of requiring prospective police officers to undergo extensive psychological assessment before they are hired, and then referring them for additional evaluations after they are hired when conditions warrant it. But this was not always the case.

In 1965, only about one-fourth of police agencies in the United States conducted any kind of psychological assessment of prospective police officer recruits. Two years later, the President's Commission on Law Enforcement and Administration of Justice (1967a), formed at a time of "increasing crime, increasing social unrest and increasing public sensitivity to both," noted that the nation's ability to effectively combat crime while achieving community trust depends on having police officers with "emotional stability, commonsense, and integrity" (p. 1). The Commission recommended that each state establish standards for "intelligence, education, personal and psychological characteristics, background or personal history, and physical characteristics" (President's Commission on Law Enforcement and Administration of Justice, 1967b, p. 73) and that psychological evaluations be conducted as a routine component of the selection process. In 2003, only two-thirds of local (i.e., city/town) law enforcement agencies used psychological evaluations for screening new officers (Hickman & Reaves, 2006). By 2007, this number grew to 72% of local police departments, including more than 98% of those serving 25,000 or more residents (Reaves, 2010). Even fewer county law enforcement agencies (62%) reported using psychological evaluations, although more than 90% of sheriffs' offices serving 500,000 or more residents required these evaluations (Reaves, 2010).

More recently, the President's Task Force on 21st Century Policing (2015) recommended evaluations of incumbent police officers, pointing out that an "officer whose capabilities, judgment and behavior are adversely affected by poor physical or psychological health not only may be of little use to the community he or she serves but also may be a danger to the community and other officers" (p. 61). This observation succinctly captures the most significant risk posed by psychologically impaired or unsuitable police officers: They endanger lives.

There are many occupations in which an impaired worker's failure to do their[2] job or to do it properly could well have a foreseeably negative impact on public safety, organizational efficiency, employer liability, and public trust, but there are few as far-reaching as the occupation of police officer. The ramifications and repercussions of a police officer's impaired functioning can result in undetected crime, unenforced felonies, and failed prosecutions, among many other injustices. Such wrongs can destroy lives, wreck families and fortunes, and endanger communities.

Yet, as bad as these consequences are, they pale in comparison to the fallout from abuses of police authority, particularly those abuses involving unwarranted and unlawful use of force, sexual assault, and other forms of unsanctioned violence. Although the true base rate of these abuses is unknown,[3] the incidence of police use of force (most of which is lawful and justified) is reported to be between 1% (International Association of Chiefs of Police [IACP], 2001) and 2% (Alpert & Dunham, 2010) of all police–citizen interactions. There is good reason to believe that most unsanctioned police violence is perpetrated by a relatively small cohort of officers (Harris, 2010), a finding consistent with Sherman's "rotten apple theory" (Sherman, 1978), which holds that exceptions to the normal pattern of professionalism and prosocial conduct by police officers are due mainly to moral or other deficits in the individual offenders rather than in the police organization or law enforcement system. It is these deficits that are among the subjects of interest in psychological evaluations.

An especially pernicious but common product of impaired police performance and unsanctioned violence is *institutional betrayal*—the result of actors affiliated with trusted and powerful institutions "acting in ways that visit harm upon those dependent on them for safety and well-being" (Smith & Freyd, 2014, p. 575). Crime victims who experience institutional betrayal also experience more severe trauma-related symptoms and generalize their mistrust of the betraying institution to others (Smith & Freyd, 2014). Acts of institutional betrayal may occur as the result of an officer's impaired psychological functioning—leading to indifference, neglect, negligence, or overt acts of abuse—but they can also be the product of unconscious associations triggered by a wide range of perceived and often irrelevant characteristics of a person, such as race, ethnicity, age, accent, or dress. A significant and growing body of empirical evidence shows convincingly that *implicit bias*—the attitudes or stereotypes that affect our understanding, actions, and decisions without awareness or intentional control—can have real-world effects on behavior, including on police officers' perceptions of threat and on decisions to use lethal force. These unconscious biases are believed to develop over the course of a lifetime, beginning at a very early age, through direct and indirect messages (Castelli, Zogmaister, & Tomelleri, 2009; Kang, 2012; Rudman, 2004), as well as through "passive observation of who occupies valued roles and devalued roles in the community" (Dasgupta, 2013, p. 237). Implicit biases also are pervasive and robust (Faigman et al., 2012; Greenwald, McGhee, & Schwartz, 1998; Kang & Lane, 2010; Nosek, Smyth, et al., 2007) and inaccessible to introspection (Greenwald et al., 2002; Kang, 2005; Nisbett & Wilson, 1977; Nosek, Greenwald, & Banaji, 2007; Nosek & Riskind, 2012; Wilson & Dunn, 2004). On the other hand, implicit biases are malleable: They can be gradually unlearned and replaced with new mental associations *if* the individual has the requisite mental and attitudinal prerequisites (Blair, 2002;

Blair, Ma, & Lenton, 2001; Dasgupta, 2013; Klauer, Schmitz, Teige-Mocigemba, & Voss, 2010). Thus, valid and well-constructed preemployment psychological evaluations can also play an important role in facilitating social justice. Our goal in writing this volume is to provide a single-source reference for information, both foundational (legal, ethical, and professional guidelines) and applied (preparation, data collection and interpretation, and report writing), necessary for conducting preemployment and fitness-for-duty evaluations of police officer candidates and employees, respectively, untethered to any particular assessment instrument.

Chapter Organization

Chapters 1 to 3 of this book are intended to establish a foundation for conducting psychological evaluations of police candidates and officers. In Chapter 1, we provide an overview of the legal framework, doctrines, and statutes that have a controlling influence on how these psychological evaluations are conducted in the United States. In Chapter 2, we discuss the functional competencies required to conduct psychological evaluations of police candidates or officers, with particular attention to "occupational competence," which includes knowledge about the essential functions of police officers, their working conditions and chain of command, and the psychological demands and stressors of police work. We transition in Chapter 3 to a consideration of the empirical foundations underlying these evaluations and the validity evidence supporting decisions about test use.

In Chapter 4, we review the information psychologists need to prepare for these evaluations. We focus on the importance of identifying the relevant forensic questions and give guidance for identifying the standard or criterion for assessing a police candidate's suitability or an incumbent officer's fitness for duty. In Chapter 5, we present methods commonly used for gathering assessment data in these evaluations, including brief descriptions of psychological tests frequently used in suitability and fitness evaluations. Chapter 6 presents models for interpreting and integrating data from the various sources of assessment information to reach a determination of suitability or fitness. In Chapter 7, we turn our attention to the written report and its various uses, including as support for later testimony.

Key Terms

Throughout this volume, we use terms that have particular meaning in the contexts of preemployment and/or fitness-for-duty evaluations but that may have different meanings in other contexts. To aid the reader, we next define these terms; any word in a definition that is also a key term is italicized.

Applicant. A person who has applied to become a police officer but has not yet satisfactorily completed the full range of *nonmedical evaluation procedures* and, therefore, has not received a *conditional offer of employment*.

Candidate. An *applicant* who has satisfactorily completed all *nonmedical evaluation procedures* and has received a *conditional offer of employment*.

Conditional Offer of Employment. A formal offer of employment following the completion of all *nonmedical evaluation procedures* that is contingent on successfully completing all *medical procedures*. It is a statutory term in the Americans With Disabilities Act of 1990 (ADA), Title I and has specific legal meaning and implications in the US.

Criterion. The statutory, regulatory, or administrative standard by which the *suitability* of a *candidate* or the *fitness* of an *incumbent* is assessed. Derivatives: **criterion standard, criteria.**

Fitness. Regarding psychological fitness, the quality of being free of an emotional or mental condition that limits the *incumbent* officer's ability to perform the essential functions of the job or poses a direct threat to the health or safety of the officer or others.

Incumbent. An individual who has been hired and is employed as a police officer.

Medical Examination. As defined by the ADA, a procedure or test that seeks information about an individual's physical or mental impairments or health. Several factors are considered by the Equal Employment Opportunity Commission (EEOC; the federal agency responsible for enforcing the ADA) to determine whether a test or procedure is a medical examination, but none is individually determinative. Medical examinations include, but are not limited to, psychological tests that are designed to identify a mental disorder or impairment.

Nonmedical Evaluation. Any evaluation procedure or inquiry that does not meet the ADA's or EEOC's definition of a *medical examination*. Examples include, but are not limited to, a civil service examination, criminal background check, oral board interview, physical agility test, and psychological assessment of normal personality traits.

Suitability. The quality of possessing or demonstrating the requisite psychological traits and characteristics to be a police officer (i.e., meeting the *criterion*). Derivatives: **suitable, qualified.** Note: In US federal employment contexts, suitability determinations refer to the consideration of specific factors as justification for finding a person unsuitable and taking a "suitability action" (see 5 C.F.R. § 731.202). For this reason, preemployment psychological evaluations of federal law enforcement officer candidates more commonly refer to the psychological "qualification," rather than suitability, of a candidate.

Notes

1. We use the term "police officers" throughout this volume to refer to all law enforcement officers who perform traditional policing functions. The term is intended to encompass city police officers, reserve police officers, deputy sheriffs, parole and probation officers, armed campus police officers, and federal law enforcement officers, among others.
2. As a plural pronoun, we recognize that *they* is traditionally (or, grammarians might insist, always) used in connection with a plural antecedent. In deference to a modern preference for gender-neutral pronouns, we also use "they" (and its derivative forms) as a singular pronoun.
3. See Corey and Stewart (2015) for a review.

PART I
FOUNDATION

The Legal Framework

1

Police psychological assessments, like all occupationally mandated psychological evaluations (OMPE Guidelines),[1] are guided by state and federal statutes and the case law promulgated by courts charged with interpreting these statutes. To be sure, competently performing these assessments requires knowledge of this foundational law. The laws pertaining to these evaluations are numerous, and their implications for practice can be nuanced. It is for this reason that our first chapter comprises a discussion of the legal foundation for police psychological assessments.

Case law often varies across states and the 11 different federal circuits that make up the federal appellate courts. When differences in case law exist between the circuits, the US Supreme Court may agree to review a case (i.e., grant *certiorari*) in order to resolve those differences. Unfortunately, this has happened seldom in this area of forensic psychology. In fact, as we will see shortly, there are several instances in which Supreme Court decisions have been neutralized by congressional mandates. So, although we will focus on mainstream opinions, practitioners need to remain vigilant for differences in relevant law in the jurisdictions in which they conduct evaluations. What is legal practice in other jurisdictions may be impermissible in your home state.

We begin this chapter with a brief discussion of relevant law and legal

BEWARE It is important that practitioners remain vigilant for differences in relevant law in the jurisdictions in which they conduct evaluations. What is legal practice in other jurisdictions may be impermissible in your home state.

procedures. Some readers already familiar with this material may wish to move past it.

English Common Law and Other Legal Terms

The term *common law* arises from medieval England when the bulk of the law developed from judicial decisions of the kings' courts. Hence, common law is also often called "judge-made law." The foundation of law in all provinces of Canada, and in all US states except Louisiana, is English common law.

Stare Decisis

Appellate courts in English common law countries follow the doctrine of *stare decisis,* Latin for "to stand by things decided," which means that when clear legal precedent exists, legal disputes and conflicts of law are resolved by adherence to the precedents set by courts of equal or higher ranking. In such cases, earlier decisions involving the same legal issues within the same jurisdiction are binding, hence the term *binding authority.* However, within a given jurisdiction, not all legal disputes have clear precedent, either because the fact pattern deviates significantly from earlier cases or because the instant case presents a new legal question. In these matters, the doctrine of *stare decisis* directs the court to consider other authoritative sources in an effort to stand by things decided. These sources are often court decisions made in other jurisdictions or countries but may also include related statutes, legal textbooks, dictionaries, or other authoritative sources of information. These alternative sources, while not binding, provide *persuasive authority* for the court's decision. For example, in appellate decisions involving interpretation of the Americans With Disabilities Act of 1990 (ADA), courts have been granted license by the statute to refer to a closely related piece of legislation—the Rehabilitation Act of 1973—as a source of persuasive authority [42 U.S.C. § 12117(b)].

Summary Judgment

Rule 56 of the *Federal Rules of Civil Procedure* provides for judgment without a trial if a party files a motion that convinces the court that there is no dispute over material facts, and established law indicates that the party asking for summary judgment is entitled to judgment.[2] The party filing the motion is usually referred to as the *moving party* or *movant*. When the movant presents a motion for summary judgment, the court views the fact pattern in the light most favorable to the other side. If the court determines that the law supports the moving party, summary judgment is granted, and that issue will not be heard in trial. On the other hand, if a factual dispute remains (courts often use the synonym, *genuine dispute*), the motion for summary judgment is denied, and the matter is referred for trial, where the dispute of fact can be resolved by the trial court or jury. We also will encounter cases in which the court renders a *partial summary judgment*, or a decision to grant/deny summary judgment *in part*. These decisions refer to the occasions in which the moving party is entitled to judgment on at least one but not all the claims.

Balancing Governmental and Private Interests

Properly done psychological assessments of job candidates and incumbents necessarily invade the privacy of the examinee. In almost every aspect of employment assessments, the examiner needs to be mindful of the tension that exists between extracting relevant personal information and respecting an employee's right to privacy.

A *penumbra* right to privacy exists in the United States and Canada, meaning that it is implied rather than explicitly articulated in either country's federal constitutions. Some states, however, have incorporated privacy protections into their state constitutions.[3] Even in states without constitutional or statutory rights to privacy, the *boundaries* of privacy have been subjected to a balancing test, in which the employee's right to privacy is weighed against other compelling interests, such as the employer's need to know about medical or psychological conditions that can affect an employee's functional abilities at work or to discover other personal information deemed necessary to fulfill the organizational mission. As early as 1987, a federal appellate court reversed the decision of a trial court that prevented the then-named US Customs Service from routinely requiring drug testing of both applicants and employees (*National Treasury Employees Union v. Von Raab*, 1987). The appellate court, siding with the employer, rejected arguments that such practice constituted (illegal) searches under the Fourth Amendment or that acquisition of positive drug findings violated one's right against self-incrimination. The court held that while the Customs Service testing program is a search "within the meaning of the Fourth Amendment, . . . because of the strong governmental interest in employing individuals for key positions in drug enforcement who themselves are not drug users and the limited intrusiveness of this particular program, it is reasonable and, therefore, is not unconstitutional" (p. 173). More recently, US Steel Corporation's practice of administering alcohol tests to probationary employees, even without cause to suspect intoxication, was permitted. The court held that, because of the dangerous working conditions in the plant and the fact that protective gear worn by employees made it difficult to assess probable cause for suspicion of intoxication, the employer's practice was job-related and consistent with business necessity (*EEOC v. United States Steel Corporation*, 2013). As we will see, similar lines of reasoning in other cases have determined that when the need for an evaluation is job-related and consistent with business necessity, the employer's interest in ordering appropriately intrusive psychological evaluations outweighs the privacy interests of employees in safety-sensitive positions. A 1988 case involving police officers of a New Jersey agency used reasoning similar to that in *Van Raab* to allow blanket drug testing to continue. The court further stated:

> The need in a democratic society for public confidence, respect and approbation of the public officials on whom the state confers that awesome power is significantly greater than the state's need to instill confidence in the integrity of the horse racing industry. . . . Accordingly, any Fourth Amendment interest is diminished because of a police officer's diminished lowered expectations of privacy. (*Policemen's Benev. Ass'n of NJ v. Washington Tp.*, 1988, p. 141)

As we continue to review case law relevant to psychological assessment practice, we will resume this discussion of privacy concerns as well as the circumstances that justify intrusions into employees' informational or autonomy privacy interests.

Employer Liability

As psychological science has developed, so has the expectation that reasonable employers will use mental health assessments to eliminate psychologically unsuitable candidates and to identify compromised employees. Depending on the fact pattern of a particular case, different legal theories can be asserted as a basis for allowing the court to grant relief when an employer negligently fails to use these resources. We will focus on three common legal theories in which an organization (or its agents) can be held civilly liable. These theories arise from § 1983 of the Civil Rights Act of 1871 and English common law theories of tort liability and *respondeat superior.*

General Tort Liability

A *tort*—a term that evolved from the Latin word *to twist*—occurs when the defendant (also known as a *tortfeasor*) engages in a wrongful act or omission that results in injury and damages to the plaintiff. In the United States and other English common law countries, the plaintiff must generally prove each of four elements. The defendant

(a) owed the plaintiff a duty,
(b) breached that duty,
(c) thereby causing injury to the plaintiff that resulted in
(d) damages to the plaintiff.

Generally, the injury to the plaintiff had to have been reasonably foreseeable by the defendant.

One of the most cited cases illustrating tort liability for failure to use psychological evaluations of police officers is *Bonsignore v. City of New York* (1981). In December 1976, Blase Bonsignore, a 23-year veteran of the New York City Police Department, shot his spouse and then killed himself. Ms. Bonsignore survived, albeit with serious and permanent injuries. Officer Bonsignore used an off-duty weapon, which he was required to carry at all times. Ms. Bonsignore sued the City on behalf of herself and her daughters and also alleged wrongful death on behalf of her deceased husband. During the trial, Ms. Bonsignore presented two theories of negligence: (a) the City should have known that Officer Bonsignore was dangerous and should have prohibited him from carrying a gun, and (b) the City was negligent by failing to psychologically evaluate and monitor him. The jury rejected the first theory but found the City negligent for failing to provide a psychological evaluation. Indeed, in *dicta* (the part of a decision in which a court offers remarks that are not part of its ruling), the court noted evidence provided by the plaintiff indicating that from 1973 to 1976, more officers killed themselves than were killed by criminals, and that during the course of Officer Bonsignore's 23-year career, he was never required to take a psychological evaluation. The appellate court found that the jury's findings were reasonable and upheld the judgment awarded to Ms. Bonsignore.

Vicarious Liability and *Respondeat Superior*

There are some instances in which an employer can be held liable *without* being at fault or without the plaintiff having to prove the injury was reasonably foreseeable. This brings us to the second theory for alleging liability against a government organization: the theory of vicarious liability. This theory involves assigning responsibility to an employer for the negligent or wrongful act of its employee, if the act occurred within the scope of employment. In the same way that the term *vicarious* refers to an experience perceived through the act of another person, *vicarious liability* is incurred by an employer through the acts of its employees. Sometimes vicarious liability is interchanged with the term *respondeat superior*: "Let the master answer" (for the acts of the master's subordinates). Vicarious liability suits often allege that the employer either negligently appointed or negligently retained the employee who harmed the plaintiff. This legal risk motivates many employers to decrease their exposure to negligence claims by conducting preemployment suitability evaluations of candidates and fitness evaluations of employees who exhibit concerning behaviors.

42 U.S.C. § 1983

The purpose of the Civil Rights Act of 1871 was to prevent public officials, and the Ku Klux Klan operating in the Southern states, from violating the constitutional rights of former slaves. Section 1983 of the act provided a mechanism for state governments or persons to be held accountable for depriving others of their federal rights. Section 1983 states, in pertinent part:

> Every person who, under color of any statute, ordinance, regulation, custom, or usage, of any State or Territory or the District of Columbia, subjects, or causes to be subjected, any citizen of the United States or other person within the jurisdiction thereof to the deprivation of any rights, privileges, or immunities secured by the Constitution and laws, shall be liable to the party injured in an action at law, suit in equity, or other proper proceeding for redress. (42 U.S.C. § 1983)

Section 1983 itself does not confer any substantive federal rights. Instead, it provides a statutory vehicle through which the plaintiff may assert that a person or governmental agency, acting under the color of law, permitted a violation of, or directly violated, an established federal or constitutional right.

Until 1978, the term *person* as used in § 1983 did not apply to municipalities or other governmental units below the state level. The definition of "person" expanded with *Monell v. New York City Dept. of Social Services* (1978). This case arose from the plaintiffs—pregnant women forced to take maternity leave before it was medically necessary—who sued the New York City Board of Education for injunctive and monetary relief (back pay).[4] The federal district court for the Southern District of New York, relying on the holding in the Supreme Court case of *Monroe v. Pape* (1961), affirmed that New York City was not a person as defined by § 1983 and, therefore, was not liable under the law to reimburse the teachers for their back pay. The plaintiffs appealed to the US Supreme Court, which considered the question of whether municipalities are persons under § 1983. In a 7–2 decision, the court reversed its previous decision in *Monroe v. Pape* and proclaimed that a municipality is a "person" and, therefore, liable when it has promulgated a policy or permitted a custom to prevail that deprives the plaintiff of their federal rights.[5] Thus, compelling pregnant employees to take leave when it was not medically necessary was deemed a constitutional injury due to a policy or custom promulgated by the school board. However, liability under § 1983 against a municipality or its agents is incurred only when the municipality or person directly caused or was deliberately indifferent to a policy or custom that resulted in the violation of a plaintiff's federal right(s).

In 1997, the US Supreme Court elaborated the criteria for proving deliberate indifference under § 1983. In *Board of Comm'rs of Bryan Cty. v. Brown* (1997), the plaintiff, Jill Brown, was the victim of excessive force by a newly hired deputy. Brown brought a suit under § 1983 and prevailed in the trial and the federal appellate courts. Bryan County appealed, arguing, in part, that a "single hiring decision by a municipal policymaker could not give rise to municipal liability" under § 1983 if that single administrative decision did not reflect a policy or custom (p. 401). The Supreme Court agreed. Justice Sandra Day O'Connor, writing the majority opinion in this 5–4 decision, wrote, "[T]he plaintiff must . . . demonstrate that, through its deliberate conduct, the municipality was the 'moving force' behind the injury alleged" (p. 404). To rule otherwise, the majority concurred, would expose municipalities to suit for injuries they did not cause. "In the broadest sense, every injury is traceable to a hiring decision. Where a court fails to adhere to rigorous requirements of culpability and causation, municipal liability collapses into respondeat superior liability" (p. 416). Given this case law, it is not surprising that some courts (e.g., *Hild v. Bruner,* 1980)[6] have found that a municipal employer's policy-based failure to conduct psychological evaluations of its police officer candidates may constitute gross negligence or deliberate indifference.

Psychologist as Agent of the Employer
Although the fact patterns in *Monell* and *Bryan County* involve cases in which the plaintiffs brought suit against a government entity, it

is important to recall that psychologists and police officials also are "persons." Since § 1983 applies to "[e]very person who, under color of any statute, ordinance, regulation, custom, or usage . . . ," deliberate acts by an agent of the employer to deprive plaintiffs of any of their federal rights can also be asserted (at least in some jurisdictions), as was the case in which a citizen brought suit against the mental health provider who conducted a preemployment evaluation on an applicant who subsequently proved to be a sexual predator (*Schaefer v. Wilcock*, 1987). Similarly, in *Jimenez v. DynCorp International* (2009), a female law enforcement candidate brought suit against a psychologist and the contracting agency for allegedly disqualifying her on the basis of her gender in violation of Title VII of the Civil Rights Act of 1964, which prohibits employment discrimination on the basis of sex, race, color, national origin, and religion. During the summary motion proceedings (written and oral arguments in response to the defendant's request that the court decide on matters submitted to it, based only on legal arguments and undisputed facts), the agency argued it should be spared liability because, if illegal discrimination did occur, it was the psychologist's fault. The court opined that Title VII (like the ADA) considers the employer to include *any* agent of the employer, and, consequently, the employer cannot sever its potential liability from that of the psychologist.

These theories of liability—tort liability, *respondeat superior*, and § 1983—are not mutually exclusive. While these theories provide various legal defenses for liability, it is also worth noting that (a) sound psychological assessment practices may decrease the probability of hiring and retaining employees who trigger § 1983 suits and other forms of liability, and (b) psychologists' inclusion as consultants to police employers, both pre- and post-hire, may also provide a defense to the charge of deliberate indifference.

Applicant, Candidate, and Employee Protections

Many of the present standard practices in police suitability and fitness evaluations, at least as they are conducted in the United States, came about as a result of Congress's passage of civil rights legislation that provided new protections for applicants, candidates, and employees. These federal laws establish the minimum protections, but readers are cautioned that some states have enacted similar laws that provide even greater protections.

Administrative Exhaustion and Legal Remedies

The federal civil rights acts we discuss next set forth procedural steps individuals must take if they believe their civil rights have been violated by their employer (or prospective employer). Some courts refer to this process as "administrative exhaustion," meaning that a suit will not be considered until these administrative steps have been taken. These steps apply to most employment discrimination cases.

Rehabilitation Act of 1973, Americans With Disabilities Act of 1990, ADA Amendments Act of 2008

These closely related civil rights statutes were enacted to prevent discrimination against people who may have an actual or perceived disability yet are able to do their jobs safely and effectively. Together, the ADA, the ADA Amendments Act (ADAAA), and the ADA's predecessor, the Rehabilitation Act, apply to the US government and other entities that receive federal funds. The Rehabilitation Act states, in pertinent part:

> No otherwise qualified individual with a disability in the United States . . . shall, solely by reason of her or his disability, be excluded from the participation in, be denied the benefits of, or be subjected to discrimination under any program or activity receiving Federal financial assistance or under any program or activity conducted by any Executive agency or by the United States Postal Service. [29 U.S.C. § 794(a)]

The ADA of 1990 extended many of the protections of the Rehabilitation Act to private employers with 15 or more employees, state and local governments, labor unions, employment agencies, and *agents* of the employer. Although the coverage afforded by the Rehabilitation Act and ADA extends to some areas that the other does not, they overlap considerably. When it comes to psychological assessment, the ADA arguably has had the greatest impact of all civil rights laws on psychological practice in the US. It mandates (a) what types of assessment approaches are permissible and (b) when they can be used. The ADA's impact on assessment practices depends on whether one is evaluating applicants, candidates, or employees.

The definitions included within the ADA and its various exceptions have been hotly debated in the nation's appellate courts. From a constitutional standpoint, the ADA is remarkable for its focus on the individual. Previous civil rights acts provided protection for an identifiable group. Unlike the Rehabilitation Act, which uses the term *handicapped* to identify a protected person, the ADA uses the term *disability* to identify those whom Congress desired to protect. Perhaps for these reasons, appellate cases on the ADA exceed the number of appellate cases on all other civil rights acts combined (Strinberg & Lowman, 1999).

The Equal Employment Opportunity Commission (EEOC) and the courts sometimes interpret the law differently. The EEOC is viewed by many jurists as being too sympathetic to employees who have disputes with their employers, whereas courts have been regarded as being too sympathetic to employers. Two examples illustrate this tension and how Congress stepped in to remedy it. The first example occurred in 1989, after the Supreme Court overturned the EEOC's interpretation of Title VII of the Civil Rights Act of 1964 in *Griggs v. Duke Power Company* (1971) and six other related decisions, including the infamous holding in *Wards Cove Packing Co., Inc. v. Antonio* (1989). Congress then pulled in the reins on the courts by passing the Civil Rights Act of 1991, which reversed *Wards Cove*.

The ADAAA is a second example of Congress overriding the Supreme Court. Congress reversed the effects of two Supreme Court decisions, *Sutton v. United Air Lines, Inc.* (1999) and *Toyota*

Motor Manufacturing, Kentucky, Inc. v. Williams (2002), and various EEOC decisions that resulted in very narrow interpretations of the terms *impairment* and *major life activity,* which collectively made it very difficult for aggrieved parties to prevail. In fact, before passage of the ADAAA, 93% of ADA cases were won by employers (Colker, 1999). The ADAAA clarified the definitions of disability contained within the ADA and Sections 501, 503, and 504 of the Rehabilitation Act. Under the ADA, a qualifying disability includes (a) a physical or mental impairment that substantially limits one or more major life activities of such individual, (b) a record of such an impairment, or (c) being regarded as having such an impairment. Under the ADAAA, an individual now meets the requirement of being regarded as having such an impairment if the individual establishes that they have been subjected to an action prohibited under the ADA because of an actual or perceived physical or mental impairment, except when the impairment is transitory (i.e., an actual or expected duration of 6 months or less; see ADAAA, Section 4).

What Is Not Covered Under the Americans With Disabilities Act?

The ADA is affirmative action legislation for those who have a qualifying disability (*Daugherty v. City of El Paso,* 1995). Persons with conditions that cannot be reasonably accommodated, problematic personality traits, brief or transitory conditions, and covered disorders that nevertheless place the employee or others at risk for substantial harm *and* cannot be reasonably accommodated are not protected by the ADA (except with respect to its procedural requirements, which in many federal circuits apply to all persons, regardless of disability status). In Chapter 4, we provide a more detailed list of conditions not covered by ADA protections.

Preemployment

Congress wanted job candidates to know when they are denied employment because of a medical condition. One of the strategies to deter discrimination based on irrelevant or nonexistent disabilities is to prevent persons from undergoing medical or psychological examinations until their nonmedical qualifications have been established and they have received a *conditional offer of employment.* Consequently, if a conditional offer is revoked after a medical examination, the candidate knows that the findings from the medical examination triggered rescission of the offer. As such, the candidate may have recourse under the ADA.

The desire to legislate accountability begins with the EEOC distinguishing between psychological evaluations that are considered medical examinations and those that are not. Specifically:

> Psychological examinations are medical if they provide evidence that would lead to identifying a mental disorder or impairment (for example, those listed in the American Psychiatric Association's most recent Diagnostic and Statistical Manual of Mental Disorders (DSM). . . . On the other hand, if a test is designed and used to measure only things such as honesty, tastes, and habits, it is not medical. (EEOC, 1995)

If, for example, psychological testing is designed to measure personality traits and does not query or examine the applicant about covered conditions, it is *not* a medical examination. However, a test designed to detect psychopathology, like the Minnesota Multiphasic Personality Inventory (MMPI) and its later versions, would be considered medical within the meaning of the ADA, according to a 7th Circuit decision (*Karraker v. Rent-A-Center,* 2005). The EEOC also provided some factors (considered alone or in combination) to help determine whether a test is medical:

1. Is it administered (or interpreted) by a healthcare professional or someone trained by a healthcare professional?

2. Is it designed to reveal an impairment of physical or mental health?

3. Is the employer trying to determine the applicant's physical or mental health or impairments?

4. Is it invasive (for example, does it require the drawing of blood, urine, or breath)?

when denied by psych, becomes "disabled" [handwritten margin note]

5. Does it measure an applicant's performance of a task, or does it measure the applicant's physiological responses to performing the task?
6. Is it normally given in a medical setting (for example, a healthcare professional's office)?
7. Is medical equipment used? (EEOC, 1995)[7]

BEWARE

When you are retained to conduct a medical examination, you must adhere to the provisions of the ADA and should decline participation if the employer has not conformed to the act. Also, if you inadvertently participate in a medical evaluation before a legal COE has been offered, the employer may be investigated by the EEOC and you may be named as a party in a lawsuit.

Accordingly, when practitioners are retained to conduct medical examinations, they must adhere to the provisions of the ADA and should decline participation if the employer has not conformed to the act. It would be easy for psychologists who are well-intentioned but ill-informed about the ADA to find that they had committed a serious violation of the ADA simply by applying standards of practice that are common in a clinical setting but prohibited in occupationally mandated psychological evaluations. We will start by reviewing the elements contained in a bona fide conditional offer of employment (COE) because if you inadvertently participate in a medical evaluation before a legal COE has been offered, the employer may be investigated by the EEOC and you may be named as a party in a lawsuit.

Applicants Cannot Be Given a Medical Examination Until They Have Received a Bona Fide Conditional Offer of Employment

The requirement that medical examinations only be given to persons who have received a conditional offer is stated in the ADA statute and was supported in some courts as early as 1996 (see, e.g., *Barnes v. Cochran*, 1996).

Appellate courts have only supported the validity of conditional job offers when they were "real." One of the leading cases on point is *Leonel v. American Airlines, Inc.* (2005). Walber Leonel and two other flight attendant applicants filed separate claims against American Airlines (AA) when their respective COEs were rescinded after their blood tests revealed they had not disclosed their HIV status or use of associated medications on a written medical questionnaire completed at the time that the blood samples were drawn. The plaintiffs, all California residents, argued that their COE was not a "real" job offer because their blood samples were collected following their interviews in Dallas, Texas (AA's headquarters) but *before* they completed a background check and without their express permission, in violation of the ADA and various privacy violations under the California Constitution and California's Fair Employment and Housing Act (FEHA). The employer countered that the blood samples were collected for the convenience of the applicants—so that they did not have to return to Dallas after the COE—and they reasoned that the plaintiffs' privacy was not unduly invaded because the blood samples were not analyzed until *after* the plaintiffs passed the background check. Besides, the employer argued, the plaintiffs were not denied employment because of their HIV status but rather because they had lied on their medical questionnaires.

The Ninth Circuit Court of Appeals then considered if a COE can be tendered even if analysis of a medical test is deferred until the background and other nonmedical inquires have been completed. The court, finding for the plaintiffs, noted that a "job offer is real if the employer has evaluated all relevant nonmedical information which it reasonably could have obtained and analyzed prior to giving the offer," citing the EEOC's published enforcement guidance as persuasive authority for its decision.[8] Furthermore, the court wrote, "to issue a 'real' offer under the ADA and FEHA . . . an employer must have either completed all non-medical components of its application process or be able to demonstrate that it could not reasonably have done so before issuing the offer" (pp. 4697–4698). The court emphasized that the ADA and the laws of California mandate the order in which medical information is obtained—not simply when it is analyzed. The court explained that real job offers involve a two-step process in which applicants are screened for nonmedical requirements first, followed by any required medical examinations. This two-step process allows applicants to know if they have been rejected for medical reasons, giving them the opportunity to challenge the business necessity of their exclusion.

As further support for its holding, the court referenced a Fifth Circuit case, *Buchanan v. City of San Antonio* (1996), which held that a COE given *before* completion of the polygraph, personal interview, and background investigation renders the medical examination premature.[9] As for AA's defense that the plaintiffs were denied employment because they lied on their medical questionnaires, the court held that the company would have been justified in rescinding the employment offer for lying on the medical questionnaire only if it had made the inquiry at the proper time. "We do not suggest that, when a medical examination is conducted at the proper time and in the proper manner, an applicant has an option to lie, or that an employer is foreclosed from refusing to hire an applicant who does" (footnote 13, p. 4699).

To help ensure that you are not involved in conducting an unlawful examination (that is, one that is done *before* a valid job offer), we recommend that you request a copy of the background investigation report or summary (other benefits of this practice are discussed in Chapter 4), and perhaps even a copy of the conditional offer of employment, before proceeding. If the employer cannot produce the background investigation, or if the COE contains a number of conditions that could reasonably be completed before the medical examination, check with the employer to make sure this requirement is understood and that all nonmedical components that could reasonably be completed before a COE have been satisfied before the candidate proceeds to the psychological evaluation. It is important to note that the ADAAA specifically states that agents of qualified employers must also comply. Thus, the evaluator and the employer are both legally responsible for adherence to this provision, whether the evaluator is an employee of the organization or is serving as an independent contractor.

Procedures to Ensure Privacy and Fair Treatment of Applicants Under the Americans With Disabilities Act

The ADA sets forth the following requirements for employers who refer applicants for a medical examination as a condition of employment:

> (a) all entering employees are subjected to such an examination regardless of disability; (b) information obtained regarding the medical condition or history of the applicant is collected and maintained on separate forms and in separate medical files and is treated as a confidential medical record; . . . and (c) the results of such examination are used only in accordance with this subchapter. (ADA, 42 U.S.C. § 12112)

These procedural requirements apply to all applicants. Well-intentioned administrators have, on occasion, asked us to perform evaluations on a subset of applicants—the ones about whom the prospective employer has concerns. We also have been asked to forward an evaluation, conducted 6 months before, to another employer that is considering the candidate for a position. While both of these requests may appear reasonable on their face, both violate the plain language of the ADA. In the first example, the psychologist is engaging in prohibited discrimination—a practice known as *disparate treatment*—because candidates suspected of harboring job-related psychopathology are treated differently from candidates not so perceived. In the second example, one is violating the confidentiality constraints imposed by the ADA by redisclosing the evaluation to another agency, even if done with the authorization of both the individual who was evaluated and the agency that initiated and paid for the evaluation.

If one candidate is subjected to a medical examination, the rest of the candidates must also be required to undergo the evaluation.[10] That said, it may be permissible to have a particular candidate take additional tests if indicated—a situation that might emerge, for example, if the psychologist suspects an impairment that cannot be ruled out by the standard preemployment battery. EEOC enforcement guidance (EEOC, 1996) states, "Where an employer has already obtained basic medical information from all entering employees in a job category, it may require specific individuals to have follow-up medical examinations only if they are medically related to the previously obtained medical information" (Question 5).[11] However, if an individual is screened out because of a disability, it must be shown that the exclusionary criterion is job-related and consistent with business necessity.[12]

BEST PRACTICE

Not all human resource managers and the attorneys they retain are well-informed about the ADA and other relevant civil rights legislation. It is therefore a useful practice to print a caveat on the first page of each preemployment evaluation report that reminds employers of mandated restrictions regarding the use of ADA-protected information.

Mindful that many human resource managers, and even the attorneys they retain, are not always well-informed about the ADA and other relevant civil rights legislation, it may be a useful practice to print a caveat on the first page of each preemployment evaluation report that reminds employers of mandated restrictions regarding the use of ADA-protected information.

The Americans With Disabilities Act and Fitness Evaluations

In order for a fitness evaluation referral to be lawful, it must be "job-related and consistent with business necessity" [42 U.S.C. § 12112(d)(4)(A)]. In general, this *business necessity standard,* as it is commonly called, is presumed to have been met when the employer has a reasonable belief, based on objective evidence, that (a) an employee's ability to perform essential job functions is impaired by a medical condition, or (b) an employee will pose a direct threat due to a medical condition.[13] In Chapter 5, we discuss in depth the various methods commonly used by psychologists to collect information in occupationally mandated psychological evaluations.

Focus on Functional Capacities

A focus on a fitness examinee's functional capacities, not diagnosis, is generally valued by appellate courts and is aligned with other types of forensic assessments. Two appellate court cases illustrate how the ADA's statutory emphasis on a job's functional requirements has been adopted by state courts, although readers are reminded that these rulings are not controlling outside their states of origin. In *Sager v. County of Yuba* (2007), the California Court of Appeal was persuaded that the psychologist hired by the employer to evaluate a deputy sheriff's fitness was correct in relying on the functional requirements enumerated in her job description and state law stipulating the preemployment suitability requirements for California peace officers. The plaintiff argued that the state's hiring standards are relevant only to whether a person should be given peace officer status, either as a new candidate or one wishing to return to a peace officer position following a break in service. The appeals court rejected this argument, noting that "it would be illogical to conclude the Legislature believed those standards disappeared once an officer began working" (p. 13).

More recently, in *Brown v. Sandy City Appeal Board* (2014), the Utah Court of Appeals ruled similarly. One of the arguments that Detective Brown raised in appealing his agency's decision to terminate his employment was that the evaluating psychologist, Dr. Mark Zelig, improperly applied California's psychological screening dimensions (discussed in detail in Chapter 4) to a Utah officer. Although the court agreed that a Utah officer is not bound by standards promulgated by other jurisdictions, it held that a Utah psychologist is permitted to be informed by standards from other jurisdictions, analogizing this use to a court's reliance on well-reasoned analyses from sister jurisdictions. The court held, "Brown significantly overstates how Zelig used the California standards. As Zelig explained in his report, his opinion of Brown's fitness for duty 'was informed by consulting published standards of psychological competence applicable to peace officers,' and the California standards included certain dimensions that applied to Brown's diagnosis" (paragraph 14).

These two cases illustrate important concepts that are discussed throughout this volume. Anchoring one's evaluation to the examinee's functional capacities or limitations stemming from a mental health condition, rather than to the diagnostic label itself, aids employers, courts, and other stakeholders in their respective decisions. It also is integral to a proposed model for data integration, which we discuss in Chapter 6. Finally, consideration of an individual's functional abilities has been emphasized by Grisso (2003), who advised psychologists conducting any evaluation of civil or criminal competency to consider the relationship between the person's mental or emotional condition and the functional requirements of the forensically relevant context.

Not Every Job Is Equal

Not all jobs are created equal: The greater the risk associated with impaired work performance, the lower the threshold for justifying a fitness evaluation referral. Business necessity and the direct threat exception are context specific. An employee's behavior may be a mere annoyance at a bake shop, but in a police or fire department, the same behavior may place the employee and others in danger. In general, an employee in a safety-sensitive position foregoes the full privacy rights and associated protections afforded to those who work in a nondangerous environment. Even before the ADA, courts were sympathetic to a police administrator's need to use psychological examinations to ensure the efficient operation of police organizations. In *Conte v. Horcher* (1977), Chief Horcher ordered Lt. Conte to undergo a psychological evaluation following Conte's involvement in a physical altercation with a citizen. The order was not disciplinary, and the police chief's authority to issue such an order was upheld by the federal circuit court of appeals. The court ruled that a physical or mental examination enables the administrator to know if a person is able to perform their job duties, and it is "also necessary to assure the effective performance of the department" (p. 154). Similarly, an employer is allowed to make more intrusive inquiries about an employee's reason for taking sick leave if that employee is assigned to a safety-sensitive position (*Transport Workers Union of America v. New York City Transit Authority,* 2004).

The contextual nature of business necessity also arose in *Watson v. City of Miami Beach* (1999), in which the plaintiff, Officer William Watson, had a long history of being antagonistic toward coworkers and supervisors. His employer ordered Watson to participate in a fitness-for-duty evaluation. He was evaluated by a psychologist, who recommended that Watson return to work with appropriate stress management counseling. Watson returned to work and then sued the police department, arguing that the City discriminated against him by relieving him from duty pending a fitness examination. The Eleventh Circuit Court of Appeals held the following:

- "In any case where a police department reasonably perceives an officer to be even mildly paranoid, hostile, or oppositional, a fitness-for duty examination is job-related and consistent with business necessity. . . . Police departments place armed officers in positions where they can do tremendous harm if they act irrationally" (p. 935).[14]
- Contrary to Watson's contention, "the ADA does not . . . require a police department to forgo a fitness for duty examination . . . until a perceived threat becomes real or questionable behavior results in injuries" (p. 935).
- In supporting its position, the court cited a passage from the EEOC Compliance Manual indicating that "periodic medical examinations for public safety positions, narrowly tailored, are consistent with business necessity" (p. 936).

The holding in *Watson* has been widely cited in other appellate decisions, including those involving prophylactic evaluations of emergency responders and private employees in safety-sensitive positions. For example, in *Brownfield v. City of Yakima* (2007), Officer Brownfield was ordered to participate in a fitness-for-duty evaluation (FFDE) when he began manifesting inappropriate anger toward his peers following a head injury. He refused, was fired, and filed suit alleging violations of the ADA and Family Medical Leave Act (FMLA). The court, following the logic in *Watson,* found that "the City had an objective, legitimate basis to doubt Brownfield's ability to perform the duties of a police officer. . . . '[W]hen a police department has good reason to doubt an officer's ability to respond to these situations in an appropriate manner, a[n] FFDE is consistent with the ADA'" (p. 1145). Therefore, the officer's refusal to participate in the examination justified the termination of his job. Another federal circuit used similar logic to uphold a police chief's referral of an officer who exhibited a wide variety of suspected psychopathology (*Franklin v. City of Slidell*, 2013).

Appropriateness of a Fitness Referral

A lower threshold for establishing business necessity in safety-sensitive positions does not eliminate the threshold. Indeed, there are cases in which the courts have held that the conduct of an employee did not rise to a level justifying the intrusiveness of a psychological inquiry. These include cases in which the referrals for examination are intended to humiliate the employee for obvious political reasons, or are made after the employee engaged in trivial behaviors or misdemeanors that do not diminish their capacity to safely and effectively perform their job. Determining the appropriateness of a fitness referral is an important topic, which we discuss in depth in Chapter 4.

One of the earliest holdings to consider the appropriateness of a mandated fitness evaluation arose when Lawrence Stewart, an English instructor at San Mateo College in Northern California, riled his administrators by participating in protests against the Vietnam War and the 1970 shootings at Kent State University (*Stewart v. Pearce*, 1973). Stewart was removed from his teaching assignment and reassigned to the library, along with being ordered to undergo a psychiatric examination. With the university administration providing no justification for the examination, Stewart filed a motion for an injunction in federal district court requiring his reinstatement, arguing that his procedural due process rights under the Fourteenth Amendment were violated by the college. The federal district trial and appellate courts sustained the injunction, remarking that an order for psychiatric examination is stigmatizing, and the college failed to provide a rational reason for its referral. Moreover, per California statute, Stewart was entitled to a hearing on the merits of the order before undergoing the examination. The court's insistence that such referrals be limited to meritorious concerns is echoed in the holding of a Michigan court that found in favor of a police dispatcher, whose referral appeared to have been motivated by office politics unrelated to her job performance (*Merillat v. Michigan State University*, 1994). To make matters worse for the defendant, the unwarranted referral opened the door for Merillat to pursue other remedies because she was regarded as having a disability under the ADA.

Merillat illustrates that one of the unintended consequences of an arbitrary and capricious referral for a fitness evaluation is to trigger employee protections that would not have been available but for the inappropriate referral.[15] The business necessity of a referral also is undermined when the referring party's motivation appears disingenuous, as evidenced when the referral is not timely or is based on unsubstantiated reports from third parties. In *Denhof v. City of Grand Rapids* (2007), for example, the appellate court found evidence that the police administration was illegally retaliating against the plaintiff for several reasons, including the chief's testimony that he believed Officer Denhof to be a danger to herself and others, "but for six more weeks, he allowed this 'dangerous' officer to patrol the streets of Grand Rapids" (no pagination).

Similarly, in the matter of *In re Williams* (2016), the Superior Court of New Jersey reversed the termination of a truck driver who refused to engage in a fitness evaluation that was ordered 8 months after the employer received an anonymous letter voicing concerns about the mental stability of the driver. The court found that the order to participate in the evaluation clearly fell short of the ADA requirement that such an examination be shown to be job-related and consistent with business necessity. In its decision, the appellate court noted the 8-month delay in taking action, as well as the township's failure to verify any of the information in the anonymous letter. The court cited EEOC enforcement guidance (2000), which lists five factors that an employer might consider in deciding whether third-party information justifies asking disability-related questions or requiring a medical examination:

(a) the relationship of the person providing the information to the employee about whom it is being provided;

(b) the seriousness of the medical condition at issue;

(c) the possible motivation of the person providing the information;

(d) how the person learned the information (e.g., directly from the employee whose medical condition is in question or from someone else); and

(e) other evidence that the employer has that bears on the reliability of the information provided.

Reasonable Accommodation Under the Americans With Disabilities Act and Rehabilitation Act of 1973: The Employer's Versus the Psychologist's Role

It is common for the organizational client to ask a psychologist to opine as to whether or how a given employee's disability or handicap can be accommodated. Outside of situations in which the impairment is so severe that reasonable accommodation clearly would not work regardless of the agency's resources, or so minor that rapid recovery can be reasonably expected, reasonable accommodation opinions are often outside of the psychologist's expertise, and they can be risky to offer. The employer-retained psychologist can, of course, describe an employee's functional abilities and limitations, and any risks that are apparent, but the ultimate responsibility for accommodation decisions falls on the shoulders of the employer (Equal Employment Opportunity Commission, 2002). Undoubtedly, one of the reasons that the EEOC offers this advice is that it is the employer who has the expertise—and the authority—to determine whether an accommodation would pose an undue hardship under the ADA.

 BEWARE

Reasonable accommodation opinions are often outside of the psychologist's expertise, and risky to offer.

Privacy Protection, Legal Discovery, and Access to Reports and Data

Assuming that the employer has articulated a legitimate need for a fitness evaluation, how much information should a psychologist or psychiatrist include in a written report? The answer to this question has prompted considerable litigation arising out of the right to privacy. Related concerns about privacy have arisen regarding the amount and types of information that the examiner may report or that the employee is required to release to their employer. Although federal mandates set the minimum standards (the floor), state laws may grant additional rights to the examinee.

The failure to adhere to state medical information privacy statutes underlies two of the most oft-cited cases on this topic: a California Court of Appeal decision, *Pettus v. Cole* (1996), and Seventh Circuit decision, *McGreal v. Ostrov* (2004). In both cases, the courts found that the fitness examiners failed to use the forms required by the respective confidentiality statutes, which would have rendered the authorized disclosure of medical information lawful. Thus, careful attention to state law pertaining to the confidentiality of medical information is vital, both for the protection of the employee's privacy interests and for the examiner's avoidance of unnecessary litigation.

BEST PRACTICE

Careful attention to state law pertaining to the confidentiality of medical information is vital, both for the protection of the employee's privacy interests and for the examiner's avoidance of unnecessary litigation.

Beyond the particular findings in the *Pettus* and *McGreal* decisions pertaining to the examiners' violations of the California and Illinois medical privacy statutes, respectively, is their illustration of the potential hazards associated with providing information not directly relevant to the fitness determination. In *Pettus,* the court was deeply concerned that the detail in the examiners' reports exceeded the commentary needed to describe Pettus's functional capacities at work. Among the nonmedical information the court cited as an unwarranted intrusion on Pettus's privacy were descriptions of the following:

> his hostile feelings toward certain current and former coworkers and supervisors; . . . his smoking and drinking patterns; a social history of his life from the time of his birth, with his family

of origin, through a marriage and divorce, to the present; and his anxious and highly emotional behavior during the interview (crying, wringing his hands, burying his face in his hands, jumping out of his chair and removing his shirt to reveal the marks on his skin from the rash medicine). (p. 441)

In *McGreal*, the Seventh Circuit Court of Appeals similarly took issue with the examining psychologist's inclusion in his written report of:

a great many details of McGreal's home life, especially regarding his relationships with his three sons, his wife, and his parents and in-laws. [The examining psychologist] also extensively reported on McGreal's version of the many incidents the department cited as problematic. [The psychologist]'s "diagnostic impression" of McGreal was that he displayed narcissistic, paranoid and histrionic traits, not rising to the level of a personality disorder. . . . In other words, McGreal suffered from no identifiable mental illness. (p. 669)

The *Pettus* court also cited public policy reasons for restricting the disclosure of private information to the minimum necessary to answer the employer's referral question:

If a health care professional were free to give an employer all the details of an employee's personal life and physical and mental health as revealed during a disability evaluation, there would be a great disincentive to full and honest disclosure by the employee. Indeed, in many cases of psychological disability, there would be a strong disincentive to the employee to seek professional help at all. Neither employees nor employers would be well served by such a rule. Employers would not get an accurate evaluation of their employees' ability to work (and entitlement to medical leave), employees would not get the benefit of a candid health assessment by the examiner, and employees would in some cases not get the health care they need to be productive workers and members of society. Our holding is, thus, firmly rooted in both the plain language of the [Confidentiality of Medical Information Act] and in sound considerations of public policy. (pp. 433–434)

Much of the information collected by the examiners in *Pettus* and *McGreal* was appropriate subject matter to explore in the respective fitness examination. The problems were in the scope and details of the written reports. We will explore these topics further in Chapters 6 and 7 in the contexts of data interpretation, data integration, and report writing.

One of the reasons it is so important to stay abreast of the statutes and case law in one's jurisdiction is that, despite the significant impact that decisions such as *Pettus* and *McGreal* have had on evolving standards of practice in fitness evaluations (e.g., American Psychological Association, 2018), they are controlling only in their respective jurisdictions. So, before writing a terse evaluation, or one limited to just a discussion of functional abilities, it is important to note that other courts have given less credence to practitioners who restrict their reports to conclusory findings. As one example, consider fitness evaluation reports reviewed by the Merit Systems Protection Board (MSPB), a quasi-judicial agency that hears appeals from employees of the US Government who are terminated or suspended without pay for 14 days or longer. This is a forum in which a clinician offering a merely conclusory report will likely do a disservice to the organizational client and the employee. In a landmark case, the MSPB established four criteria for weighing the credibility of an expert report:

(a) whether the opinion was based on a medical examination;
(b) whether the opinion provides a reasoned explanation for its findings as distinct from mere conclusory assertions;
(c) the qualifications of the expert rendering the opinion; and
(d) the extent and duration of the expert's familiarity with the treatment of the appellant (*Bahm v. Department of the Air Force*, 1988, p. 8).

These criteria also affected the plight of Collister Slater (*Collister Slater v. Department of Homeland Security*, 2008), who was employed as a police officer in the Federal Protective Service, Immigration and Customs Enforcement. He was removed from his position when an agency-retained physician determined that he had serious medical problems. Slater appealed. The hearing officer was not impressed with brief letters that Slater produced stating that he was medically qualified to perform his duties, characterizing these submissions as "having very little probative value. They are entirely conclusory, devoid of any medical documentation or explanation in support of their conclusions" (p. 16). Slater produced another report, which was described as "a thorough, detailed, and relevant medical opinion addressing the medical issues of the agency's removal action" (p. 16). Placing considerable weight on the report that documented the reasoning behind the medical opinions, along with the absence of any direct medical testimony during the hearing, the hearing officer found that the employing agency failed to meet its burden of showing that "the appellant has a disqualifying medical condition or that it poses a reasonable probability of causing substantial harm" (p. 17). Consequently, Slater was restored to his former position.

Much of the case law we have reviewed thus far arose in contexts in which there was conflict or mistrust between the employee and employer. On the other hand, we have received many referrals in which a fitness evaluation is clearly indicated and with which the employee agrees. When there is a high level of mutual trust between the employee and employer, the employee often asks that personal information supporting the psychologist's findings and conclusions also be included in the summary report, believing that the employer has their best interest at heart and will use the information to facilitate reasonable accommodations or grant other considerations. Although information that goes beyond conclusory statements may be helpful for the employee and organization, or improve the probative value of a report, an evaluating psychologist should be careful: After information is released, it cannot be recalled.

Additional Aspects of Privacy

Expectations of privacy should also be considered when disclosing written reports of occupationally mandated psychological evaluations to third parties. Another important aspect of privacy involves discovery requests that may arise from tort ligation, typically involving reports and records generated in the course of a suitability or fitness evaluation. In such cases, a reasonable expectation of privacy can also control the release of information obtained from a prior mental health examination. Indeed, the leading case on patient–therapist privilege arose from a US Supreme Court case (*Jaffee v. Redmond,* 1996) in which the plaintiff in a wrongful death case attempted to discover the psychotherapy records of Officer Redmond, who had used deadly force. When the officer did not authorize the release of her records, the jurors received an instruction from the trial court judge, advising them to consider the nonproduction of records in the worst possible light toward Redmond, strongly suggesting to the jury that Redmond had something to hide. In this holding, the US Supreme Court formally recognized the patient–psychotherapist privilege and ordered that Redmond be given a new trial without the prejudicial jury instruction.

Similarly, in a Florida case (*Gavins v. Rezaie,* 2017), a plaintiff alleging excessive force sought to compel Officer Aryo Rezaie and the City of South Miami to release the officer's preemployment psychological evaluation records, hoping they would enhance the plaintiff's excessive force claim. The defendants objected for a number of reasons, including Rezaie's claim that he believed that its contents would remain confidential. Citing *Jaffee,* the court ruled that Rezaie's expectation of privacy was sufficient to bar release of the report. In denying the plaintiff's motion, the court also relied on *Caver v. City of Trenton* (2000), in which a New Jersey court held that police candidates had an expectation of privacy, and to rule adversely to the defendant would be detrimental to public policy. Adopting the finding of the *Caver* court, the Florida court held:

> The Court recognizes that the public has an interest in knowing whether their police are mentally fit for the job, but disclosure of actual psychological records is not necessary and would have a chilling effect on frankness between patient and psychologist. If police officers are not completely honest when speaking to a mental health professional, it will make it more difficult for the mental health professional to accurately evaluate the mental status of a police officer, and to ensure public safety. (2000, p. 163)

Accordingly, the court found that the officer had a reasonable expectation of privacy and denied the discovery motion on this basis.

Employer Access to Private Healthcare Records

An employer's access to private healthcare records is an issue that may arise during suitability and fitness evaluations. As you may recall, the examiner conducting a postconditional offer examination of a police candidate may request any medical records deemed relevant. On the other hand, after an employee is hired, if the employee refuses a request to disclose those records, the issue is typically resolved utilizing a balancing test that weighs the employer's interest in obtaining the records against the employee's right to privacy.

Employers and psychologists have generally been supported in their requests for medical records when they can articulate a reasonable need and the scope of the requested records is limited (EEOC, 2011).[16] The case that provides perhaps the clearest discussion of a balancing test between explicit Fourth Amendment rights to freedom from unreasonable searches and seizures (and implied rights to privacy) may be *Yin v. State of California* (1996).

Cecelia Yin worked as a tax auditor for the State of California Employment Development Department. In the 5 years preceding this action, Yin used significantly more sick leave than her peers, and she also fell below average in the number of audits completed and the amount of additional tax liability she discovered. In February 1994, after a long stint of absences from work, her supervisor asked her to submit to a state-selected physician for an independent medical examination (IME). Yin refused, retained a lawyer, and filed suit against the state, asking the court to bar her employer from requiring her to release her medical records, participating in an IME, or disciplining her for not doing so.

The federal district court concluded that the request for an IME to determine whether Yin had a disability was permitted under the ADA's business necessity standard and, furthermore, that it did not violate her Fourth Amendment rights. Yin appealed to the Ninth Circuit, which addressed the question of whether compelling an employee "with a prolonged and egregious history of absenteeism and a record of on-the-job illnesses to undergo a fitness-for-duty medical examination" (p. 866) violated either the ADA or her rights under the Fourth Amendment.

The court held that a government employer's intrusion on an employee's Fourth Amendment rights does not require probable cause, as would be the case in a criminal investigation, but a balancing test, in which the reasonableness of the search is determined by "weighing the privacy interests of the individual against the government's interest in the search" (p. 870). In applying this balancing test, several factors (other than probable cause) were considered. These included Yin's long history of illness, her participation in a collective bargaining agreement that allowed necessary medical examinations, and her decreased work productivity. The court emphasized that these factors *diminished* (but did not eliminate) her right to privacy, with the result being that the government prevailed in the balancing analysis and that the demand for her records and participation in an IME was deemed lawful.

Similarly, the holding in *Thomas v. Corwin* (2007) upheld the termination of a Kansas City civilian police employee who refused to execute a release of information allowing the department-retained psychologist to obtain the specific medical records he believed were necessary to complete the evaluation. The appellate court noted that the "medical examination or inquiry is no broader or more intrusive than necessary"[17] (p. 528) and the employee's "refusal to cooperate with the reasonable requirements of her FFD evaluation and her violation of KCPD's rules of conduct provided the defendants with legitimate, nondiscriminatory reasons to terminate [her]" (p. 529).

In *Thompson v. City of Arlington* (1993), a federal appellate court went even further, granting the police department administration the right to ongoing access to Officer Thompson's medical records, even after she passed a fitness evaluation conducted by a psychologist retained by the City. The court held that the employer had a legitimate interest in monitoring the mental health of Thompson. Regarding the fact that their appointed psychologist found Thompson fit for duty, the court stated, in part:

Defendants were not obligated to defer to the opinions of the mental health specialist as to whether Plaintiff was fit to return to regular duty. Those opinions would be but factors competent officials of City could take into account in making their decision. Total reliance on opinions of the healthcare providers would carry with it the obvious risk of deception caused by therapeutic-type recommendations, made in the interest of the patient rather than the goal of insuring that the objectives of the police department have been satisfied. . . . [The] City and its officials, who have special knowledge of the factors that enter into whether a particular person should serve as a police officer, are better equipped than healthcare providers, or other healthcare experts, to determine whether plaintiff should return to regular duty. (pp. 1147–1148)

The court thus held that the City's intrusion into the plaintiff's medical records was "reasonably warranted for the achievement of a compelling governmental interest that [could] be achieved by no less intrusive, more reasonable means" (p. 1151).

On the other hand, an administrative decision to not disclose records to a psychologist carries its own set of risks. In an unpublished decision, *Colon v. City of Newark* (2006), the City was found liable under a § 1983 claim when it failed to disclose relevant disciplinary history to the examining psychologist charged with conducting a fitness evaluation, which occurred *before* the constitutional injury was inflicted. The federal appellate court refused to reverse the jury's verdict that found the City of Newark liable for the beating of the plaintiff, Carlos Colon, who was incarcerated when Officer Bergus beat him in the face and stomach and put him in a choke hold. At the time of this event, Bergus was working in an unarmed position in the jail because he had been accused of domestic violence. Before being assigned to the jail, he underwent a fitness evaluation by a psychologist, who found him fit for duty. However, this opinion "was rendered without benefit of Bergus' previous psychological evaluations or past history of disciplinary charges and proceedings" (no pagination), including a past accusation of domestic violence and another episode of assault. The examining psychologist indicated that, if he had known this background information, "he would have recommended . . . that Bergus be restricted to a desk job where he would not interact with the public, receive counseling for six months, and then a re-evaluation" (no pagination).

It is important to advise our organizational clients that, despite the validity of psychological assessment methods, and consistent with the "best practice" standard, we also must rely on relevant collateral information to understand the individual we are examining. For this reason, we always ask the referring agency for past performance ratings and any record (e.g., investigative findings) of misconduct. In considering these cases together, psychologists are advised to always request the examinee's pertinent personnel and medical records held by the employer and, if they cannot obtain them, declare these omissions as a limiting factor in their report.

BEST PRACTICE

We advise psychologists to always request the examinee's pertinent personnel and medical records held by the employer and, if you cannot obtain them, declare these omissions as a limiting factor in your report.

The Right to Access One's Own Personal Health Information

Personal health information is an integral part of any police suitability or fitness evaluation. When applicants, candidates, or employees seek to access those records from the examiner, whether limited to the written report or inclusive of the underlying records and assessment data, knowledge of state and federal statutes pertaining to a person's right to access their own personal health information is essential.

Health Insurance Portability and Accountability Act, Privacy Rule, Title 45, Subtitle A, Subchapter C, Part 164, Subpart E

This legislation was signed into law in 1996 by President Clinton. The main objectives of the Health Insurance Portability and Accountability Act (HIPAA) were to remove the preexisting

condition clause from insurance policies (i.e., to facilitate portability), to prevent fraud and abuse, and to achieve "administrative
simplification." It is under this third objective that federal privacy provisions were created that would establish rules for the use
and disclosure of protected health information. The law affected
providers who either store or transmit healthcare information
electronically. Such healthcare providers are considered "covered
entities" under the law.

HIPAA's control is limited to covered entities, which
excludes the employer—an important point for evaluators to note.
Therefore, unless other local laws or agreements (such as a collective bargaining agreement) prohibit or control the release of information, the employer may provide the examiner with medical
records it has collected for an employee, including those kept in a
separate medical file, because the employer is normally not a covered entity and the examiner is acting as its agent.

As the law was being implemented, some forensic authorities
presented well-thought-out arguments that HIPAA does not apply
in those instances in which one is providing a forensic evaluation for
a court or an administrative agency (Connell & Koocher, 2003).
After all, according to this argument, the forensic provider is not
providing healthcare, the employer is the paying party, and the
purpose of such evaluations is to render an analysis of functional
abilities relevant to the job, not to diagnose. The problem with this
reasoning is that HIPAA does not distinguish between treatment
and forensic or other evaluative services. Instead, HIPAA indicates
that after a healthcare provider has stored or transmitted health
information electronically (e.g., insurance forms), they become a
covered entity, regardless of the other types of service they may
perform. Therefore, it appears that almost all psychologists who
would be called on to perform suitability or fitness evaluations are
covered entities.[18]

HIPAA grants the right of an individual to inspect or obtain a
copy of protected health information with several exceptions. The
exceptions that are most likely to arise in the course of an occupationally mandated psychological evaluation are subdivided into
unreviewable and reviewable grounds for denial.

UNREVIEWABLE GROUNDS FOR DENIAL

Under this category, there are five exceptions. The three exceptions most likely to present to a psychologist or psychiatrist providing employment evaluations are

(a) information compiled in reasonable anticipation of, or for use in, a civil, criminal, or administrative action or proceeding [§ 164.524(a)(ii)];

(b) protected health information that is contained in records subject to the Privacy Act, 5 U.S.C. § 552a, if the denial of access under the Privacy Act would meet the requirements of that law [§ 164.524(2)(iv)][19]; and

(c) protected health information obtained from someone other than a healthcare provider under a promise of confidentiality if the access requested would be reasonably likely to reveal the source of the information [§ 164.524(2)(v)].

REVIEWABLE GROUNDS FOR DENIAL

HIPAA procedures for reviewable denials of requests to release protected health information allow "the individual . . . to have the denial reviewed by a licensed healthcare professional who is designated by the covered entity to act as a reviewing official and who did not participate in the original decision to deny" [§ 164.524(4)]. This category contains three exceptions. The single exception under this category likely to present during an employment evaluation occurs when:

> The protected health information makes reference to another person (unless such other person is a healthcare provider) and a licensed healthcare professional has determined, in the exercise of professional judgment, that the access requested is reasonably likely to cause substantial harm to such other person. [§ 164.524(3)]

Practitioners who deny access to records for one of the various "reviewable grounds for denial" are required to refer the review to a licensed healthcare professional for a decision on the request [§ 164.524(d)(4)]. If a practitioner receives a request for access, they generally have 30 days to permit access or to issue a written explanation for the denial of access, or to offer an explanation as to why more time is needed to respond [§ 164.524(b)]. HIPAA also provides that a covered entity:

> may provide the individual with a summary of the protected health information requested, in lieu of providing access to the protected health information or may provide an explanation of the protected health information to which access has been provided, if: (A) the individual agrees in advance to such a summary or explanation; and (B) the individual agrees in advance to the fees imposed, if any, by the covered entity for such summary or explanation. [§ 164.524(c)(2)(iii)]

A test user should also note that, under another provision of HIPAA [42 U.S.C. 1320d-1 § 1172(e)], test materials (e.g., question booklets or test manuals) may not be subject to release to the extent that they comprise confidential commercial information or a trade secret.

BEWARE

Respond to an examinee's request for disclosure of their records within 30 days, even in those cases in which it appears that the request is exempted by law.

BEST PRACTICE

Before releasing information to a third party, advise the examinee and the retaining party of the request or subpoena because those parties may have a legitimate independent right to resist the request or demand.

We urge the evaluator not to ignore requests for disclosure of their data, even in those cases in which it appears that the examinee's request is exempted by law. As noted earlier, whether an exemption applies or not, failure to respond timely to a request (e.g., within 30 days under HIPAA) may expose the examiner to additional penalties and costs. Of course, before a psychologist releases such information to a third party, the subject of the evaluation and the retaining party should be advised of the request or subpoena because those parties may have a legitimate independent right to resist the request or demand. It is important to consider that it is still a matter of unsettled law as to whether an employee can waive particular federal access rights when they initially consent to the evaluation. If you receive a records request and HIPAA applies to your professional practice, we recommend reading the pertinent HIPAA sections in their entirety, advising the organizational client of the request, and considering a consultation with legal counsel—who is retained to act in *your* interests—before releasing the records.

State Confidentiality Acts

State confidentiality acts may grant greater access than HIPAA requires. Recalling that federal statutes set the floor, some states have allowed access to materials that are otherwise exempted by HIPAA from disclosure requirements. When it comes to access to records generated by a licensed healthcare practitioner, the definition of "patient" becomes broader than that

> **BEWARE**
>
> If you receive a records request and HIPAA applies to your professional practice, we recommend reading the pertinent HIPAA sections in their entirety, advising the organizational client of the request, and considering a consultation with legal counsel—who is retained to act in *your* interests—before releasing the records.

provided under various tort liability theories, and often includes individuals being evaluated by a psychologist. As one example, in *Cleghorn v. Hess* (1993) the Nevada Supreme Court ruled that police officer candidates are "patients" under Nevada Revised Statute § 629.061 and, therefore, are entitled to access records associated with the suitability evaluation.

Freedom of Information Statutes

The federal Freedom of Information Act (FOIA; 5 U.S.C. § 552) is legislation designed to promote openness in government by granting the citizenry access to federal government records. In police psychology, this act (along with its state progenies) is encountered most often in the context of job candidates who have been rejected for safety-sensitive positions based on the outcome of their psychological evaluations. In such cases, they have argued that FOIA laws authorize access to the psychological evaluation and underlying test data. While the federal FOIA is applicable to federal agencies, many states have enacted similar legislation, which often parallels the federal statute. Like HIPAA, access under FOIA is not absolute and includes a number of exceptions to access. Under the federal act, if a request for information is rejected by the reviewing agency, those with legal standing can appeal to the federal district court, which adjudges the request de novo.[20]

One of the widely recognized exceptions to access pertains to "examination data." It is common for the agency to argue that release of the material is contrary to public policy because the information, if disseminated, would give other candidates for the position an unfair advantage in future examinations. State and federal courts have reached different opinions on this question (e.g., *Patton v. Federal Bureau of Investigation*, 1985; *Schroeder v. City of Detroit*, 1997; *Stamford v. Freedom of Information Commission*, 1999).

Discovery Under Administrative Proceedings

Employees, unlike applicants and candidates, have a property interest in their position, and the US Supreme Court has held that government employees are granted a due process right to a pretermination hearing upon receiving notification that they are subject to termination or serious disciplinary action (*Cleveland Board of Education v. Loudermill*, 1985). This hearing allows the employee to hear the "charges" against them and to present their side of the story—that is, to present evidence that refutes or mitigates the allegations. In a *Loudermill* hearing, a fitness-for-duty report may be one of the pieces of evidence that the agency provides the employee in support of the proposed action.

Attorney–Client Privilege

Attorney–client privilege may trump all of these statutes (in most states). There may be occasions in which a practitioner is retained to reevaluate an aggrieved candidate or employee, or to evaluate the work of another mental health expert who performed an employer-mandated evaluation. In such cases, and whenever possible, we recommend that the psychologist be retained by the attorney, not by the examinee. Psychologists retained by an attorney are typically working under attorney–client privilege, which is not waived until the attorney makes the decision to do so or engages in some other action that dissolves the privilege.

While working under an attorney–client privilege, the attorney controls the dissemination of information that you have obtained. The attorney–client privilege is so highly regarded in the United States that in most states it trumps mandatary reporting requirements, such as those that are triggered when a healthcare provider learns of child or elder abuse, or by duty to warn or protect statutes (e.g., *Elijah W. v. Superior Court*, 2013).

BEST PRACTICE

There may be occasions in which you are retained to reevaluate an aggrieved candidate or employee, or to evaluate the work of another mental health expert who performed an employer-mandated evaluation. In such cases, and whenever possible, we recommend that you be retained by the attorney, not by the examinee.

Genetic Information Nondiscrimination Act, Title II

The Genetic Information Nondiscrimination Act of 2008 (GINA), Title II (pertaining to employers) prohibits, with few exceptions, the collection of genetic information of applicants, candidates, and employees by government agencies, private employers with 15 or more employees, or their agents. While the ADA focuses on preventing discrimination based on an individual's *manifest* impairment or conditions regarded as a disability, GINA seeks to prevent discrimination on the basis of conditions that have the genetic *potential* to occur.

Psychologists and those who conduct medical examinations are bound by a broad definition of genetic information that includes not only the results of genetic tests, but also the medical history of family members by blood or adoption [29 C.F.R. Part 1635.3(b)].[21] Based on this definition, covered entities shall not request, require, or purchase genetic information about an applicant/candidate or employee. GINA exempts information about an individual's (or their family member's) age or gender, or a disclosure that an individual presently has a disease (which may be protected by the ADA).[22] Even though family history for psychiatric disorders may be more predictive of psychiatric impairment than many psychological test scores, Congress granted no exception for those evaluating job candidates or employees engaged in highly dangerous or other safety-sensitive professions.

There are six exceptions in which an employer (or its agent) can legally receive genetic information, although such information still cannot be used to make employment decisions. The three exceptions most pertinent to a practitioner conducting a suitability or fitness evaluation include

(a) inadvertent acquisition, also known as the "water fountain exception" (such as when an employee is overheard telling a coworker about genetic information) and when an employee discloses genetic information in the course of requesting reasonable accommodation;

(b) information disclosed in the course of applying for benefits under the FMLA, if kept in a separate file by the employer; and

(c) inadvertent acquisition from sources like public media or reading a news story (e.g., obituary of family member), but only if the employer does not use pubic media to search for such information.

Although complaints under GINA are relatively rare (Rothstein et al., 2015), violators often end up paying hefty fines or judgments (e.g., *Lowe v. Atlas Logistics Group Retail Services*, 2015). In our practices, we have instituted several measures to foster compliance with GINA. We explicitly instruct candidates and incumbents not to provide any psychiatric or medical history about their relatives. These admonitions are printed on the disclosures and biographical

BEST PRACTICE

We have instituted several measures to foster compliance with GINA. We explicitly instruct candidates and incumbents not to provide any psychiatric or medical history about their relatives. These admonitions are printed on the disclosures and biographical forms candidates complete before the evaluation.

forms candidates complete before their evaluations. Even after these admonitions, we sometimes still have to remind examinees not to provide this information when they have made unprompted disclosures. When we receive such disclosures, we do not record them other than to note that GINA-prohibited information was inadvertently acquired.

The EEOC also recommends that when evaluators seek medical records, they advise the records custodian that the evaluation is for employment purposes and, therefore, to redact or withhold all family medical or family psychiatric history. Despite these advisements, almost all healthcare providers send us GINA-prohibited material. Our experience does not appear to be unique. Rothstein et al. (2015) observed that medical providers rarely redact genetic information. Accordingly, when we have occasion to request medical records for employees or candidates, we include the following admonishment, which contains language copied verbatim from the EEOC website:

> The Genetic Information Nondiscrimination Act of 2008 (GINA) prohibits employers and other entities covered by GINA Title II from requesting or requiring genetic information of an individual or family member of the individual, except as specifically allowed by this law. To comply with this law, we are asking that you not provide any genetic information when responding to this request for medical information. "Genetic information" as defined by GINA, includes an individual's family medical history, the results of an individual's or family member's genetic tests, the fact that an individual or an individual's family member sought or received genetic services, and genetic information of a fetus carried by an individual or an individual's family member or an embryo lawfully held by an individual or family member receiving assistive reproductive services.[23]

A covered entity that uses language such as this has an affirmative defense under 29 C.F.R. Part 1635.8 that the receipt of genetic information was inadvertent, as long as it is not used to make employment decisions.

Family Medical Leave Act

The FMLA of 1993 allows up to 12 weeks of unpaid medical leave within any 12-month period. To be eligible for federal FMLA benefits (state leave statutes may include more liberal eligibility criteria), the employee must have been employed for 1 year and worked at least 1,250 hours in the past 12 months. The act covers government and private employers with at least 50 employees. The employee is able to take leave to assist themselves or another family member with pregnancy, adoption, or foster care. To obtain leave, an eligible employee must present a certification completed by the employee's healthcare provider that describes (a) the date the health condition or illness commenced, (b) the likely duration of the condition, (c) relevant medical facts that support the diagnosis/condition, and (d) a statement attesting that, because of the medical condition, the employee is unable to perform essential job functions. Upon returning to work, the employee is "entitled to be restored to his or her position of employment or an equivalent position" [29 U.S.C. § 2614(a)(1)]. An employer may require an employee taking FMLA leave to provide certification from the employee's healthcare provider that the employee is able to resume work, as long as this requirement is uniformly imposed on other employees and the policy is not superseded by a collective bargaining agreement [29 U.S.C. § 2614(a)(4)]. This certification is frequently referred to as a "return-to-work letter" and typically includes a statement that the medical condition has resolved or improved and that the employee is able to perform the essential job functions.

In *Albert v. Runyon* (1998), Deborah Albert, who worked for the US Postal Service as a district manager in the Boston area, developed depression and commenced FMLA leave in September 1997. Her psychologist advised the Postal Service that Albert was able to return to work as of December 1, 1997. The human resources manager, however, deemed the return-to-work letter to be inadequate and ordered Albert to participate in a fitness evaluation conducted by an employer-designated physician *before* reinstatement. Albert objected, arguing that the Postal Service had no authority to order such an examination. Albert brought suit in US

District Court in the District of Massachusetts, asking that she be restored to her job and that a permanent injunction prohibit the Postal Service from requiring a fitness evaluation.

The court held that the psychologist's certification was sufficient because it contained the requisite elements for FMLA eligibility, and that Albert must be reinstated per the plain language of the statute. However, the court also concluded:

> she is not entitled to the full scope of relief she has requested. The FMLA cannot support a permanent injunction preventing the Postal Service from ever conditioning her employment on such an examination. Once Albert returns to work, the Service may order her to undergo a fitness-for-duty examination if it has sufficient reason under the ADA/Rehabilitation Act and its own agency regulations. (p. 69)

Sufficient reasons under which an employer may order further evaluation *after* reinstating an employee include the following:

1. The employer "has reason to doubt the validity of the provider's certification" (p. 61)—noting, however, that the criteria justifying doubt about the validity of medical certification are "not well-established" (p. 65).
2. The employer can establish that a fitness evaluation would have been ordered had the employee not taken leave.
3. The employee's "post-reinstatement behavior provides a reason for doing so" (p. 66).

In a more recent court case (*White v. County of Los Angeles*, 2014), investigator Susan White argued that her return-to-work certification was sufficient to alleviate the need for a fitness evaluation that was anticipated before she took FMLA leave. White secured a permanent injunction preventing her employer from requiring a medical reevaluation of her based on her prior conduct, or from charging her with insubordination for failing to comply with the medical reevaluation. The County appealed, and the appellate court addressed the question of whether White's return-to-work certification foreclosed the employer's right to obtain an evaluation after her reinstatement. The court affirmed that ordering the employee for a second opinion evaluation is not permitted until the employee is reinstated, but such reinstatement could be accomplished by putting White back on the payroll and duty-stationing her at home pending the outcome of the independent fitness evaluation. "The question presented by the instant case is whether, if the employer is not satisfied with the employee's health care provider's certification, the employer may restore the employee to work, but then seek its own evaluation of the employee's fitness for duty at its own expense. We conclude that it may" (p. 694). A separate California law stipulates certain qualifications for psychologists and psychiatrists who perform suitability or fitness evaluations of California peace officers, and the court held that the employer is not required to accept a return-to-work letter from a treating healthcare provider who does not meet those minimum qualifications.[24] We discuss these requirements further in Chapter 2.

Albert v. Runyon and *White v. County of Los Angeles* offer some important considerations. The FMLA will not shield the employee who uses the act to escape a fitness evaluation. The law clearly indicates that an employer is authorized to order an evaluation if the need is job-related and consistent with business necessity, based on events that occur either before or after taking FMLA, but this can occur only *after* the employee has been reinstated. We have encountered employers that refer employees for fitness evaluations *before* they have been reinstated from FMLA leave, without awareness that they are violating the law. Accordingly, we recommend that the examining psychologist specifically ask if the employee is on FMLA leave. If so, the evaluation must be deferred until the employee has been reinstated to their former (or equivalent) position, even if this involves being on paid assignment at home.

Federal Employment Contexts—5 C.F.R. Part 339

This mandate is applicable to federal employees who work under the auspices of the US Office of Personnel Management (OPM), which includes various law enforcement agencies, such as Federal Protective Service, Immigration and Customs, Department of

Veterans Affairs Police, and Marshals Service. In such cases, 5 C.F.R. Part 339.301(e) permits employees to be referred for a psychological or psychiatric evaluation under either of two circumstances:

(a) when a general medical examination reveals "no physical explanation for behavior or actions that may affect the safe and efficient performance of the applicant or employee, the safety of others, and/or the vulnerability of business operation and information systems to potential threats"; or

(b) a psychiatric examination or psychological assessment is specifically called for in a position having medical standards or subject to a medical evaluation program established under this part.

Psychological assessment authorized by either of these conditions "may only be used to make inquiry into a person's mental fitness as it directly relates to successfully performing the duties of the position without significant risk to the applicant or employee or others, and/or to the vulnerability of business operation and information systems to potential threats" [5 C.F.R. Part 339.301(e) (2)]. Any report of such an assessment "must be made available to the applicant or employee" [5 C.F.R. Part 339.305(a)].

Uniformed Services Employment and Reemployment Rights Act

Curran, Holt, and Afanador (2017) estimate that 20% of police officer applicants have prior military experience. Under the Uniformed Services Employment and Reemployment Rights Act (USERRA), qualified veterans are eligible for four basic entitlements:

(a) reemployment after military service (38 U.S.C. § 4312);

(b) reinstatement to the same position "or a position of like seniority, status and pay" (38 U.S.C. § 4313);

(c) freedom from discrimination by an employer because of their military service (38 U.S.C. § 4311); and

(d) not being fired without cause during the first year of reinstatement (38 U.S.C. § 4316).

When the employer believes that a returning service member may be harboring psychological issues that could affect that person's ability to safely and effectively execute their civilian duties, the law is clear: Similar to the employer's obligation under the FMLA, a returning service member must be reinstated to their former position before an employer can order them to participate in any medical or psychological examination (e.g., *Petty v. Metro. Gov't of Nashville-Davidson County*, 2008).[25]

BEST PRACTICE

We recommend that the examining psychologist specifically ask if an employee remains on USERRA or FMLA leave. If so, the evaluation may need to be deferred until the employee has been reinstated to their former (or equivalent) position, even if this involves being on paid assignment at home.

Civil Rights Acts of 1964 and 1991

The Civil Rights Act of 1964 is also a labor law, which bars employment discrimination based on race, religion, sex, or national origin. It applies to public or private employers with 15 or more employees. The Civil Rights Act of 1964 also gave birth to the EEOC, which developed guidelines to help identify discriminatory practices in employment situations. One form of discrimination is called *disparate impact,* which protects employees from an employment process that discriminates against one of the protected classes, even without the *intent* to discriminate. The doctrine of disparate impact should not be confused with *disparate treatment,* which involves intentionally inflicted discrimination on persons belonging to a protected class.

In an alleged case of disparate (or adverse) impact in hiring decisions, the initial burden of production is on the plaintiff to demonstrate a statistical disparity between the employment rate of the protected and unprotected classes. If the statistical disparity is demonstrated, the burden then shifts to the defendant (employer), who can either show that the statistical analysis was erroneous or, if the practice does discriminate, that it is valid (i.e., job-related) and consistent with business necessity (see also *Griggs v. Duke Power*

Co., 1971). After this defense is offered, the burden shifts back to the plaintiff to show that alternative measures could be equally effective in addressing business necessity without having a disparate impact.

Psychologists can usually minimize the risk of protracted litigation, along with the shifting burdens of production, by (a) avoiding disparate impact on persons from protected classes, and (b) using a battery composed of tests and measures with demonstrated validity (and an absence of adverse impact) within the context that they are being used.

Despite the intent of Title VII of the Civil Rights Act of 1964, it was infrequently applied. In 1989, the death knell came to Title VII with Congress's disagreement with the US Supreme Court's holding in *Wards Cove v. Atonio* (1989), which shifted the burden of proving business necessity from the employer to the employee. An additional driving force for amending the Civil Rights Act of 1964, according to Tenopyr (1996), arose from a US Department of Labor practice during the 1980s in which the scores of applicants on the General Aptitude Test Battery were adjusted upward for African Americans to equate with the means of whites. When news of this practice reached Congress, language was included in the Civil Rights Act to prohibit this practice. As a result, Congress passed the Civil Rights Act of 1991, which also amended Title VII by adding:

> It shall be an unlawful employment practice for a respondent, in connection with the selection or referral of applicants or candidates for employment or promotion, to adjust the scores of, use different cutoff scores for, or otherwise alter the results of, employment related tests on the basis of race, color, religion, sex, or national origin. (§ 106)

This is significant because psychologists conducting suitability evaluations now must avoid use of psychological tests that rely on gender- and race-specific norms.

Accordingly, psychologists engaged in employment or promotion evaluations should ensure that their assessment batteries include tests with demonstrated validity for the purpose for which they are being used. Tests that do not allow the option of using combined-gender norms, or that use separate racial norms, should be avoided in matters of hiring or promotion. It is also important to note that there is no language in Title VII that prohibits the use of gender-based norms when used outside of hiring and promotional purposes. Accordingly, a test that uses gender-specific norms may be appropriate in a fitness evaluation and does not appear to be illegal in this context because examinees in fitness evaluations are not "applicants or candidates for employment or promotion."

BEST PRACTICE

Psychologists engaged in employment or promotion evaluations should ensure that their assessment batteries include tests with demonstrated validity for the purpose for which they are being used.

Notes

1. Our use of this term is identical to its meaning in the *Professional Practice Guidelines for Occupationally Mandated Psychological Evaluations* (OMPE Guidelines, American Psychological Association, 2018). It encompasses evaluations using any procedure, inquiry, or test that seeks information about an individual's physical or mental impairments or health and includes, but is not limited to, psychological tests that are designed to identify a mental disorder or impairment.

2. Throughout this volume we refer to the *United States Rules of Civil Procedure and Rules of Evidence*, which are promulgated by the US Supreme Court and apply to federal court proceedings. Although many states and English common law countries have similar rules—oftentimes adopted verbatim from the federal model—the reader is reminded that rules in local jurisdictions may be different in important ways from the federal rules.

3. Alaska, Arizona, California, Florida, Hawaii, Illinois, Louisiana, Montana, South Carolina, and Washington have explicit privacy provisions in their state constitutions (National Conference of State Legislatures, 2017).

4. An *injunction* is a court order that compels a person to carry out a certain act—in this case ordering the Board of Education to desist from forcing women to take leave before it was medically necessary.

5. The Supreme Court rarely reverses itself. In this case, Justices Rehnquist's and Burger's joint dissent was based on their concern that, in light of the number of cases the court had sustained supporting the

1961 decision in *Monroe v. Pape,* the majority's decision abandoned the doctrine of *stare decisis* (the doctrine of precedent).

6. See also *Minton v. Guyer* (2014) and *Woods v. Town of Danville, WV* (2010).

7. These factors apply to post-offer, preemployment evaluations only when used to deny employment to a qualified person with a disability.

8. *ADA Enforcement Guidance: Preemployment Disability-Related Questions and Medical Examinations* (1995, Question 15).

9. The appellate court noted, "While Buchanan did sign an acknowledgment in May of 1992 that he was receiving a conditional offer of employment, the document itself makes clear that the offer was not conditioned solely on a medical examination, but was instead conditioned on successful completion of 'the entire screening process,' which included 'physical and psychological examinations, a polygraph examination, a physical fitness test, an assessment board, and an extensive background investigation'" (p. 199). The lower court awarded Buchanan $300K in damages and attorney's fees—not a modest judgment based on 1996 prices.

10. 42 U.S.C. § 12112(d)(3) (1994); 29 C.F.R. § 1630.14(b) (1998).

11. At least two federal appeals courts have supported the EEOC's position. In a Seventh Circuit decision, the court held that "additional medical tests do not render the offer insufficient" (*O'Neal v. City of New Albany,* 2002, p. 1009). More recently, the Ninth Circuit held that requiring follow-up medical evaluations (paid by the employer, not the candidate) when medically related to information obtained from all candidates "would appear to be a necessary implication of allowing employers to conduct medical examinations—it would be an odd and incomplete medical exam that could not include follow-up inquiries or testing based on red flags raised in the initial exam" (*EEOC v. BNSF Railway Company,* 2018, p. 19).

12. 42 U.S.C. § 12112(b)(6)(1994); 29 C.F.R. § 1630.10 and 1630.14(b) (3)(1998).

13. See the EEOC Enforcement Guidance response to Question 5, https://www.eeoc.gov/policy/docs/guidance-inquiries.html.

14. The US Supreme Court has noted the psychological demands placed on peace officers, even when discussing subject matter *not* related to employee issues. In a case involving a claim of excessive force by police, the Supreme Court remarked, "The calculus of reasonableness must embody allowance for the fact that police officers are often forced to make split-second judgments—in circumstances that are tense, uncertain, and rapidly evolving—about the amount of force that is necessary in a particular situation" (*Graham v. Connor,* 1989, pp. 397–398).

15. An "arbitrary and capricious" act has been defined by one court as "one that is willful and unreasonable, without any consideration of the

facts and in total disregard of the circumstances" (*Metropolitan School District of Martinsville v. Mason*, 1983).

16. After an individual begins working, an employer may only ask disability-related questions or require medical examinations that are job-related and consistent with business necessity [29 C.F.R. § 1630.14(c)]. Generally, this means that an employer may only obtain medical information when it reasonably believes that an employee will be unable to perform the job or will pose a direct threat due to a medical condition. Medical information also may be obtained to determine whether an employee with a nonobvious disability is entitled to a requested reasonable accommodation or satisfies the criteria for using certain types of leave, such as leave under the Family and Medical Leave Act or under the employer's own sick leave policy. In all of these instances, however, the information sought *must be limited in scope.*

17. This finding by the court undoubtedly was supported by the fact that Dr. Harris requested a very narrow range of Thomas's medical records (i.e., those from May 22 to July 10, 2001). As the EEOC states in its enforcement guidance (2000), "in most situations, an employer cannot request an employee's complete medical records because they are likely to contain information unrelated to whether the employee can perform his/her essential functions or work without posing a direct threat" (p. 12).

18. Practitioners who do not store or transmit healthcare information electronically, while certainly an oddity today, are also unlikely to be able to evade HIPAA's Privacy Rule. This is because the law provides the federal floor of privacy protection, below which no state or local jurisdiction is permitted to descend. Practitioners who ignore these protections simply because they are not covered entities under the law may still be subject to tort claims or other causes of action under state law.

19. This act has control only over federal agencies. In such a case, protected records would include "testing or examination material used solely to determine individual qualifications for appointment or promotion in the Federal service, the disclosure of which would compromise the objectivity or fairness of the testing or examination process" [5 U.S.C. § 552a(k)(6)].

20. *Standing* and *de novo* are terms with legal significance. Standing is sometimes referred to as *locus standi*, and is the doctrine whereby a party must demonstrate sufficient connection with the issue or harm in order to challenge the action. The term *de novo* means "anew" or, more practically, "new trial," and thus, in the previous example, the aggrieved party and the agency must present their claims and evidence anew without regard to any determination made by the agency that has the test data.

21. Rothstein et al. (2015) note that the definition of a family member "does not mention spouses but explicitly covers dependents, including those by marriage or adoption (i.e., step and adopted children)"

referencing 29 C.F.R. § 1635.3 (2014, p. 557). We remain gun-shy about inquiring about spouses' medical history until the law becomes more settled in the appellate courts.

22. We realize that we are preaching to the choir when we observe the *huge* literature that finds significant correlations between family or genetic history and subsequent behavior problems (e.g., Milne et al., 2009). On the other hand, excluding candidates based solely on their family medical history is undoubtedly going too far. As an illustration, a law in Hong Kong prohibited applicants who had a parent with serious psychopathology from entering the police or fire services. Applicants in Hong Kong filed suit, and the law was overturned (Wong & Lieh-Mak, 2001).

23. See https://www.eeoc.gov/laws/regulations/gina-background.cfm.

24. California Penal Code § 832.05 stipulates that law enforcement employers "shall utilize a person meeting requirements set forth in subdivision (f) of Section 1031 of the Government Code, applicable to emotional and mental examinations, for any emotional and mental evaluation done in the course of the department or agency's screening of peace officer recruits or the evaluation of peace officers to determine their fitness for duty." This means that the requirements for psychologists conducting fitness evaluations in California are identical to those for preemployment screening. See California's *Peace Officer Psychological Screening Manual* (Spilberg & Corey, 2019) for a detailed discussion of those requirements.

25. Some federal agencies (e.g., Federal Bureau of Investigation, Central Intelligence Agency, or National Security Agency) are required by 38 U.S.C. § 4315 to establish protections for returning service members comparable to USERRA.

Functional Competencies   **2**

Professional standards and practice guidelines highlight the importance of practicing only within one's area of competence. But for many practitioners the difficulty in applying this principle lies in defining those competencies necessary for effective practice in a recognized specialty.

In all professions, the "half-life of knowledge" (Dubin, 1972)—an estimate of the time it takes a practicing professional, in the absence of any new learning, to become roughly half as knowledgeable or competent as needed to practice in their field (Neimeyer, Taylor, Rozensky, & Cox, 2014)—rapidly diminishes as the rate of new knowledge production increases. Neimeyer et al. estimated that the half-life of knowledge in forensic psychology, which was calculated to be 7.37 years in 2014, would decrease to 6.58 years by 2024. For police and public safety psychology, they estimated a decrease to 6.56 years from a half-life of 7.78 years. Thus, competency is not static and must be maintained through continuous study, training, and consultation.

BEST PRACTICE

Competency is not static and must be maintained through continuous study, training, and consultation.

Understanding professional competence is clouded by the absence of a universally accepted definition. Epstein and Hundert (2002) proposed that competence is the:

> habitual and judicious use of communication, knowledge, technical skills, clinical reasoning, emotions, values, and reflection in daily practice for the benefit of the individual and community

being served. Competence builds on a foundation of basic clinical skills, scientific knowledge, and moral development. (p. 226)

Others view professional competence as residing on a continuum. At one end, competence is equated with the minimal skills needed for licensure, representing an enforceable standard of professional conduct (Barnett, Dahl, Younggren, & Rubin, 2007). In this way, professional competence is consistent with the definition of competence used in the civil and criminal justice systems, where competence is present if one possesses the minimum capacity to knowingly and intelligently make a legal decision. On the opposite end of the continuum, competence is viewed as an aspirational goal, reflecting the desire and efforts of professional psychologists to continually improve their skill set and judgment as they strive to become better practitioners.

The *Ethical Principles of Psychologists and Code of Conduct* (EPPCC) of the American Psychological Association (APA, 2017) places the responsibility of determining competence squarely on the individual psychologist, but this view has not been universally accepted. In criticizing the self-assessment duty, some (Johnson, Barnett, Elman, Forrest, & Kaslow, 2013) have cited research showing that judgments about one's competence are not entirely objective because those who lack the requisite skills or knowledge are the *least* likely to be aware of their deficiencies. This irony has been recognized in many fields of professional endeavor and has been described as the *Kruger-Dunning effect*, which observes that those who are:

> poor performers often suffer a double curse. First, limitations in their expertise cause them to make many mistakes. Second, those exact same limitations prevent them from accurately recognizing just how mistaken their own choices are and how superior the choices of others might be. (Sheldon, Dunning, & Ames, 2014, p. 125)

Johnson et al. (2013) proposed that professionals form networks of colleagues and other relationships in order to provide peer feedback and ongoing critiques of one's work. There are several members of the Police Psychological Services Section of the International

Association of Chiefs of Police who have followed their advice and formed peer groups for this purpose (Corey, Trompetter, & Ben-Porath, 2013; Zelig & Trompetter, 2016).

Regardless of how competence is defined, practitioners must determine that they possess it before accepting a professional engagement. This should not be a problem if one has considerable training in and experience with the subject matter. It is also easy to identify those situations in which the subject matter is clearly beyond one's competence, where the practitioner knows that they do not have the experience or training to proceed. The most difficult referrals reside in the gray area, where our experience or training is limited, but the deficit might be remedied by further study or consultation with trusted and experienced peers. These gray-area situations require the most careful deliberation before accepting the referral. Mindful that the definition of competence is often situationally defined, and that self-assessment can be clouded by personal blindness or self-serving interests, we suggest using Checklist 2.1: Competency Self-Assessment, to help consider requests for services that lie in the gray area just described.

BEST PRACTICE

Regardless of how competence is defined, determine that you possess it before accepting a professional engagement.

CHECKLIST 2.1
COMPETENCY SELF-ASSESSMENT

☐ *Checkbox 1: Do I understand the applicable standards of care and standards of practice that apply to the contemplated referral?*

Heilbrun, DeMatteo, Marczyk, and Goldstein (2008) distinguished between standard of care and standard of practice. The *standard of care* is defined by a court charged with delineating the minimal acceptable level of professional performance. Falling below that standard can result in malpractice liability.[1]

On the other hand, *standards of practice* are determined by members of the profession. These standards are also described as the *industry standard* or *best practices*. Failure to conform to a standard of practice does not generally result in malpractice exposure or sanctions from one's licensing body unless the breach also violates ethical standards.

There have been occasions when we have encountered sloppy work done by professionals who argued they are *not* forensic or police psychologists and thus should be excused for their lack of adherence to applicable professional guidelines. Although adherence to standards of practice may be considered aspirational, the modern trend in professional psychology is to oblige all psychological practitioners to incorporate best practices in a particular task, regardless of their professional identity. Indeed, the most recent edition of the *Specialty Guidelines for Forensic Psychologists* (SGFP; APA, 2013) states, in pertinent part, "Application of the Guidelines does not depend on the practitioner's typical areas of practice or expertise, but rather on the service provided in the case at hand" (p. 7). Thus, professionals performing services in an area of specialty practice are expected to adhere to the standard of care and strive to use best practices, regardless of how they characterize their professional identities as psychologists. Accordingly, one should restrict oneself to professional activities in which they can articulate the standards of care and practice. Being knowledgeable of the various practice standards documents cited at the end of this chapter is a reasonable starting point.

☐ *Checkbox 2: Do I understand the essential functions of the position relevant to the contemplated referral?*

When asked to conduct an occupationally mandated psychological evaluation, our task is to evaluate the compatibility between an examinee's functional abilities and the demands of the position or assignment. It is doubtful that there is any forensic practitioner capable of competently addressing *all* referral questions that may arise in the context of *all* occupationally mandated evaluations. For example, the practitioner who is highly qualified to assess a candidate's suitability for an entry-level police officer position may not have the expertise to assess the suitability of an experienced officer to work a particular special assignment, such as deep undercover work or investigating child exploitation cases.[2] This is why it is important to be aware of the essential job functions and psychological demands of the position and not rely on intuition or media sources. When practitioners have a good understanding of the demands that accompany a given position or assignment, they can better determine if they have the skill set to evaluate an examinee's ability to safely and effectively perform those duties.

☐ *Checkbox 3: Do I have the assessment skills and tools to address the clinically relevant topic in a contemplated evaluation?*
It can be anticipated that, in the course of providing various employment-based evaluations, one will encounter referrals for which the practitioner may lack the knowledge or proper assessment tools to comprehensively assess the examinee. All sorts of issues may present, ranging from psychotropic medications to sleep disturbances, neuropsychological impairment, or other medical issues that may reside outside of one's expertise or scope of practice. Similarly, evaluating psychiatrists may need a psychologist to perform psychometric testing. In such cases, the practitioner should determine if they need to refer the matter to another professional or if the evaluation can be competently performed by using another specialist as a consultant.[3]

☐ *Checkbox 4: If I accept the referral, will my lack of experience or training cause me to be too cautious or hesitant to form a decisive opinion?*
Sometimes when practitioners venture into unfamiliar territory, they compensate by approaching the subject matter too cautiously. The resulting hesitancy or overcautiousness may prevent the formation of a decisive opinion, which would otherwise have been available to a more experienced practitioner. Accordingly, if one feels significant trepidation because of lack of familiarity with an area of practice, it is appropriate to pass on the referral or proceed with the assistance of an experienced colleague.

Conducting an Impartial, Unbiased Evaluation

Limiting involvement only to cases in which the practitioner can be impartial is another aspect of competency. It is our

BEST PRACTICE

Professionals performing services in an area of specialty practice are expected to adhere to the appropriate specialty guidelines, regardless of how they characterize their professional identities as psychologists.

2
chapter

> **BOX 2.1** Be unbiased and impartial but offer a forceful presentation of data when appropriate
>
> When conducting forensic examinations, forensic practitioners strive to be unbiased and impartial, and avoid partisan presentation of unrepresentative, incomplete, or inaccurate evidence that might mislead finders of fact. This guideline does not preclude forceful presentation of the data and reasoning upon which a conclusion or professional product is based (APA, 2013, SGFP Guideline 1.02, p. 9).

> **BOX 2.2** Fitness-for-duty guidelines and impartiality
>
> The examiner strives to remain impartial and objective and to avoid undue influences by any of the parties involved in the case (IACP, 2018a, Guideline 7.4).

job to make judgments based on relevant, reliable, and empirically based findings. Bias is different. By definition, bias represents the inclusion of systematic error based on irrelevant factors and may result in faulty conclusions and partiality. Bias comes in many forms. We will discuss the overlapping categories of explicit bias, cognitive bias, and implicit bias.

Explicit Bias

Explicit bias is the easiest to identify because it encompasses those forms of bias about which we are consciously aware. We have both declined participation in various referrals because of awareness of our explicit biases, either toward the referral source or the examinee. Obviously, we decline such cases because it places the evaluation at risk for an outcome based on a biased predisposition against or in favor of one of the parties. Failure to recuse oneself when holding an explicit bias not only is unfair to at least one of the parties but also can make it difficult to support the examiner's summary opinion if it is challenged. For

BEWARE

Failure to recuse oneself when holding an explicit bias is unfair to at least one of the parties and also can make it difficult to support the examiner's summary opinion if it is challenged.

example, in the matter of *Denhof v. City of Grand Rapids* (2007), the appellate court faulted a police chief for retaining a psychologist to perform a fitness evaluation when it was abundantly clear that the psychologist had already formed an opinion about Officer Denhof's fitness before he evaluated her. Another less obvious danger of working on a case in which one has a conscious bias is the risk of overcorrecting to avoid that bias. If one has to make a concerted effort to compensate for bias, one should strongly consider recusal.

There may also be other situations in which the evaluator does not hold bias, but an examinee may perceive differently. It can be helpful to ask the examinee if they perceive that the examiner has any conflict of interest. In this manner, some of the perceptual issues can be dealt with before the evaluation proceeds too far.[4]

Cognitive Errors and Bias

Other forms of bias are inherent in our thinking and may even be adaptive in negotiating our living environment. However, when cognitive biases enter the assessment arena, they introduce systematic error. As summarized in the *Professional Practice Guidelines for Occupationally Mandated Psychological Evaluations* (OMPE Guidelines; APA, 2018), *cognitive biases* fall into overlapping categories that include, but are not limited to

(a) *anchoring bias,* in which first impressions about a person are disproportionately weighed;

(b) *confirmatory bias,* which describes the selective search for evidence supportive of one's hypothesis at the expense of disregarding information contrary to the hypothesis;

(c) *allegiance* (also known as *adversarial* or *affinity) bias,* in which one favors the retaining party by disregarding evidence contrary to the retaining party's position; and

(d) *attribution error,* where undue weight is given to an examinee's disposition rather than relevant situational characteristics when making the assessment.

To illustrate how insidious bias may be, consider the research on allegiance bias carried out by Murrie, Boccaccini, Guarnera, and Rufino (2013). These researchers distributed a case file of a hypothetical defendant to participants attending a workshop on the administration of the Psychopathy Checklist—a tool commonly used by forensic psychologists to assess the construct of psychopathy, usually in criminal defendants or inmates. Murrie et al. found that workshop participants gave more favorable scores to the hypothetical defendant if they were told that the referral source was a defense attorney than when the subjects were told the client was a prosecutor. The only difference in the files was the attributed referral source.

Although it may be impossible to eliminate all forms of cognitive bias completely, various commentators (e.g., Borum, Otto, & Golding, 1993) have offered strategies to mitigate their effect when conducting forensic evaluations. It is important for evaluators to educate themselves regarding forms of cognitive bias in order to build mitigation strategies into their assessment approach.

Implicit Bias

In Chapter 1 we discussed the importance of avoiding referrals for fitness evaluations when it is clear that the referral source is motivated by political or other factors irrelevant to the examinee's fitness for duty. Similarly, we should also acknowledge that we all hold *implicit biases*—biases about which we have little or no awareness (Bertrand & Duflo, 2016; Nosek, Hawkins, & Frazier, 2011).

It is impossible to compensate for a bias about which one is unaware, yet implicit bias can have an extremely deleterious impact on our work product. Our colleagues in internal medicine have studied how implicit biases held by healthcare providers can result in substandard care. In a 15-year retrospective study that looked at medical interventions for New York State residents suffering from peripheral vascular disease secondary to diabetes, black patients were significantly more likely than white patients to be treated with amputation rather than an alternative salvage procedure (Stapleton et al., 2018). To attribute such practice to overt racism overlooks the likelihood that these decisions were made by conscientious healthcare professionals who would honestly deny such bias and, furthermore, assert that they were acting in the best interest of their patients when considering treatment alternatives. Research has indicated that minority group members may hold the same intragroup implicit biases as their majority group counterparts (Nosek, Banaji, & Greenwald, 2002).

Corey (2018) reviewed the literature as it pertained to the malleability of implicit bias. He cited an extensive literature indicating that implicit biases can be gradually unlearned and replaced with nonbiased associations, particularly with those who also show qualities of mindfulness, high levels of executive functioning, metacognitive ability, and self-regulation without excessive self-control. Corey further advocated the intentional selection of police officer candidates who have the cognitive resources to mitigate the deleterious effects of implicit biases because a growing body of research shows that biases are most malleable in persons with high levels of metacognitive ability. In Chapter 5, we return to this topic when we discuss promising psychometric approaches (including several easy-to-administer executive functioning measures) to identify and screen out those most likely to hold immutable implicit biases.

Checklist 2.2: Bias Self-Assessment may help us address the explicit and implicit biases we may hold. Some of these questions are easy to answer; others require considerable reflection, self-assessment, insight, and perhaps collaboration with a trusted colleague.

CHECKLIST 2.2
BIAS SELF-ASSESSMENT

☐ Do I track my outcomes over time to see if there are differences based on biographical, lifestyle, cultural demographics, or other factors that are irrelevant to adaptive functioning in the workforce?

☐ Do I have any type of multiple relationships with the organizational client or the examinee in the present or the foreseeable future? Of course, not all multiple relationships are ethically prohibited: "Multiple relationships that would not reasonably be expected to cause impairment or risk exploitation or harm are not unethical" (APA, 2017, Section 3.05).

☐ If I receive a fitness evaluation referral of an employee whom I previously evaluated, do I hold a bias based on the outcome of the previous evaluation? Past experience may introduce bias, but this is not inevitable.

☐ Am I concerned that my fitness conclusion may be influenced by an employee's popularity or political standing in the organization?

☐ Do I have any concern that my findings may affect whether I receive subsequent work from this organizational client? Will that concern shape how I conduct the evaluation or the opinions I reach?

☐ Do I believe that all people with a mental illness are categorically unable to perform the work of a police officer? Am I aware that not all psychological deficits limit one's ability to perform essential job functions?[5]

☐ Does an examinee engage in behaviors or a lifestyle that I find objectionable? If so, am I able to set aside my values and evaluate the aspects of the examinee that are relevant to their ability to safely and effectively perform essential job functions?

☐ Am I so worried about being biased toward one side or the other that I may fail to pursue legitimate areas of inquiry or clinical exploration?

Checklist 2.2 is not exhaustive. We encourage readers to construct their own checklist based on their self-assessment of vulnerability to bias.

Psychological Evaluator Competencies

Spilberg and Corey (2019) identified eight professional competencies required for effective practice in conducting preemployment psychological evaluations of police candidates. These competencies are incorporated by reference in California

Code of Regulations, Title 11, Section 1955(a)(2), which requires psychological evaluators who conduct evaluations of California peace officer candidates to be competent in each area. Corey and Ben-Porath (2018) also applied these competencies to fitness-for-duty evaluations of incumbent officers. We list them next and discuss important aspects of each.

1. Assessment Competence

Definition: *Ability to properly gather, analyze, and integrate the full range of pertinent assessment data* (e.g., *personal health records, background investigation and other personal history information, psychological testing, clinical interview, and observations) to reach a determination of psychological suitability/fitness to exercise the powers of a police officer.*

Competence in this area begins with an understanding of the importance of relying on multiple sources of information in these and all other forensic mental health assessments. Evaluations of police officers and candidates are high-stakes assessments for the person being evaluated, the employing or hiring agency, fellow officers, and the public. In the more litigious area of fitness evaluations, they also present high stakes for the psychologist conducting the evaluation, and, as with all forensic evaluations, competence is the foundation of good risk management.

In preemployment evaluations, candidates are generally motivated to present themselves favorably. Indeed, owing to the substantial vetting (e.g., background investigation) of candidates before the conditional offer of employment, police candidates tend to be better adjusted and more virtuous than the general population, which can present a challenge when interpreting underreporting validity scales (i.e., measures of positive impression management or defensiveness).[6] Reliance on multiple sources of information, with a focus on corroboration (SGFP Standard 9.02), aids in distinguishing between accurate and deceptive self-presentations, reduces the likelihood of erroneous determinations of suitability or fitness due to false-positive or false-negative test results, and enhances validity when data from one or more sources are unreliable. As discussed in the Standards:

The availability of information on multiple traits or attributes, when acquired from various sources and through the use of various methods, enables professionals to assess more accurately an individual's psychosocial functioning and facilitates more effective decision making. When using collateral data, the professional should take steps to ascertain their accuracy and reliability, especially when the data come from third parties who may have a vested interest in the outcome of the assessment. (p. 155)

In Chapter 5, we discuss further the data collection methods used in both suitability and fitness evaluations.

2. Clinical Competence

Definition: *Ability to assess the impact of an individual's emotional or mental condition, and normal and abnormal personality traits and adaptation, on performance as a police officer.*

As implied by this competency, the mere existence of a mental health disorder does not preclude safe and effective performance as a police officer. For example, a candidate or incumbent may have a chronic anxiety or mood disorder, attention-deficit/hyperactivity disorder, posttraumatic stress disorder, or adjustment disorder, the symptoms of which are well managed and not job-limiting. This is the reason that the Americans With Disabilities Act of 1990 (ADA) requires an "individualized assessment" of the ability of a person to perform a particular job, "one which focuses on the medical condition's actual effect on the specific" candidate or employee (*EEOC v. Hussey Copper Ltd*, 2010). Determinations that a person with a mental or emotional impairment is unable to perform the essential functions of a position and/or poses a direct threat in that position must be based, not on subjective judgments, but on the best available objective evidence. This principle is also reflected in the OMPE Guidelines (APA, 2018), which encourage psychologists "to support conclusions about the job relevance of a psychological condition with established scientific and professional knowledge" (Guideline 4). It also is consistent with the strongly worded admonition in *Chevron v. Echazabal* (2002), in which the US Supreme Court required the medical examiner to produce "a reasonable medical judgment that relies on the most current medical knowledge and/or the best available objective evidence, and upon an expressly individualized assessment of the individual's present ability to safely perform the essential functions of the job" (p. 85).

Normal-range personality traits, such as conscientiousness, assertiveness, or constraint, also exist on a continuum, and their behavioral expressions are often contingent on context and other factors. The central task of assessment in preemployment psychological evaluations (normal-range traits are generally not at issue in fitness evaluations) is to determine how the candidate's personality affects or is likely to affect their performance as a police officer. Some candidates, for example, may be shy or socially avoidant in nonwork settings but are nevertheless able to perform adequately in professional roles—much like a stage actor or comedian may be introverted off-stage but dynamically entertaining "in role." Competence in this area requires the psychologist to have a working knowledge of the psychological requirements of the position and the range of variability in normal and abnormal functioning that can exist without jeopardizing performance as a police officer.

3. Communication Competence

Definition: *Ability to communicate the necessary and appropriate findings, conclusions, and recommendations in a manner that is clear and useful to the referring party and that conforms to jurisdictional and institutional requirements.*

In most forensic evaluations, particularly those in which a written report is directed to an employer about a job candidate or incumbent, discerning judgment must be used when deciding what information will be disclosed, as we discussed in Chapter 1. These evaluations necessarily involve gathering considerable amounts of private information, not all of which the employer needs to know. The potential for misuse of private health information is especially high. Including in written and oral reports "only information germane to the purpose for which the communication is made" (EPPCC, Standard 4.04) is an established ethical standard.

2
chapter

Similarly, SGFP Guideline 11.04 encourages forensic practitioners "to limit discussion of background information that does not bear directly upon the legal purpose of the examination or consultation" and "avoid offering information that is irrelevant and that does not provide a substantial basis of support for their opinions, except when required by law."

Beyond restricting the disclosure of private information, competent communication also requires avoiding jargon and assiduously linking opinions to the relevant criteria for determining suitability or fitness. Chapter 7 provides more specific guidance on writing reports that address the needs of the hiring or employing agency and facilitate testimony in any future litigation or administrative proceeding.

4. Jurisprudence Competence

Definition: *Knowledge and application of statutory, regulatory, and case law pertinent to evaluations of police officers and candidates.*

Evaluations of police suitability and fitness are driven not only by clinical considerations but also, as we showed in Chapter 1, by legal ones. Practitioners new to this area of work need not be intimidated by the substantial legal foundation required in this area of practice. The statutes, regulations, and case law cited in Chapter 1 are resources not unlike test manuals and peer-reviewed research literature. When practitioners are familiar with these resources, they facilitate practice rather than inhibit it. On the other hand, ignorance of these resources puts the practitioner at risk not only of legal jeopardy but also of reaching opinions and conclusions that are erroneous, unreliable, irrelevant, and, therefore, unhelpful to the retaining party.

5. Procedural Competence

Definition: *Knowledge and application of the psychological assessment procedures meeting jurisdictional requirements, organizational needs, and professional standards of practice.*

Procedural integrity in preemployment evaluations requires that they be conducted consistently across all candidates for a given agency, and all evaluations of police suitability and fitness require conformance to legal and professional standards and institutional requirements. An essential procedural component for psychological evaluations in any context is the acquisition of informed consent (or assent) before the start of the evaluation.

BEST PRACTICE

An essential procedural component for psychological evaluations in any context is the acquisition of informed consent (or assent) before the start of the evaluation.

In some jurisdictions, there are requirements to use certain tests or types of tests, or to conduct the interview only after written testing has been administered and analyzed. These and other assessment procedures are discussed in Chapter 5.

2
chapter

6. Psychometric Competence

Definition: *Understanding of psychological test properties, including test validity, reliability, base rates, test norms, and group differences, and the ability to select appropriate tests for evaluating psychological suitability/fitness and to make proper, accurate inferences from test score results.*

This competence is often referred to as *assessment literacy*—knowledge about testing that supports valid interpretation of test scores for their intended purposes, including knowledge about test development, test score interpretations, threats to valid score interpretations, score reliability and precision, test administration, and use.[7] Assessment literacy is most easily acquired with respect to a particular assessment instrument through careful review of its interpretive and technical manuals, relevant peer-reviewed studies, and texts providing interpretive guidance.

Practitioners seeking to develop assessment literacy in connection with other instruments can avail themselves of manuals and other texts made available by the test publisher or distributor, as well as by continuing education opportunities, many excellent examples of which are offered by the American Academy of Forensic Psychology.[8] The California Commission on Peace Officer Standards and Training also accredits training courses that pertain specifically to competencies in conducting psychological evaluations of police candidates, and these are listed on its website.[9]

7. Standards Competence

Definition: *Knowledge and application of ethical principles and standards, and professional standards and guidelines, pertinent to psychological assessments of police officers and candidates.*

In any area of specialty practice, adherence to relevant standards and professional guidelines is one of the most important strategies for risk management. Standards are mandatory and may be accompanied by an enforcement mechanism. In contrast, professional practice guidelines suggest or recommend specific professional behavior, endeavor, or conduct for psychologists. Guidelines are not mandatory; they are aspirational and "aim to facilitate the continued systematic development of the profession and to promote a high level of professional practice by psychologists" (APA, 2015, p. 828). At the end of this chapter, we briefly summarize several sources of standards and guidelines particularly relevant to evaluations of police suitability and fitness.

8. Occupational Competence

Definition: *Knowledge of the essential job functions of police officers, their working conditions and chain of command, and the psychological demands and stressors inherent in the police officer position.*

Each of the seven previously discussed competencies is routinely acquired through postgraduate and continuing education and training. Occupational competence, however, requires obtaining knowledge from outside of psychology. In the remainder of this chapter, we provide a brief overview of knowledge relevant to this competence.

The Role of Police Officers in Contemporary Society

The APA (2018) OMPE Guidelines encourage psychologists who conduct occupationally mandated evaluations to obtain an "understanding of the job description and psychologically relevant demands and working conditions of the position [as] a necessary foundation for judgments about the examinee's ability to perform the essential functions of the position" (p. 191). Toward that end, we next discuss information that suitability and fitness examiners should know as a foundation for conducting these evaluations, followed by a brief discussion of contemporary challenges facing police.

What a Police Psychologist Should Understand About Police Organizations

Police organizations come in many different sizes, and their organizational structures range from the small town police departments, like the Frenchtown Borough (New Jersey) Police Department with a chief of police and three or four patrol officers, to large urban agencies, like the New York City Police Department with a complex organizational structure and nearly 40,000 police officers in 20 operational bureaus and 77 precincts. Following is a brief description of US police agencies, their organizational features, and common police officer work assignments.

DEMOGRAPHICS OF LAW ENFORCEMENT ORGANIZATIONS IN THE UNITED STATES

The most authoritative source of information regarding the demographics and personnel of law enforcement organizations in the United States is the Bureau of Justice Statistics.[10] Reaves (2015), a statistician for the Bureau of Justice Statistics, provided the data on the personnel composition of US law enforcement agencies in 2013, based on surveys collected from the nation's police departments. In summary, Reaves reported the following:

- There were approximately 17,000 law enforcement agencies in the United States, of which 15,388 were state or local agencies. Federal agencies are broadly divided into military, civilian, and tribal agencies.
- The total number of sworn officers employed by those agencies was 724,690. While the *mean* size of the average US agency was 47, the *modal* size was 10 officers (due to the size of large police departments, e.g., New York City, Chicago, and Philadelphia). Only 5% of the nation's agencies had more than 100 officers.

- 12% of officers were female, more than double the amount of female officers reported in 1987.

- In addition to sworn officers, almost all agencies employ civilians in various support services, such as dispatching, recordkeeping, and, in many agencies, crime scene evidence collection and analysis. While support personnel were not as likely to be subject to preemployment screening, probably because they are not required to make deadly force decisions, most of them work in information-sensitive positions.[11]

ORGANIZATIONAL FEATURES OF LAW ENFORCEMENT AGENCIES

The chief of police is the head of municipal police agencies. This person is typically appointed by the mayor, city council, city manager, or a police commission and usually does not have the protection of a merit system. Similarly, a deputy chief or assistant chief is typically appointed by the chief from within the police department. If the chief or deputy chief was employed by the agency before their appointment to that position and they are relieved of those duties, they typically return to their former (civil service) position within the police department.

In county law enforcement, the sheriff is the chief law enforcement officer and is the only elected police official in the United States. Sheriff's offices typically have the responsibility to patrol and investigate crimes in non-incorporated areas or in incorporated jurisdictions that contract for their services. They also provide court protection services and usually run the county jail.

The management structure of all law enforcement organizations is paramilitary, with a rank structure that designates the chains of command and authority. For a civilian professional to maintain an ongoing relationship with law enforcement agencies, it is important to respect this structure. This often involves channeling communication through the person designated to receive information.

WORK ASSIGNMENTS WITHIN LAW ENFORCEMENT AGENCIES

An important consideration in understanding the role of a police officer in a municipal, county, or state agency is the size of the agency. Since the modal size of a police agency in the United States is 10 officers, most sworn members are generalists who may engage in activities ranging from patrol and traffic enforcement to criminal investigation. In agencies that hire 100 or more sworn officers, specialized units are the norm, and the work of any particular officer is more circumscribed.

In these larger agencies, uniformed officers are typically assigned to a patrol division, in which the focus is the suppression of crime, preliminary investigations, and building relationships with the community. Other uniformed officers may be assigned to traffic enforcement, where they typically investigate accidents and enforce the traffic code. In these agencies, patrol officers do not usually engage in traffic enforcement, except in those cases in which they observe flagrant violations in their presence or when they conduct traffic stops as a mechanism for determining if the traffic violator is involved in more serious activity. Regardless of one's assignment in a uniformed division, officers are expected to use discretion and judgment in selectively enforcing various laws. It is not enough to learn the criminal code; an essential job skill is having the judgment to know when and how it should be applied.

Those who work in a uniformed position typically have days off during the week or during only part of a weekend. They often work on legal holidays. Uniformed officers work in shifts, exposing them to a major stressor in police work—sleep and circadian rhythm disturbance (Violanti, 2018).

In many agencies, after a uniformed officer has had sufficient street experience, the officer may apply for positions in investigative areas or may be directly recruited by supervisors who have become aware of their reputation and their abilities in conducting preliminary investigations. Working in a specialized investigation unit, such as property crimes, crimes against children, or bomb squad, allows police officers to pursue an area in which they may hold particular interest or have a preexisting skill. They typically work business hours, with weekends and holidays off. However, investigators assigned to major crimes may respond to the scene of a newly discovered crime, even before the patrol officers have completed their preliminary investigation. Such investigators are subject to being called out to investigate a crime 24 hours a day,

7 days a week. This can be a stressful burden on detectives and their families, causing some to view their prior assignment as a uniformed patrol officer as "the good ol' days." In some cases, investigators may eventually request a transfer back to a uniformed assignment. Those who have worked as investigators in larger agencies might also report that one of the advantages of working in patrol, which they may not have appreciated earlier in their career, is the fact that once a shift is over, they typically have no responsibility to follow up on investigations because the cases usually are referred to someone else in an investigative unit. Indeed, many investigators who are assigned to person (as opposed to property) crimes, such as sex crimes or homicide, feel that they are always working because it is difficult to let go of those serious events even after they leave the office.

Some agencies recruit uniformed or plain clothes officers to work in special assignments. These various activities may include titles such as school resource officer, Special Weapons and Tactics (SWAT), canine (dog handler), and undercover assignments. Some agencies may consult a psychologist to help them match these positions with the most compatible candidates. In providing such input, it is important that the psychological consultant not rely on general assumptions about what a position entails because often this information is obtained from the media—and is frequently incorrect or relies on stereotypes. This further underscores the importance of the psychological consultant gaining a first-hand understanding of the demands of the position. This can be accomplished by reviewing relevant research, undertaking formal job analyses, and speaking with subject matter experts.

The value of an onsite visit, or "shadowing" officers in these special assignments, also should not be overlooked. Such an experience will often provide invaluable insights into the demands of those positions. Indeed, Mark Twain's aphorism, "A man who carries a cat by the tail learns something he

BEST PRACTICE

In helping employers match candidates to special assignments, it is important that you not rely on general assumptions about what a position entails because often this information is incorrect or relies on stereotypes.

can learn in no other way," is particularly true for the psychologist who wishes to have a clear picture of what police officers do. For example, members of Special Weapons and Tactics (SWAT) teams not only are required to be in top physical condition but also, upon arriving at a SWAT callout (such as during a riot, hostage situation, or terror attack), must maintain a high level of vigilance for prolonged periods, sometimes in adverse weather conditions. They have to be comfortable functioning as members of a team within an environment in which independent, uncoordinated decision-making could be very detrimental to the mission. Such demands may not be apparent to the clinician who views these positions from the outside. Accordingly, a psychologist who assists in filling vacancies on a SWAT team, and who accompanies these officers on callouts, would probably appreciate the importance of selecting candidates who have a track record of team participation, along with excellent attention span, focus, and executive functioning abilities. This is not a good environment for officers who have attention deficits or low tolerance for boredom.

Each of the special assignments mentioned thus far has varying demands for different psychological attributes. Some special assignments come with greater psychological risks than others. For example, officers assigned to investigate child pornography, vice operations, or other forms of undercover work may benefit from policies that restrict the length of time in those assignments. Unfortunately, success in one of these assignments may also require considerable technical training and experience to become proficient—creating a tension between developing expertise versus limiting an officer's exposure to environments that are particularly psychologically noxious. Given the concern that all police work is psychologically hazardous, *The President's Task Force on 21st Century Policing* (2015) called for police departments to perform yearly mental health checkups on their sworn officers, a practice that has not been widely implemented.

When a psychologist conducts an evaluation to select individuals for special assignments, there is a particularly important consideration. If one uses tests or asks interview questions that trigger the EEOC's definition of a medical examination (see Chapter 1), the candidate must be conditionally approved (analogous to a conditional offer of employment) before the evaluation can take place.[12]

Contemporary Challenges in Policing

Pinker (2018) makes the case that people are living longer, healthier, freer, and happier lives, and society's formidable problems will eventually be solved by reason, science, and humanism. Let's hope so, but meanwhile police work has never been more challenging. These challenges are too numerous to adequately treat in this volume, but those we mention have compelling implications for police officers and the psychological factors underlying their suitability and fitness.

Hales and Higgins (2016) observed that policing can be understood to have *instrumental* and *symbolic* roles. The former has to do with issues such as crime reduction, public safety, and prosecution of offenders; the latter is concerned with public perception of safe communities, as well as trust and confidence in, and the legitimacy of, the police profession. These roles, and public perceptions of how successful police are in performing them, are increasingly in conflict because of social change. One such change is reflected in "noncrime demands" on police, which are estimated to account for about 80% of police calls for service (Hales & Higgins, 2016). These calls result mainly from failures in other social service delivery and criminal justice systems, such as mental health, drug, and alcohol treatment; housing; public schools; the courts; and correctional institutions. As the instrumental police role broadens, the number of noncrime contacts with citizens increases. But when responding to noncrime calls for service involving the mentally ill, the homeless, and parties in dispute, the potential for violent escalation also increases, which undermines public assessment of police officers in their symbolic role. A half-century ago, sociologist Egon Bittner (1970) wrote about this inherent dilemma in a police officer's use of coercive force:

> [W]hatever the substance of the task at hand, whether it involves
> protection against an undesired imposition, caring for those who
> cannot care for themselves, attempting to solve a crime, helping

to save a life, abating a nuisance, or settling an explosive dispute, police intervention means above all making use of the capacity and authority to overpower resistance. . . . There can be no doubt that this feature of police work is uppermost in the minds of people who solicit police aid or direct the attention of the police to problems, that persons against whom the police proceed have this feature in mind and conduct themselves accordingly, and that every conceivable police intervention projects the message that force may be, and may have to be, used to achieve a desired objective. (p. 40)

This inherent conflict in instrumental roles (where coercive force is valued) and symbolic roles (where it is not) is displayed publicly and dramatically in Internet and news media videos of police officers shooting unarmed juveniles and nonwhite subjects. In response, the public has understandably demanded greater police accountability.[13]

Two trends have emerged from these demands. The first is a growing focus on *de-escalation* and *nonescalation* in noncrime contacts. Police officers are now increasingly expected not only to discern when force is required, and to employ only the minimum necessary amount of it, but also to act in ways that negate the need to use force at all. Police administrators also have instituted policies that often result in police officers walking away from noncrime contacts that simply do not justify the risk of escalated tensions that could lead to actions requiring coercive force.

A second trend is the implementation of training designed to correct for implicit bias, which we discussed earlier in this chapter as a risk for evaluator bias. Researchers (e.g., Dasgupta, 2013; Kang & Lane, 2010; Roos, Lebrecht, Tanaka, & Tarr, 2013) have discovered that automatic and unconscious negative attitudes toward members of nominal (and often devalued) groups (e.g., racial minorities, the poor or homeless, the seriously mentally ill) can be gradually unlearned and replaced with new mental associations, but only in persons having the necessary attributes. These consist primarily of executive functions, such as self-awareness, metacognitive ability, working memory, the ability to "mentalize" or form "theory of mind" (i.e., interpersonal perspective-taking), self-regulation, and an internal motivation to promote social justice. Importantly, these same cognitive and attitudinal qualities also facilitate de-escalating and nonescalating behaviors, and point to potentially important areas for assessment in police candidates and officers. Anxiety and mood disorders can have a debilitating effect on self-regulation, and high levels of chronic and acute stress can deplete mental capacity and working memory. Just as "free space" or available rapid-access memory is needed for a computer to carry out its operations, mental capacity and working memory are needed for humans to self-reflect, mentalize others' thinking, and perform the complex tasks of self-regulation.

Standards and Guidelines That Inform Evaluator Competencies

What follows is a brief summary of six standards and guidelines documents that are especially pertinent to evaluations of police suitability and fitness. Each of these documents is periodically reviewed by the disseminating group; therefore, it is important to ensure that you have the current versions.

1. *Professional Practice Guidelines for Occupationally Mandated Psychological Evaluations* **(OMPE).** The OMPE Guidelines (APA, 2018) is the first APA policy document addressing recommended practices in both preemployment and fitness-for-duty evaluations. The 13 guidelines are organized under three headings: (a) preparing for an OMPE, (b) conducting an OMPE, and (c) communicating OMPE findings.

2. *Preemployment Psychological Evaluation Guidelines* **(PPE Guidelines).** These guidelines reflect the consensus of the Police Psychological Services Section of the International Association of Chiefs of Police (IACP, 2014). The more than 200 members of the IACP Police Psychological Services Section make up the largest membership group of police psychologists in the United

States and Canada. The most recent version of the PPE Guidelines was ratified by the section in 2014, and they were approved and published by the IACP Board of Directors in 2015. The 46 practice guidelines are organized by 14 headings: (a) purpose, (b) limitations, (c) definitions, (d) examiner qualifications, (e) job analysis, (f) disclosure, (g) testing, (h) interview, (i) technology considerations, (j) background information, (k) reports, (l) use of the evaluation, (m) follow-up, and (n) appeals and second opinions. The PPE Guidelines define a preemployment psychological evaluation as a "specialized examination to determine whether a public safety applicant meets the minimum requirements for psychological suitability mandated by jurisdictional statutes and regulations, as well as any other criteria established by the hiring agency" (p. 1).

3. *Fitness-for-Duty Evaluation Guidelines* (**FFDE Guidelines**). As with the PPE Guidelines, the FFDE Guidelines (IACP, 2018a) were developed by the Police Psychological Services Section of the IACP. The most recent version of these guidelines was ratified by the section in 2018, and they were approved and published by the IACP Board of Directors in 2019. The 65 FFDE practice guidelines are organized under 12 topics: (a) purpose, (b) limitations, (c) definition, (d) threshold considerations, (e) examiner qualifications, (f) multiple relationships and conflicts of interest, (g) referral process, (h) informed consent and authorization to release information, (i) evaluation process, (j) report and recommendations, (k) technological considerations, and (l) third-party observers and/or recording devices. An aspect of the IACP PPE and FFDE guidelines that distinguishes them from the other guidelines referenced in this chapter is that they are reviewed for possible revision every 5 years, whereas APA guidelines, for example, are sunsetted or revised after a period of 7 to 10 years.

4. *Preemployment Clinical Assessment of Police Candidates: Principles and Guidelines for Canadian Psychologists* **(CPA Guidelines).** The CPA Guidelines (Canadian Psychological Association, 2013) contain a list of psychological dimensions for use in evaluating police candidates that is very similar to those published by California POST (Spilberg & Corey, 2019). The principles and guidelines are intended to balance "organizational and societal needs with the rights of the candidates and the professional standards of the psychologist" (p. 3). The document comprises two sections: the Statement of Principles, which identifies best practices in preemployment psychological screening of police candidates, and a set of Guidelines for Users, which consists of consensus-based guidelines developed by Canadian practitioners.

5. *Specialty Guidelines for Forensic Psychology* **(SGFP).** The SGFP (APA, 2013) is the only APA-approved set of guidelines that addresses a single specialty in professional psychology. The guidelines are intended to apply to any psychologist who reasonably expects to, agrees to, or is legally mandated to provide expertise on an explicitly psycholegal issue. Inasmuch as psychological evaluations of police officers and candidates are generally guided by a legally defined (i.e., by statute, regulation, administrative rule, or case law) criterion or set of criteria, they are properly conceptualized as forensic practice. That these evaluations also fall into another area of specialty practice—police and public safety psychology— does not alter their forensic nature any more than does the fact that treatment of children falls under both the clinical psychology specialty and the clinical child and adolescent specialty. The 59 SGFP guidelines are grouped under 11 headings: (a) responsibilities, (b) competence, (c) diligence, (d) relationships, (e) fees, (f) informed consent, notification, and assent, (g) conflicts in practice, (h) privacy, confidentiality, and privilege, (i) methods and

procedures, (j) assessment, and (k) professional and other communications.

6. *Standards for Educational and Psychological Testing* (**Standards**). The Standards (2014) is published jointly by the American Educational Research Association, American Psychological Association, and National Council on Measurement Education. Although it is self-described as a set of *standards,* they are not enforceable by the sponsoring organizations. However, the Standards has repeatedly been recognized by regulatory authorities and courts as generally accepted professional guidance that test developers and users of tests follow. As noted in the introduction to the Standards, "Compliance or noncompliance with the *Standards* may be used as relevant evidence of legal liability in judicial and regulatory proceedings. The Standards, therefore, merits careful consideration by all participants in the testing process" (p. 2).[14] Consequently, despite the lack of an enforcement mechanism built into the Standards, they comprise important guidance.

Concerning Board Certification in Police and Public Safety Psychology

Police and public safety psychology is recognized by the APA as one of only 17 specialties in professional psychology. In 2011, the American Board of Police and Public Safety Psychology (ABPPSP) became an affiliated specialty board of the American Board of Professional Psychology (ABPP), which has been certifying specialists in psychology since 1947 and is the only multiple-specialty board certification organization recognized by the APA. Licensed psychologists desiring to demonstrate their competency in the four domains of this specialty (i.e., assessment, intervention, operational support, and organizational consultation) must first meet generic requirements of the ABPP and then satisfy additional specialty board requirements of the ABPPSP. Those candidates who satisfy this initial credential review are invited to submit a written practice sample (containing, among other requirements, two work samples for the purpose of demonstrating specialist-level competence). Successful candidates are then invited to sit for a 3-hour oral examination conducted by a panel of three ABPPSP-certified specialists. Practitioners who are interested in learning more about what is expected of specialists in each of the four domains of practice in police and public safety psychology will find it useful to review the *ABPPSP Examination Manual* for a detailed listing of the functional competencies.

There are many ways for a police psychologist to achieve and demonstrate competence, but board certification by the ABPPSP has several distinct advantages:

1. Its international reputation for high standards attests to consumers and peers alike that the psychologist has met those standards.
2. It facilitates interstate practice because many states waive a number of examination requirements for ABPP-certified psychologists applying for licensure.
3. It provides an opportunity for psychologists to have their work reviewed by their peers.
4. It establishes the board-certified psychologist in a community of other specialists who work collaboratively to promulgate professional standards and guidelines and who engage in a wide range of activities that collectively shape the specialty.

Each of us is board certified by the ABPPSP and the American Board of Forensic Psychology. We encourage all psychologists who practice in police and public safety psychology to visit www.abpp. org and consider the rewards of board certification.

Notes

1. Malpractice claims are relatively rare events in the lives of forensic psychologists, partly because there is no *corpus* of case law that clearly defines the standard of care. This results in an absence of an enforceable standard of care in forensic mental health assessments (Heilbrun et al., 2008).

2. For examples, see Krause (2009), who discusses the psychological demands of working undercover, and Powell, Cassematis, Benson, Smallbone, and Wortley (2014), who discuss the perils facing officers who work with internet child exploitation.

3. It may be difficult to find an allied specialist who is also knowledgeable about important legal and organizational parameters that must be followed when conducting a fitness evaluation. For this reason, we have periodically collaborated with consultants who have the needed expertise. In such cases, we may use them as a consultant, or we may write a jointly authored report.

4. For example, on a biographical form completed by examinees before testing and interviewing, they might be asked the following two questions: "To your knowledge, has the evaluator ever had any past contact with you or someone close to you?" and "Do you know of any conflict of interest the evaluator may have in performing this evaluation?" Examinees who answer either question in the affirmative may then be asked for details.

5. We have had a number of informal conversations with various law enforcement officers, whom we were *not* evaluating, who shared their own stories of experiencing mental illness. Many of these officers were reputed as high-functioning and successful. From these early conversations, we discovered that we had formed a bias in which we assumed that mental illness always resulted in some loss of functional ability in this high-stress and demanding job. These experiences underscored for us the reality that not all people with psychopathology manifest with *functional* impairments at their job or elsewhere.

6. See Corey and Ben-Porath (2018) and Detrick and Chibnall (2014) for a comprehensive treatment of this topic.

7. *Standards for Educational and Psychological Testing* (2014), p. 216.

8. See http://aafpforensic.org/workshops/.

9. See https://www.post.ca.gov/approved-cpe-courses.aspx.

10. See https://www.bjs.gov/.

11. While most nonsworn personnel are hired without psychological screening, it is important to recognize that dispatching in a large police department may be one of the most demanding occupations in terms of executive functioning and stress regulation. Indeed, analyses performed by the California Peace Officer Standards and Training (POST) Commission led to passage of 11 C.C.R. § 1959, which stipulates that dispatchers are subject to precisely the same background investigation dimensions, which closely mimic the POST Psychological Screening Dimensions for peace officers.

12. See Corey, D. M. (2007). Analysis of the ADA as it pertains to medical examinations of police officers applying for special assignments. *AELE Monthly Law Journal, 501*(7). http://www.aele.org/law/2007-07MLJ501.pdf

13. We are mindful that countless encounters occur every day in which police officers use exquisite crisis intervention skills to prevent encounters from ending tragically. However, there is no dispute that unwarranted excessive force responses can have a profound impact on the direct victims, public, and other officers who abhor unprofessional conduct in their colleagues.

14. American Educational Research Association, American Psychological Association, & National Council on Measurement Education. (2014). *Standards for educational and psychological testing.* Washington, DC: American Educational Research Association.

Empirical Foundations

Preemployment suitability evaluations of police officer candidates have been criticized for having "no nationally recognized and generally followed set of recommendations as to what questionnaire(s) or evaluative protocols" to use for these evaluations (Dantzker, 2011, p. 276). Detrick (2012) countered this criticism by noting that nationally recognized protocols do exist for these evaluations; these protocols stipulate that such tests "should have documented reliability, validity, and other empirical evidence supporting their use in the preemployment evaluation of public safety applicants" (International Association of Chiefs of Police [IACP], 2014, Guideline 7.1). However, Detrick also observed that there are "relatively few inventories that possess the[se] characteristics" and, in any event, "promoting utilization of only a few select instruments for a specific purpose . . . might well impede scientific inquiry" (2012, p. 162).

For more than 100 years, beginning with Lewis Terman's 1916 study of the Stanford-Binet IQ Test's utility in evaluating police applicants to the San Jose (California) Police Department (Terman et al., 1917; Trompetter, 2017), a notable legacy of scientific inquiry has established a solid foundation of evidence underlying psychological evaluations of police officer suitability and fitness. This research has focused predominantly on two questions:

- What psychological constructs are implicated in police officer suitability and fitness?
- What assessment instruments provide valid measures of these constructs?

We review in this chapter the particularly relevant published, peer-reviewed studies addressing both questions.

Psychological Constructs Implicated in Police Officer Suitability and Fitness

Spilberg and Corey (2019) described the published literature as reflecting two approaches to understanding police personality, "roughly organized into attributes of good performers and attributes associated with counterproductive and/or ineffective behavior" (p. 41). Research involving positive attributes has consistently identified traits such as agreeableness, assertiveness/extroversion, conscientiousness/responsibility, dependability, emotional toughness (freedom from anxiety, hostility, and psychological distress), flexibility/adaptability, independence/achievement orientation, integrity, intellectual efficiency, self-discipline/self-control, social confidence/self-assuredness, social sensitivity, tolerance, and well-being (e.g., Aamodt, 2004; Claussen-Rogers & Arrigo, 2005; Cuttler & Muchinsky, 2006; Detrick & Chibnall, 2013; Hargrave & Hiatt, 1989; Hogan, Hogan, & Roberts, 1996; Lorr & Strack, 1994; Sarchione et al., 1998). Studies of negative attributes have targeted counterproductive work behaviors such as excessive force, sexual misconduct, sexual harassment, substance abuse, insubordination or other supervisory problems, embezzlement, deceitfulness, driving problems, inappropriate verbal conduct, blackmail, bribery, theft, lying, kickbacks, personal violence, revenge, discrimination, fraud, absenteeism, internal affairs investigations, missing court, and citizen complaints (e.g., Sarchione et al., 1998; Sellbom, Fischler, & Ben-Porath, 2007; Son, Davis, & Rome, 1998; Tarescavage, Brewster, Corey, & Ben-Porath, 2016; Tarescavage, Corey, & Ben-Porath, 2015, 2016; Tarescavage, Corey, Gupton, & Ben-Porath, 2016; Tarescavage, Fischler, et al., 2016).

The California Peace Officer Standards and Training (POST) Commission set out more than 20 years ago to generate and validate a set of "psychological screening dimensions" for use in evaluating prospective police officers. To accomplish this objective, the California POST Commission carried out two independent research efforts, described in detail by Spilberg and Corey (2019). The first phase involved a comprehensive review of job analysis information to identify personality-related traits and behaviors pertinent to police officer performance and systematic and inter-active feedback from hundreds of stakeholders to synthesize the findings into a coherent set of psychological screening dimensions (see Table 4.1 in Chapter 4). The second phase of research in-volved a meta-analysis of more than 1,700 studies on psychological predictors of police officer behaviors yielding more than 6,000 va-lidity coefficients. The goal of the meta-analysis was to assess the em-pirical support for the POST Psychological Screening Dimensions as constructs for predicting police performance. Spilberg and Corey (2019) summarized the outcomes of the two independent research phases as providing "convincing evidence that each of the POST Psychological Screening Dimensions reflect[s] integral constructs underlying and responsible for peace officer job perfor-mance" (p. 87).

3
chapter

These screening criteria represent the most comprehensive effort to date to identify the psychological traits, behaviors, and competencies associated with police performance. Indeed, in a national survey of the assessment protocols and procedures used by police psychologists in evaluating police officer candidates (Corey, 2016), 78.6% of the respondents reported using the POST Psychological Screening Dimensions as at least a portion of their criterion standard. Notably, nearly two-thirds (65.1%) of respondents from outside of California also reported using these selection criteria. These criteria also are used in fitness-for-duty evaluations to aid in assessing the impact of an incumbent officer's mental impairment on their work performance. This is discussed further in Chapter 4.

While cautioning that the purpose of the POST meta-analysis was to determine the criterion validity of the screening dimensions, rather than the validity of specific tests for measuring those dimensions, Spilberg and Corey (2019) observed:

Responsibility for providing validity evidence on specific instruments rests primarily with the test publishers. Such evidence should include proof that test scales measure what they say they measure. For the purposes of peace officer psychological screening, that proof should include evidence of a relationship between the test's scales and the constructs embedded in the POST Dimensions, as well as other peace officer work behaviors and outcomes of interest. (p. 87)

We turn next to this proof.

Measuring Job-Relevant Psychological Constructs: Validity Evidence

We focus our discussion in this chapter on examples of research related to the most commonly used instruments in these contexts (Blau, 1994; Corey, 2016; Dantzker, 2011). Brief descriptions of these instruments are provided in Chapter 5 (see Table 5.4). We limit our review to studies published in peer-reviewed journals and pertaining only to version(s) of the test currently supported by the test's publisher (e.g., California Psychological Inventory–434 [CPI-434], Minnesota Multiphasic Personality Inventory–2 Restructured Form [MMPI-2-RF], Minnesota Multiphasic Personality Inventory–2 [MMPI-2], and Personality Assessment Inventory [PAI]).

A Few Words About Validity

Tests are often referred to as "valid," although it is the *inferences drawn from test scores* that are actually validated. Two types of inferences are typically supported by validity studies: those associated with a targeted construct, such as anxiety or dominance, and those associated with a behavior or outcome of interest, such as job termination or citizen complaints. Test scores are used to infer information about an individual's personality and psychological functioning, as well as about potential problems associated with those findings. Both types of inferences require validity evidence, and effective use of tests requires that the examiner be familiar with the instrument's research findings in order to properly interpret the test. (See Chapter 6 for guidance on test interpretation.) Inadequate familiarity with a test's validity evidence can lead to interpretive errors, both Type I (making an inference that *is not supported* by the evidence) and Type II (failing to make an inference that *is supported* by the validity research).

BEWARE Inadequate familiarity with a test's validity evidence can lead to interpretive errors: making an inference that *is not supported* by the evidence, and failing to make an inference that *is supported* by the validity research.

One of the most important factors limiting validity research in preemployment screening involves restricted range in both test scores and outcome measures. Since police candidates become more homogeneous as employers remove those with undesirable characteristics, it becomes increasingly difficult to demonstrate predictive validity— because there is little variability in research subjects, especially among those who "pass" the psychological evaluation and are hired. The only foolproof remedy to this conundrum is to administer an assessment battery and hire every applicant early in the process, before the group becomes too homogeneous. Of course, doing so would be both reckless and unethical. Consequently, the more useful (and ethical) approach is to choose tests with expected validity, administer them to police candidates, study the behavior of qualified candidates who are subsequently hired, and apply contemporary statistical methods (e.g., Hunter and Schmidt, 1990) to evaluate the tests' utility in predicting meaningful post-hire behavior. Collectively, a test's cumulative body of validity evidence comprises what Cronbach (1988) referred to as the "validity argument" supporting a test's use for a particular purpose: an evolving rationale supporting the plausibility of inferences drawn from a test score with appropriate evidence (Kane, 1992).

Test Revisions and Generalization of Validity Evidence

Many of the assessment instruments used today to evaluate police officer candidates are revisions of a prior version. In some cases, a test publisher will continue to support the previous version of a test for a period of time while the newer version is studied and gains acceptance in the professional community, after which the publisher will discontinue its sale. In other instances, a test publisher will make significant changes to a test that has amassed a large body of validity evidence and discontinue its use before publishing evidence of the newer version's validity. Such was the case, for example, with the Inwald Personality Inventory (IPI; Inwald, Knatz, & Shusman, 1982), a self-report personality inventory described by its author as "the first comprehensive personality inventory that was designed and validated specifically for public safety officer selection" (Weiss & Inwald, 2018, p. 192). After its introduction in 1980, the IPI gained considerable empirical support for its construct and criterion validity (e.g., Chibnall & Detrick, 2003; Detrick, Ben-Porath, & Sellbom, 2016; Detrick & Chibnall, 2002; Detrick, Chibnall, & Rosso, 2001; Inwald & Shusman, 1984; Knatz, Inwald, Brockwell, & Tran, 1992; Tarescavage, Fischler, et al., 2015). In 2011, however, the Inwald Personality Inventory-2 (IPAT; Stubenrauch & Young, 2015) was published and the IPI was phased out. In contrast to the IPI's 310 items and 25 content scales, the IPI-2 contains 202 items, one validity scale, and 16 content scales, which comprise a "reorganization of the remaining items into new discrete scales based upon their content to eliminate the item overlap that existed on the original IPI scales."[1] Despite these significant revisions to the test—as well as the inclusion of predictions based on discriminant function equations of a test taker's likelihood of meeting expectations as a police recruit in four field performance areas—no peer-reviewed studies have been published on the IPI-2's construct or criterion validity. Similarly, although there are a number of published, peer-reviewed studies demonstrating the predictive validity of the fourth and earlier editions of the Sixteen Personality Factor Questionnaire (16PF) in assessing police suitability (e.g., Drew, Carless, & Thompson, 2008; Fabricatore, Azen, Schoentgen, & Snibbe, 1978; Lorr & Strack, 1994), none exist at the time of this

INFO

Except for scales that were left unchanged or are highly correlated with one another, validity does not generalize from one version of a test to another. Indeed, the greater the changes to a test, the greater the need for proof that the revised version measures (and predicts) what it purports.

writing for the two current versions of the test, the fifth and sixth editions.

Substantive changes to the items in any test preclude total reliance on the prior version's validity evidence. Instead, new evidence must be gathered to demonstrate the revised test's construct and criterion validity (Butcher, 2000). Validity generalization procedures (e.g., Schmidt & Hunter, 1977) may justify using a test to evaluate candidates in a position similar, but not identical, to those targeted by the underlying studies, but validity does not generalize from one version of a test to another, except for scales that were left unchanged or are highly correlated with one another. Indeed, the greater the changes to a test, the greater the need for proof that the revised version measures (and predicts) what it purports.

California Psychological Inventory–434

Multiple studies published over the past 30 years have demonstrated the utility of the CPI in predicting relevant outcomes in police officers. We cite only those studies that included the current (434-item) version of the CPI, which was published in 1995.[2] Sarchione, Cuttler, Muchinsky, and Nelson-Gray (1998) compared the preemployment CPI-434 scores of police recruits who were disciplined for misconduct against those of a matched control group of police recruits. Their analyses showed that composite scores on the Responsibility, Socialization, and Self-Control scales predicted membership in the misconduct-disciplined group, with moderate effect sizes. Varela, Boccaccini, Scogin, Stump, and Caputo (2004) conducted a meta-analysis that included 78 studies and more than 11,000 subjects, which found the CPI to be a reliable predictor of post-hire behavior in police officers; however, not all of the studies included in this meta-analysis involved the CPI-434.

Extending the work of Sarchione et al. (1998), Cuttler and Muchinsky (2006) studied associations between the preemployment CPI-434 scores of hired police candidates and post-hire outcomes by comparing a sample of officers who were disciplined for misconduct with a matched nonoffending control group. The authors reported that officers who were not disciplined for misconduct scored significantly higher (i.e., more positively) than the disciplined sample on the Responsibility, Socialization, and Self-Control scales, although the effect sizes were small despite statistical corrections for range restriction (i.e., disattenuated correlations).[3]

More recently, Roberts, Tarescavage, Ben-Porath, and Roberts (2018) examined associations between pre-hire CPI-434 and prorated MMPI-2-RF scale scores (calculated from responses to the original MMPI using a technique first reported by Tarescavage, Corey, & Ben-Porath, 2016). The authors reported a number of significant findings regarding various CPI scales, including that the Dominance and Independence scale scores were positively correlated with excessive force problems and control of conflict; scores on Capacity for Status were negatively correlated with verbal communication, problem-solving, and decision-making and were positively correlated with reliability; and lower Socialization scores correlated with poor relations with coworkers, alcohol abuse, and dishonesty/lack of integrity. Importantly, the authors also demonstrated that the CPI-434 and MMPI-2-RF—measures of normal and abnormal personality functioning, respectively—complement one another by contributing incrementally to predictive validity over and above what either test demonstrated alone.

Roberts and Johnson (2001) developed a CPI-434 score report, the *CPI Police and Public Safety Selection Report* (CPI-PPSSR), which includes a number of features and special scales described in Chapter 5. Among these features are eight Suitability Risk Statements (Johnson & Roberts, 2001) that are calculated from undisclosed regression equations, six of which correlate with self-reported life history problems, one with a "poorly suited" rating from the post-offer psychological evaluation, and another that correlates with the "probability of involuntary departure." Fischler (2004) was the first researcher to report associations between pre-hire CPI-PPSSR scores and post-hire performance of police officers. He found that lower scores on Self-Control and Work Orientation, and higher scores on the "poor suitability" equation (constructed as a predictor of a candidate's likelihood of being rated as poorly suited on the basis of a psychological evaluation) and two equations corresponding with life history problems, correlated with sustained internal affairs complaints. He also reported other CPI-PPSSR correlations with citizen complaints and involuntary termination.

In the previously discussed study by Roberts et al. (2018), the authors also reported a strong association between a "special purpose" scale, Integrity (constructed to predict police candidates lying about recent illegal drug use), and poor verbal communication, reliability, general appearance, relations with coworkers, relations with citizens, control of conflict, and problem-solving and decision-making. Among other findings, the authors also reported significant correlations between low Amicability and poor verbal communication, as well as between high Hostility and poor verbal communication and relations with citizens.

Minnesota Multiphasic Personality Inventory–2 Restructured Form

Sellbom, Fischler, and Ben-Porath (2007) studied associations between the MMPI-2 Restructured Clinical (RC) Scales (Tellegen et al., 2003)—which are also included in their original form on the MMPI-2-RF[4]—and post-hire outcomes in a large sample of police officers. Using disattenuated correlations that corrected for range restriction, the authors found that the RC Scales, particularly RC3 (Cynicism), RC4 (Antisocial Behavior), RC6 (Ideas of Persecution), and RC8 (Aberrant Experiences), outperformed the MMPI-2 Clinical Scales in predicting post-hire outcomes such as deceptiveness, citizen complaints, excessive use of force, rude behavior, failure to take responsibility for mistakes, displaying a bad attitude toward members of the public, being uncooperative toward supervisors, being a defendant in civil litigation, abuse of police authority, and termination for cause. Sellbom et al.'s research, which also employed relative risk ratios to demonstrate the importance and utility of using cutoff scores substantially lower than the traditional threshold for clinical significance (65T), ushered in a "paradigm shift" for subsequent research in this area, including the use of range restriction corrections and of subclinical cutoffs (Ben-Porath, Corey, & Tarescavage, 2017, p. 56). A year after publication of the important Sellbom et al. study, the MMPI-2-RF was released (Tellegen & Ben-Porath, 2008/2011). In the ensuing years, there have been more published, peer-reviewed research studies on the validity of the MMPI-2-RF in police suitability evaluations than any other psychological test now in use, including its predecessor version, the MMPI-2.

Detrick and Chibnall (2014) examined the impact of demand characteristics on MMPI-2-RF scale scores by comparing scores produced during high-stakes suitability evaluations (in which the test was used to determine candidates' suitability to be hired) with those produced in a low-stakes context at the end of the academy, where the results were of no consequence. Consistent with expectations, the authors found that the low-stakes subjects generally produced higher scores on the substantive scales (i.e., they admitted to more problems), but this pattern was mediated by scores on the two underreporting scales (L-r and K-r), such that test takers with higher L-r scores were more likely to underreport behavioral dysfunction and cynicism, in contrast to test takers with higher K-r scores, who were more likely to underreport emotional dysfunction and cynicism.

Detrick, Ben-Porath, and Sellbom (2016) examined associations between scale scores on the MMPI-2-RF and IPI administered concurrently to a police candidate sample. Their findings were largely consistent with theoretically hypothesized expectations and "add to a growing body of studies (reviewed by Ben-Porath, 2012) that establish the construct validity of the MMPI-2-RF substantive scales" (p. 94).

Tarescavage, Brewster, Corey, and Ben-Porath (2015) studied associations between pre-hire MMPI-2-RF scores and post-hire performance ratings of a sample of male police officers. These authors found, in particular, that MMPI-2-RF scores from the emotional dysfunction domain were substantially correlated with post-hire measures of emotional control and stress management problems; scores from the thought dysfunction domain were associated with problems involving marksmanship and predicting situational outcomes; scores from the behavioral dysfunction domain correlated with integrity and substance use problems; and scores from the interpersonal functioning domain were associated with problems involving performance under stressful conditions, assertiveness and social interactions, and oral communications.

Tarescavage, Corey, and Ben-Porath (2015) examined associations between MMPI-2-RF scores in a pre-hire sample of candidates hired by the Portland (Oregon) Police Bureau and documented performance problems during field training. As in the previous study, the authors found robust (and generally expected) relationships between various measures of post-hire performance problems and MMPI-2-RF scores in the emotional dysfunction, thought dysfunction, behavioral dysfunction, and interpersonal functioning domains.

Tarescavage, Corey, Gupton, and Ben-Porath (2015) replicated the Portland study (Tarescavage, Corey, & Ben-Porath, 2015) with members of the Honolulu Police Department and found many of the same correlations reported in the former study. However, the authors reported the unexpected finding that scores on the MMPI-2-RF behavioral dysfunction domain (particularly BXD, RC9, and DISC-r) were negatively correlated with failure to engage subjects, reflecting the fact that low scores on these scales were associated with excessive behavioral inhibition. In a subsequent study, Corey, Sellbom, and Ben-Porath (2018) explored these findings in greater depth in a large sample of police officers who had previously been screened using the MMPI-2-RF, and confirmed that very low scores on BXD, RC9, and DISC-r are indeed associated with difficulties performing under ambiguous, high-stress, and rapidly evolving conditions, which the authors hypothesized to be attributable to behavioral overcontrol and inhibition.

Tarescavage, Fischler, Cappo, Hill, Corey, and Ben-Porath (2015) examined associations between MMPI-2-RF scale scores and selected scales and indices from the CPI-PPSSR and the IPI. They found expected correlations affirming the construct validity of the tests' respective scales. For a subsample of subjects for whom post-hire performance data were available, the authors found associations between MMPI-2-RF scale scores and performance problems that, as with the other studies just cited, indicate the validity of subclinical elevations in pre-hire MMPI-2-RF substantive scale scores in predicting a wide variety of performance and off-duty conduct problems in police officers.

Tarescavage, Corey, and Ben-Porath (2016) used an archival dataset of largely MMPI protocols gathered by Boes, Chandler, and Timm (1997), and re-scored using an innovative prorating procedure to estimate MMPI-2-RF scores. They found that several estimated MMPI-2-RF substantive scale scores were meaningfully correlated (using statistical corrections for range restriction and with small to medium effect sizes) with integrity violations and disciplinary infractions. In addition, estimated scale scores from the emotional, thought, and behavioral dysfunction domains were positively correlated with a wide range of performance problems (e.g., excessive force, supervisory problems, conduct unbecoming, failure to attend court).

Minnesota Multiphasic Personality Inventory–2

When the MMPI-2 was published in 1989, a number of published studies had already established its predecessor, the MMPI, as a standard component of assessment batteries used in screening police candidates (see, e.g., Azen, Snibbe, & Montgomery, 1973; Beutler, Storm, Kirkish, Scogin, & Gaines, 1985; Blum, 1964; Marsh, 1962; Saxe & Reiser, 1976). Since the release of the MMPI-2, which included an updated normative sample, substantially fewer published studies have reported on its validity in predicting post-hire outcomes in police officer samples. To some extent, a study by Hargrave, Hiatt, Ogard, and Carr (1994) may have heralded this dearth of research when the authors reported that, in a comparison of MMPI and MMPI-2 protocols concurrently administered to a sample of incumbent police officers, the two versions could be expected to yield comparable results. Although Hargrave et al. noted the need for validity research focused specifically on the MMPI-2, few researchers responded to their call to action.

Boes, Chandler, and Timm (1997) examined pre-hire MMPI and MMPI-2 scores of 439 police officers known to have engaged in a serious integrity violation (i.e., known offenders) from 69 police agencies across the United States and compared them with a matched control sample. They reported that subjects in the known-offender group scored higher on Clinical Scale 4 and on the L Scale in comparison to control subjects. (This dataset was reanalyzed by Tarescavage, Corey, & Ben-Porath [2016], who showed that prorated MMPI-2-RF scores outperformed the MMPI or MMPI-2 in predicting offender-group membership.)

Brewster and Stoloff (1999) conducted a retrospective examination of successful and problematic officers, finding that disqualifying candidates with any MMPI Clinical Scale score of 65T or higher would have led to the preemployment rejection of candidates who later engaged in counterproductive behavior. Castora, Brewster, and Stoloff (2003) studied the scores of four aggression-related scales (Ho, ANG, HOS, and O-H) on the MMPI-2, which was administered post-hire to 80 incumbent police officers in two police departments, to assess their utility in predicting supervisory ratings of aggressive behavior. The authors reported "no significant correlations between any of the MMPI-2 scales and any of the supervisor ratings" (p. 3).

Detrick, Chibnall, and Rosso (2001) examined correlations between MMPI-2 and IPI scale scores. They found that MMPI-2 Clinical Scale and IPI scale scores were moderately correlated in expected ways, but only when using non–K-corrected Clinical Scale scores. Similar findings by Sellbom, Fischler, and Ben-Porath (2007), as previously discussed, contributed to MMPI-2 experts recommending against the continued use of K-corrected clinical scores in preemployment evaluations (Graham, 2012; Greene, 2011).

Personality Assessment Inventory

Weiss, Rostow, Davis, and DeCoster-Martin (2004) explored associations between the pre-hire PAI scores of 800 Louisiana law enforcement officers and their performance after 1 year of service. The authors reported significant correlations between scores measuring aggression (AGG), antisocial behaviors (ANT), and impression management (both positive [PIM] and negative [NIM]), and post-hire problems. For example, Physical Aggression (a subscale of AGG) was found to correlate with frequency of weapon use, termination, and insubordination toward superiors.

Weiss, Hitchcock, Weiss, Rostow, and Davis (2008) examined associations between pre-hire PAI scores on the Borderline, Drug, and Alcohol Scales, and subsequent performance of 643 police officers. Using discriminant function and multiple regression equations, the authors concluded that scores on these three scales did not predict post-hire performance. They did not report findings related to other PAI scales.

Lowmaster and Morey (2012) explored associations between pre-hire PAI scale scores and post-hire performance (supervisory ratings of job performance, integrity problems, and abuse of disability status) in a sample of 85 law enforcement officers. The authors reported modest correlations for all domains, although "predictive validity was moderated by defensive response style, with greater predictive validity observed among less defensive responders" (p. 254).

Other Personality Tests Used in Police Suitability Evaluations

Although not commonly used in screening police candidates (see Chapter 5), there is much peer-reviewed research on the validity of the revised version of the NEO Personality Inventory (NEO PI-R; Costa & McCrae, 1992) in predicting police performance (e.g., Chibnall & Detrick, 2003; Detrick & Chibnall, 2019; Detrick, Chibnall, & Call, 2010; Detrick, Chibnall, & Luebbert, 2004). However, the current version of the test is the NEO PI-3 (McCrae & Costa, 2010), for which, at the time of this writing, there are no published peer-reviewed studies of its validity in assessing police suitability.

The Matrix-Predictive Uniform Law Enforcement Selection Evaluation (M-PULSE) Inventory (Davis & Rostow, 2008) is the second psychological assessment instrument (after the IPI) to use police candidates as its sole normative sample (Ellingwood, Williams, Sitarenios, & Solomon, 2018). These authors describe this test as "contextualized" (i.e., using job-specific items, such as, "I like that cops . . .") and "actuarial" (i.e., mechanically predicting on-the-job performance liabilities). Although the authors reported that the findings "supported the reliability, factor structure, and lack of gender or ethnic bias of the M-PULSE" (p. 1), the study included no data linking the test results to post-hire performance. In discussing this limitation, the authors wrote, "Predictive validity should be a priority in evaluating law enforcement screening measures, but the time and resource commitments required from law enforcement agencies poses a significant challenge, due to the low base rates of officer liability and other logistical issues" (p. 13). Thus, more than a decade after publication of the M-PULSE, no peer-reviewed studies report the predictive validity of the instrument.

Empirical Studies Involving Measures Used in Fitness-for-Duty Evaluations

As we discuss further in the next chapter, fitness evaluations are fundamentally clinical assessments conducted for the purpose of assessing job-relevant mental impairment and capacities. Consequently, psychologists are tasked with choosing test instruments that have been validated to assess clinical constructs relevant to the particular individual being examined and the functional abilities in question. Such choices are necessarily supported by validity evidence derived from broad clinical samples, rather than from police officer subjects. When assessing for posttraumatic stress disorder (PTSD), for example, a clinician may choose to administer the MMPI-2-RF, the MMPI-2, the PAI, the Detailed Assessment of Posttraumatic Stress (Briere, 2001), or other measures assessing either broad psychopathology constructs or PTSD specifically, such as the structured interview-based Clinician-Administered PTSD Scale for DSM-5 (CAPS; Weathers et al.,
2018). Thus, the relevant empirical foundation for the selection of assessment instruments used in fitness evaluations consists of the validity argument supported by research involving a diverse set of clinical populations rather than from police officers alone. Nonetheless, in recognition of

BEST PRACTICE

The relevant empirical foundation for the selection of assessment instruments used in fitness evaluations consists of the validity argument supported by research involving a diverse set of clinical populations rather than from police officers alone.

the role that context can play in influencing test responses (e.g., Arbisi, Ben-Porath, & McNulty, 2006; Bornstein, 2011; Detrick & Chibnall, 2014; Walfish, 2010), a practitioner may find utility in comparing the test scores of an officer examined in a fitness evaluation to other police officers assessed in that context.[5]

Notes

1. See   http://lib.post.ca.gov/Publications/PsycScreeningManual/IPI-2.pdf.
2. A 260-item version of the CPI (CPI-260) was published in 2002. At the time of this writing, no studies have been published on the validity of the CPI-260 in the context of police evaluations.
3. This statistical technique, developed by Hunter and Schmidt (1990) and first applied by Sellbom et al. (2007) to test validation involving police candidates, alters the standard deviation (SD) of the predictor variable to approximate that of the target population. The SD of the research sample is significantly smaller than the target population (i.e., all police officer candidates, both qualified and unqualified), which artificially attenuates (lowers) the true correlation. For example, in a study of police candidates subsequently hired as recruit trainees at the Honolulu Police Department, Tarescavage et al. (2015) reported that the MMPI-2-RF Higher-Order Scale EID (Emotional/Internalizing Dysfunction) correlated with a post-hire performance measure of Assertiveness/Control Problems Under Stress Conditions ($r = 0.17$), but when corrected for range restriction, the correlation rose to $r = 0.29$.
4. David Corey is coauthor of the MMPI-2-RF *Police Candidate Interpretive Report* (PCIR; Corey & Ben-Porath, 2014). As such, he receives royalties on the sale of the report and its derivative products.
5. Corey and Ben-Porath (2018) provide tables depicting the means and standard deviations (presented separately for male and female subjects) for the 51 scales of the MMPI-2-RF administered to police officers during fitness evaluations.

PART II
APPLICATION

Preparation for the Evaluation

4

Doing the necessary legwork before conducting a police suitability or fitness evaluation cannot be overemphasized. Proper preparation requires the examiner to understand three areas of information related to the specific evaluation:

- the "legitimacy" of the referral,
- the relevant demands and working conditions of the examinee's position, and
- the criterion standard for determining whether the examinee is psychologically suitable or fit for duty.

We next discuss these preparatory requirements, along with a few additional ones, for evaluations of both suitability and fitness.

Legitimacy of the Referral

The responsibility for ensuring the legitimacy of the referral lies ultimately with

BEST PRACTICE

Doing the necessary legwork before conducting a police suitability or fitness evaluation cannot be overemphasized.

the employer, not the examiner. However, given the high stakes involved in these evaluations, an examiner's acceptance of a referral for which there is no legal justification (or which is legally prohibited) can result in costly litigation and harm to both the examinee and the organizational client. We next describe the steps an examiner can take to assess the legitimacy of a referral and, at the same time, gather information that will be necessary for a valid evaluation.

Legitimacy in Suitability Evaluation

As we discussed in Chapter 1, a preemployment suitability evaluation is permitted by the Americans With Disabilities Act of 1990 (ADA) only if *all* entering employees are subjected to such an examination or inquiry regardless of disability—and only if it *follows* a bona fide offer of employment (that is, an offer given after the employer has completed all nonmedical components and contingencies in the application process that can reasonably be completed). The *Occupationally Mandated Psychological Evaluations* (OMPE) Guidelines (American Psychological Association [APA], 2018) admonish psychologists "to confirm with the referring party that a conditional offer of employment [COE] has been tendered before conducting the evaluation" (p. 189). One way to confirm the legitimacy of a suitability evaluation is to receive a narrative summary of the hiring agency's background investigation of the candidate before conducting the evaluation. This ensures not only that the timing of the evaluation is lawful (meaning that it follows the collection and analysis of the reasonably obtainable nonmedical information) but also that you have the collateral information needed to conduct the most reliable and valid assessment. Another method we discussed in Chapter 1, particularly with agencies that do not routinely complete background investigation reports before the COE, is to request a copy of the COE to ensure that it does not include nonmedical requirements that may render it invalid.

Legitimacy in Fitness Evaluations

The legitimacy of a fitness evaluation referral is determined by its job-relatedness and consistency with business necessity [42 U.S.C. § 12112(d)(4)(A)]. As noted by the OMPE Guidelines,

"Understanding how the employer has met this 'business necessity standard,' and the objective evidence giving rise to it, can contribute to a more complete understanding of the goals of the evaluation and the psychologist's ability to meet them" (p. 190). Corey (2011) recommends a "prereferral conference" with the referring party to obtain this information before agreeing to conduct the evaluation. Doing so also enables you to understand the objective facts underlying the referral and to decide if a fitness evaluation is indicated and whether the subject matter falls within your areas of competence. For example, a referral based on observations of a sudden change in cognition may require competence in neuropsychological assessment, and unless you are qualified to conduct such evaluations, there should be a referral to (or collaboration with) a qualified neuropsychologist.

BEWARE

A preemployment suitability evaluation is permitted by the ADA only if *all* entering employees are subjected to such an examination or inquiry regardless of disability—and only if it *follows* a bona fide offer of employment (that is, an offer given after the employer has completed all nonmedical components and contingencies in the application process that can reasonably be completed). In contrast, the legitimacy of a fitness evaluation referral is determined by its job-relatedness and consistency with business necessity.

4
chapter

A prereferral conference also allows for consideration of an alternative timing of the fitness evaluation. Employers sometimes refer a police officer for a fitness evaluation concurrent with an internal affairs or other administrative investigation. Although this may be necessary (as when there is reason to worry that the officer poses a risk of suicide or a danger to others), often the evaluation is better delayed until the facts of the investigation have been determined (and shared with the examiner) and when the employer is prepared to return the officer to duty pending the outcome of the evaluation. Equally important is the opportunity that the prereferral conference can provide for assessing whether the examiner is able to be impartial, which is a fundamental ethical standard governing all evaluations (Otto, Goldstein, & Heilbrun, 2017).

Referral Letter

After a psychologist has conferred with the referral source and confirmed the legitimacy of a mandatory fitness evaluation, it is a good policy to request a formal referral letter. This is typically written by the referring supervisor or human resource officer, or sometimes the employer's legal counsel, and describes the objective reasons for the organization's concern that the employee's performance is impaired because of a known or suspected psychological or cognitive disorder. Stated differently, the referral letter should address one or both of the elements of business necessity articulated in the ADA. These two elements are

- reasonable cause to suspect that the employee has a mental impairment that substantially limits their ability to perform the essential functions of the position, or
- reasonable cause to suspect that the employee has a mental impairment that may pose a significant risk of harm to self or others in the workplace.[1]

A referral letter also helps limit the scope of the evaluation, so the inquiry is no broader or intrusive than necessary. In those cases in which the referral appears appropriate, the psychologist may wish to review a draft of the referral letter and provide editorial feedback. A letter that is nebulous or only vaguely describes the objective evidence underlying the employer's concern does little to further the efforts of providing a relevant evaluative process that is designed to explore the potential causes of the behaviors that generated the concern.

Although it is ideal for the referral source to provide an objective nexus between impaired performance/threat *and* a suspected psychological or cognitive condition, the burden of demonstrating this evidence is not equal across all industries: the burden decreases as the safety-sensitivity of the position increases. Recall from Chapter 1 that, in *Watson v. City of Miami Beach* (1999), the federal district court held that when:

> a police department reasonably perceives an officer to be even mildly paranoid, hostile, or oppositional, a fitness for duty

examination is job-related and consistent with business necessity. . . . Police departments place armed officers in positions where they can do tremendous harm if they act irrationally [and, moreover,] the ADA does not require a police department to forego a fitness for duty examination to wait until a perceived threat becomes real or questionable behavior results in injuries. (p. 935)

Similar fact patterns and holdings are found even in settings outside of law enforcement, such as with paraprofessionals who provide direct patient care (e.g., *EEOC v. Amego, Inc.,* 1997).

The referral letter should be provided before the evaluation begins. The employer often shares the referral letter with the employee, which increases the transparency of the evaluation. An appropriately crafted letter may provide assurance to both the psychologist and the employee that the evaluation is not pretext for a fishing expedition or some other prohibited motive, such as when a "retaliatory referral" is made for the purpose of stigmatizing or discrediting the employee (Gold et al., 2008, p. 10). Indeed, you may also recall from Chapter 1 the Ninth Circuit case of *Stewart v. Pearce* (1973), in which a referral for a mental health evaluation was used to stigmatize a college professor who engaged in political activities contrary to the views of the administration.

When a practitioner receives a referral for a fitness evaluation, there is often great urgency. The employee is typically on paid administrative leave or in a restricted duty position pending the outcome of the evaluation. The need is especially acute in smaller agencies when the absence of even one officer places a significant burden on staffing and community safety. It is tempting to hastily proceed through these preliminaries because of the employer's sense of urgency. In doing so, one can experience considerable hardship down the road if the referral was illegitimate, the psychologist and employer did not consider other reasonable alternatives, or the psychologist was ill-suited to perform the evaluation.

> **BOX 4.1** Applicable guideline: The referral letter
>
> It is recommended that the employer's referral to the examiner include a description of the objective evidence giving rise to concerns about the employee's fitness for duty and any particular questions that the employer wishes the examiner to address. It is also recommended that the referral, and the basis for it, be documented in writing, either by the agency or the examiner (IACP, 2018a, Guideline 7.4).

Occasions When a Fitness Referral Is Inadvisable

In the course of the initial prereferral conference, it is possible that the psychologist and referring party will determine that a fitness evaluation is not appropriate. Rostow and Davis (2004) discussed a number of scenarios in which they conclude that a fitness evaluation is inadvisable. These include the following:

1. *Criminal conduct is suspected.* If the employee is suspected of criminal conduct, a fitness evaluation should not be done (or at least should be deferred) until the legal issue is resolved. Indeed, Rostow and Davis (2004) opine, "FFDEs [fitness-for-duty evaluations] are primarily for the purpose of salvaging good officers who need assistance, not in protecting or rehabilitating criminally inclined officers. Where little is to be gained from the viewpoint of potential officer rehabilitation, the FFDE is usually questionable" (p. 152).

   Similarly, an FFDE should not be used when the psychologist suspects its purpose is to obtain evidence that can be used in a criminal investigation involving officer misconduct. Doing so also may be inconsistent with the protections afforded law enforcement officers by the US Supreme Court decision in *Garrity v. New Jersey* (1967), in which the court held that law enforcement officers and other public employees have the right to be free from compulsory self-incrimination in criminal matters. This decision gave birth to the *Garrity warning*, which is administered by investigators to police officer suspects in internal and administrative investigations in a similar manner as the *Miranda warning* is administered to suspects in criminal investigations. Following a Garrity warning, a police officer can be ordered to participate in an internal or administrative investigation and give a statement, and the officer's statements (or silence) can be later used against the officer in disciplinary hearings and civil lawsuits, but not in criminal prosecution.

2. *Annoying employees.* Rostow and Davis (2004) contend that when the referral presents as an effort "to dispose of a marginal or annoying officer whose behavior has not changed substantially in recent times, an FFDE is usually inappropriate" (p. 153). Our most common experience in this regard involves the problem officer working for a new manager who is not tolerant of the long-standing problematic behavior. In most circumstances, such issues should be addressed with administrative remedies and resources. On the other hand, Rostow and Davis qualify this recommendation by stating, "FFDEs are most useful in the examination of officers who are showing new uninviting or inappropriate behavior or notable worsening of previous conduct" (p. 153).

3. *Obscene language.* In *Maplewood v. Law Enforcement Labor Service* (1996), an arbitrator concluded that obscene language communicated by an officer over the radio is not, by itself, sufficient to mandate a fitness evaluation of the "expressive officer."

4. *Grievances, lawsuits, or targeting a specific officer.* A psychologist should exercise caution when accepting a referral for a fitness evaluation of an officer who is presently engaged in a grievance or lawsuit against the employer. Although an emotionally disturbed officer may initiate actions with little substantive basis, the psychologist should avoid involvement when there is a strong indication of political or retaliatory motivation. Similarly, Rostow and Davis (2004) advise psychologists to be cautious of fitness referrals based on violations of

conduct rules that are being selectively enforced toward one employee and not toward other apparent violators.

In addition to the warnings listed by Rostow and Davis, we have encountered some of our own contraindicated referrals that we will add to the list. Sometimes it is a situation in which an employee has an emotional, yet normal reaction to a critical incident. One of the most common situations in which this occurs is when we are asked to do a fitness evaluation of an officer involved in a justified shooting. Being distraught and upset in such a situation is a normal reaction and should not be pathologized (Zelig, 1998). Moreover, the International Association of Chiefs of Police (IACP; 2018b) *Officer-Involved Shooting Guidelines* cautions practitioners and employers not to assume that a fitness evaluation is necessary for an officer experiencing normal reactions to trauma. Some employers may have policies that routinely require psychological evaluations of all officers who have been involved in shootings and other critical incidents. Although doing so would be inconsistent with the aforementioned IACP guidelines, it would not appear to violate ADA law, at least as interpreted by the district court in *EEOC v. U.S. Steel* (2013). Still, such evaluations would not comprise a fitness evaluation, as defined by the IACP (2018a) FFDE guidelines, because such an evaluation would not result from "(1) objective evidence that the employee may be unable to safely or effectively perform a defined job and (2) a reasonable basis for believing that the cause may be attributable to a psychological condition or impairment" (Guideline 3.1).

Another ill-advised fitness referral involves cases in which the employee is referred for evaluation but is not ordered to participate. If participation is optional, it is hard to envision a situation in which the grounds for referral could meet the business necessity threshold.

Mayer and Corey (2017) also delineated the basis for considering the justification for various types of fitness referrals, with a considerable focus on statutory and case law in support of their opinions. Undoubtedly, the experienced practitioner reading this section could expand the list of particular scenarios in which they

> **BOX 4.2** Applicable guideline: FFDE referrals for officer-involved shootings or other critical incidents are generally not appropriate
>
> Officers' fitness for duty should not be brought into question simply by virtue of their involvement in a shooting or other critical incident. Post-shooting and other critical incident psychological interventions are separate and distinct from any fitness-for-duty assessments or administrative or investigative procedures that may follow. This does not preclude an agency from requesting a formal fitness-for-duty evaluation based upon objective concerns about an officer's ability to perform his or her duties due to a suspected medical or psychological condition. However, the mere fact of being involved in a shooting does not necessitate such an evaluation prior to return to duty (IACP, 2018b, Guideline 6.10).

determined that a fitness evaluation was inappropriate. One commonality with many of these inappropriate referrals is that they all fail to demonstrate a nexus between a reasonably suspected emotional or cognitive condition and a functional impairment on the job.

Relevant Demands and Working Conditions

Both suitability and fitness evaluations require the examiner to be familiar with the relevant demands and working conditions of the position for which the individual is being evaluated. The OMPE Guidelines underscore that "understanding the job description and psychologically relevant demands and working conditions of the position is a necessary foundation for judgments about the examinee's ability to perform the essential functions of the position" (p. 191). As we noted in the previous chapter, suitability and fitness determinations rest not only on findings that an individual has certain problematic traits or impairments but also on the impact of those findings on the person's ability to safely and effectively perform the essential functions of the job.

Reviewing the position description and underlying job analysis is always a good place to start. Although large departments often include job descriptions as part of their civil service regulations, it

BEST PRACTICE

Both suitability and fitness evaluations necessitate familiarity with the relevant demands and working conditions of the position for which the individual is being evaluated.

is unusual for a small police department to have the resources to develop the elaborate, empirically based, and often expensive job task analyses conducted by our industrial and organizational psychology colleagues. In fact, most job or position descriptions are authored by a human resource professional or a committee. Guion (1991) pointed out that a job analysis need not be a complicated or expensive undertaking: "[J]ob analysis is any procedure used to develop insights into job components: things people do on a job, resources they draw on in doing them, and organizational implications of doing them well or poorly" (p. 331). Although the ADA does not require a job analysis to specify essential job functions (Rennert, 2004), the necessity of identifying the essential job functions and the knowledge, skills, and abilities required is reinforced in applicable IACP practice guidelines.

It is also important to recognize, as we discussed at length in Chapter 2, that there can be great variability in the work of a police officer across agencies and assignments. A police officer in a rural four-person police department faces significantly different job demands and working conditions than an officer in a major urban department. Similarly, when conducting a fitness evaluation, the examiner will need to be familiar with the job demands of the *particular* position (including any ancillary assignments) to which the officer is assigned (e.g., school resource officer, homicide detective, tactical unit). Interviews and ride-alongs can provide useful information about the unique requirements and stressors of a particular position that may set it apart from the more common patrol officer functions.

These activities also can help distinguish essential or critical job functions from marginal and less critical duties, along with identifying the knowledge, skills, and abilities required for the position. Interviewing field training officers and asking them what they view as the strengths and weaknesses of past hired recruits

BOX 4.3 Applicable guideline: Know the demands of the position

5.1. Information about the required duties, responsibilities, working conditions, and other psychologically relevant job characteristics should be obtained from the hiring authority prior to beginning the psychological evaluation. This information should be directed toward identifying skills, behaviors, attributes, and other personal characteristics associated with effective and counterproductive job performance.

5.3. The examiner should consult with the hiring authority regarding agency-specific risk management concerns, and seek clarification as to whether the evaluation should go beyond the identification of unsuitable candidates to include information about other specific selection criteria and/or specialized characteristics not covered in the job-analytic data referenced in 5.1 (IACP, 2014).

may further assist the psychologist in designing evaluations to help identify candidates who lack the attributes most needed by their community and department.

The importance of preparation through the acquisition of job knowledge relevant to a particular agency and assignment is equally true for fitness evaluations of incumbent officers. As we discuss in Chapter 5, assessing the suitability of a candidate or fitness of a police officer requires understanding how the psychological characteristics of the individual link with the demands specific to the position in the hiring/employing agency. Grisso (2003) has argued that all forensic mental health assessments should include an analysis of the interaction between an individual's functional abilities (and deficits) and the demands faced by that person in a particular context. As such, knowing the functional and contextual requirements of the specific position in the employing agency is essential.

The Criterion Standard

We next discuss the criterion standard used in both suitability and fitness evaluations. But before we begin our discussion of the criterion standard used in the preemployment assessment of a police officer candidate's psychological suitability for the position, it is useful to place the evaluation in the context of the broader selection process.

4
chapter

The Context of the Suitability Evaluation

Obtaining employment as a law enforcement officer takes considerable time to complete, from application to swearing-in, depending on the size and requirements of the agency. The hiring process typically includes three stages. In the first stage, it is determined whether the applicant meets the basic requirements (e.g., absence of a disqualifying arrest record, minimum age, passing a physical agility test). During this stage, the applicant may also take written and/or oral examinations, which may yield rankings used to assign the applicant a position on a civil service or eligibility list.

If the applicant meets the basic qualifications and is positioned sufficiently high on the eligibility list, they advance to the second stage, which consists of the background investigation (typically including interviews with personal references, coworkers and supervisors, neighbors, and other collateral informants) and a polygraph examination. In some agencies, a psychologist may be retained to perform a pre-offer screening assessment, in which applicants complete biographical forms and/or normal-range personality tests designed to identify those most likely to have the traits and character associated with success in law enforcement. In US agencies, this evaluation should not contain ADA-prohibited medical questions—inquiries that must be deferred until after a conditional offer of employment has been tendered. The splitting of psychological evaluations into nonmedical (pre-COE) and medical (post-COE) stages has been referred to as a "bifurcated model" (Corey, 2008; Jones, Cunningham, & Dages, 2010).

One important variable that influences the number of applicants cut from the first and second stages is the ratio of applicants to vacancies. This, in turn, is influenced by the starting salary and the reputation of the agency, among other factors. The more applicants there are for a given position, the more selective the agency can be before advancing candidates to the more expensive selection processes used in the second and third stages. Indeed, agency administrators engage in a balancing act between setting the standards for entry criteria as high as possible and ensuring an adequate pool of applicants. When entrance requirements include a college degree, previous law enforcement experience, or prior state certification,[2] any benefit that might be gained from setting higher entrance standards could be lost if it renders the applicant pool so small that the agency is unable to be highly selective. Indeed, an agency with 10 vacancies may be able to hire 10 superior recruits more easily from 200 applicants with a high school degree than from an applicant pool of 50 applicants with a 4-year degree.[3]

Those who survive the second stage may advance to the third stage and receive a conditional offer of employment. Because it is reasonable to assume that some candidates will be lost to the medical and psychological examinations, and others will take positions with other agencies, the Equal Employment Opportunity Commission (EEOC) has permitted public safety employers to give more conditional offers than positions so that they can develop a pool of eligible candidates. As a result of these different dynamics, a psychologist who screens for various agencies, even in the same geographical area, is likely to notice differences in the overall quality of candidates across agencies.

The Criterion Standard in Suitability Evaluations

The evaluator's role in either selecting or screening candidates is not unlike that of a quality control (QC) inspector in a traditional fruit-packing business. After the fruit is picked by field workers and deposited in bins, the product advances on a conveyor belt to the QC inspector, which in this analogy is played by the screening evaluator. The inspector has no role in picking the fruit. Instead, the fruit gradually proceeds along the conveyor belt to be packed by other workers for delivery to the grocery store, restaurant, or other consumer unless it is removed by the inspector for failure to meet the QC standards. Examining psychologists, like QC inspectors, are responsible not for deciding what selection criteria to use (although they can and should share relevant criterion options and recommendations with the employer), but rather for applying those standards to their task.

4
chapter

BEST PRACTICE

Like all occupationally mandated psychological evaluations, the focus of a suitability evaluation is driven by the *criterion standard*.

Like all occupationally mandated psychological evaluations, the focus of a suitability evaluation is driven by the *criterion standard*. Indeed, it is the most basic forensic question in police suitability and fitness evaluations. Without knowing the criterion, the examiner cannot identify the methodology needed to conduct the evaluation or how to analyze the assessment data, select the relevant findings, formulate opinions, and communicate the results of the evaluation. In psychological suitability evaluations of police candidates, the criterion standard:

> may be derived through review of a job analysis conducted by the hiring organization or by a global job analysis conducted by a professional/trade association or regulatory agency. For others, the standards may be defined by statute, regulation, or policy, or they may be inferred from the job description, job classification documentation, and/or knowledge of the working conditions associated with the position in question. (APA, 2018, OMPE Guideline 2, p. 190)

We continue our analysis of the criterion standard in suitability evaluations by exploring the statutes and mandates promulgated in various states and provinces.

ILLUSTRATIVE DEFINITIONS OF PSYCHOLOGICAL SUITABILITY

Many jurisdictions have established statutory and/or regulatory criteria for defining a psychologically qualified police officer. These provisions set the floor, or the minimum suitability standards.[4] In the United States, these mandates are passed by the legislature; in Canada, the standards are promulgated by the Provincial Chiefs of Police Associations, who are delegated this task by the Provincial Solicitor General or, at least in one case (Ontario Association of Chiefs of Police), in collaboration with the provincial Ministry of Community Safety and Correctional Services. These mandates vary widely in their specificity and approach in reflecting the respective originator's aspirations for the qualifications of law enforcement officers within their jurisdictions. Frequently, the criterion standard is stated in the local agency's civil service regulations.

Corey and Borum (2013) reported at the time of their writing that 38 states had established preemployment or precertification requirements for the emotional, mental, or psychological health, functioning, fitness, or suitability of police officers in their respective jurisdictions. After analyzing each state's published requirements, they found that the most common standard (in 17 of the 38 states) was an *exclusionary* one that prohibited the hiring of a person having an emotional or mental condition that might adversely affect the person's ability to exercise the powers and duties of the position. Thirteen states at the time had adopted *inclusionary* criteria, often described in overly broad terms (e.g., Colorado's requirement of "fitness to serve as a peace officer" or North Carolina's stipulation that the person be "mentally and emotionally suitable to properly fulfill the responsibilities of the position"). Kentucky and Maine offered more detailed constructs, such as assertiveness, self-confidence, the ability to accept criticism, and the ability to get along with others (Maine). Three states (Alaska, California, and Delaware) established hiring standards for police officers that include both exclusionary and inclusionary criteria.

4
chapter

Although the Corey and Borum (2013) analysis provided a useful overview of the state-by-state selection criteria in effect at the time, it is already out of date. New statutes and regulations have been passed, and others have been revised. It is important that evaluators stay informed about the requirements in their respective jurisdictions and stay abreast of any changes over time.

Those in jurisdictions that have yet to legislate selection standards can take solace in a Bureau of Justice Statistics survey report noting that 98% of police departments serving populations of 25,000 or more use some form of psychological screening (Reaves, 2011). Yet, even if a statute mandates consideration of certain aspects of psychological suitability (e.g., emotional stability), it will not necessarily specify *how* that criterion is ascertained. For example, Utah's statute (Utah State Code Section 53-6-211) focuses on grounds for decertification and thus *implies* what mental traits are needed for certification. However, it does not require that a preemployment psychological evaluation be conducted. Rather, the hiring authority has the responsibility to declare that the candidate or officer meets all of the requirements for initial and ongoing certification, including those subsumed under mental health.

A notable exception to the vagaries of most state mandates is the research conducted by the California POST Commission to identify the psychological demands of law enforcement work and to codify those demands into psychological screening standards. California Government Code § 1031(f) and its implementing regulations (POST Commission Regulation 1955)[5] set standards regarding the qualifications of examining psychologists and minimal standards for the psychological examination. More specifically, psychologists or psychiatrists who perform these evaluations must have 5 years of post-doctoral experience and meet biennial continuing education requirements specific to maintaining competency in police candidate screening [11 C.C.R. § 1955(a)]. Other licensed professionals are not allowed to conduct these evaluations. California POST also publishes a comprehensive psychological screening manual that contains applicable regulations, research, and sample forms (Spilberg & Corey, 2019).[6] Thus, California POST "provides the most detailed and comprehensive set of statutes, administrative rules, and agency regulations pertaining to psychological screening" (Corey & Borum, 2013, p. 251) of police candidates and has established strong precedent for a national standard.

California requires that police officers be evaluated both to ensure they are "free of any physical, emotional or mental condition that might adversely affect the exercise of the powers of a peace officer" [California Government Code § 1031(f)] and to "otherwise ensure that the candidate is capable of withstanding the psychological demands of the position" [11 C.C.R. § 1955(a)]. But even these combined criteria give little guidance for understanding the kinds of personality traits and characteristics expected to impede successful performance or result in counterproductive behavior as a police officer. To fill that gap, the California POST Commission requires that police candidates be evaluated against a set of 10 *Peace Officer Psychological Screening Dimensions* (Table 4.1). These

Table 4.1 | California POST Psychological Screening Dimensions

Psychological Screening Dimension	Associated Traits and Competencies
Social competence	Tactfulness, awareness of the impact of one's own words and behavior on others, interest and concern for the feelings of others, respectfulness and sensitivity toward all members of society.
Teamwork	Cooperative working relationships with others, subordinating personal interests in deference to the organizational mission, doing one's share of the work, not letting differences get in the way of working together.
Adaptability/flexibility	Adjusting to unplanned events, using discretion in enforcing regulations and applying policies, working steadily without immediate oversite, accommodating different styles of supervision.
Conscientiousness/ dependability	Diligence, reliability, conscientious work patterns, punctuality, perseverance in the face of obstacles and adverse working conditions, careful attention to details, following through on commitments.
Impulse control/attention to safety	Avoiding impulsive and/or unnecessarily risky behavior, showing regard for the safety of oneself and others, thinking things through (including consequences) before acting, exercising self-control and restraint while being able to act under ambiguous, high-stress, and rapidly evolving situations requiring a response.
Integrity/ethics	Honesty, trustworthiness, conformance with laws and organizational procedures, using police powers only for lawful purposes and never for personal gain or exploitation.

4
chapter

Table 4.1 | Continued

Psychological Screening Dimension	Associated Traits and Competencies
Emotional regulation/stress tolerance	Maintaining emotional and behavioral composure, especially during time-critical emergency events, while using force, and in other stressful situations. Accepting criticism without excessive defensiveness. Exercising proper self-care so as to be able to cope resiliently with intense and chronic stress, sleep deprivation, and other physical and emotional hardships.
Decision-making/judgment	Ability to size-up situations and take the appropriate action. Ability to quickly assess what is relevant and important, and to use that information to make good decisions. Prioritizing competing demands.
Assertiveness/ persuasiveness	Ability to persuade others to adopt a desired course of action and, when necessary, to take charge and control. Ability to engage people under both routine and dangerous conditions, resist intimidation, and use force to maintain or restore safety.
Avoiding substance abuse and other risk-taking behavior	Avoiding conduct, including the misuse of alcohol and other chemical substances, that can negatively affect personal functioning, on and off the job, as well as community confidence in the police.

dimensions, the methodology used to identify them, and how suitability can be assessed for each are described in detail in the California POST *Peace Officer Psychological Screening Manual* (Spilberg & Corey, 2019). As Detrick and Chibnall (2013) observed, because the California POST dimensions "specify validated, behaviorally defined police officer psychological attributes and associated positive and counterproductive work behaviors," they "provide a template for translating clinical findings into job-related concerns and issues" (p. 373), even in jurisdictions outside California.

LOCAL RULES OR EXPECTATIONS

The content and scope of psychological evaluations may also be subject to local rules or agreements. A collective bargaining agreement may dictate certain parameters, although such conditions are far more likely to be present in the course of a fitness evaluation than in a preemployment evaluation. One way to address unexpected contingencies is to have the agency review and approve the evaluating psychologist's procedures. This may prevent a situation in which the local jurisdiction assumes that the psychologist is following a requirement, custom, or practice that is uncommon or idiosyncratic to the local agency or jurisdiction and unknown to the evaluating psychologist. One of the best ways to obtain this understanding is by offering an informed consent document to the hiring agency—a topic we discuss in detail in Chapter 6.

PERSONALITY TRAITS AND CONDITIONS NOT COVERED BY THE AMERICANS WITH DISABILITIES ACT

There are several conditions that are not covered by the ADA. Accordingly, a psychologist conducting a pre-offer evaluation can make inquiries about the following topics:

4
chapter

1. *Questions that are not expected to yield information about a disability.*
2. *A person's drinking habits, but not if the questions can reveal an alcohol use disorder.*
3. *Current illicit drug use, but not past drug abuse or addiction.*

We know of no bright line defining when the candidate or employee is considered a current or former user. The modern trend seen in various appellate court decisions requires evidence of permanent cessation of drug use. For example, in *Shafer v. Preston Memorial Hospital Corporation* (1997), a nurse anesthetist was caught diverting fentanyl for her own use. Her employer placed her on leave, helped her find a rehabilitation program, and then fired her the day she graduated from the inpatient portion of her rehabilitation program. The nurse sued Preston Memorial, claiming that since she was no longer using, her fentanyl addiction constituted a protected disability under ADA. Preston Memorial did not dispute that addiction was covered by the ADA but argued that the plaintiff was still considered to be engaged in current drug use, given the recency with which she used fentanyl. The court researched Congress's legislative history[7] when the ADA was being written and concluded that Congress wanted to avoid a narrow definition of "current use." The court held that the ADA "does not require that drug user have a heroin syringe in his arm or a marijuana bong to his mouth at the exact moment" to preclude protection under the act (p. 278). Similarly, in *Baustain v. State of Louisiana* (1996), the court upheld the termination of an employee who had stopped using marijuana 7 weeks prior, concluding this was insufficient time to avoid being considered a current drug user. It thus appears that former users will not be afforded ADA protection until they have a track record of at least long-term abstinence.

4. *Transvestism, transsexualism, pedophilia, exhibitionism, voyeurism, gender identity disorders not resulting from physical impairments, or other sexual behavior disorders; compulsive gambling, kleptomania, or pyromania; and "homosexuality and bisexuality are not impairments and so are not disabilities* as defined in this part" (Appendix, Part 1630.3). Examiners should be mindful, however, that laws in local jurisdictions may bar discrimination on the basis of these and other conditions not protected by the ADA.

5. *Pregnancy* [Appendix Section 1630.2(h)] is not a protected disability. However, any medical complication arising from pregnancy is a covered condition. Here, too, state law may afford protections for pregnancy that federal law does not.

6. *A mental impairment that poses a direct threat to self or others* is also not a covered condition if it cannot be neutralized with reasonable accommodation.

7. *Personality traits* (but personality disorders may be covered under ADA).

The definition of an impairment also does not include common personality traits such as poor judgment or a quick temper where these are not symptoms of a mental or psychological disorder. Environmental, cultural, or economic disadvantages such as poverty, lack of education, or a prison record are not impairments. Advanced age, in and of itself, is also not an impairment [29 C.F.R. Part 1630.2(h); 29 C.F.R. Part 1630, Appendix].

The Criterion Standard in Fitness Evaluations

Suitability criteria for initial qualification generally apply throughout the tenure of a police officer. As such, they are relevant not only for determining preemployment suitability but also for evaluating the psychological fitness of incumbents. Although it is generally agreed that the focus of fitness evaluations is whether the officer has a mental condition or impairment that renders the officer "unable to safely or effectively perform a defined job" (IACP, 2018a), suitability standards may be useful in this analysis. Two state appellate cases (*Brown v. Sandy City Appeal Board*, 2014; *Sager v. County of Yuba*, 2007) illustrate this point; both courts held that the California POST Psychological Screening Dimensions provide useful guidance for assessing the requisite competencies that may be diminished by the symptoms and behaviors associated with a police officer's mental impairment.

The applicability of preemployment standards across the career of a police officer does not negate the central importance of first determining whether the officer has a mental health impairment. Absent such an impairment, the threshold requirement for being unfit for duty cannot be met. Corey and Ben-Porath (2018) presented a model for data integration in fitness evaluations, which we discuss in more depth in Chapter 6, but it warrants some attention here in order to further explicate the fitness criterion.

Recall from our discussion in Chapter 1 that the ADA prohibits an employer from mandating a medical examination or inquiry of an employee except when there is objective evidence leading to a reasonable belief that the employee is unable to perform the essential functions of their position, or poses a direct threat, *due to a mental impairment*. With this mandate in mind, Corey and Ben-Porath (2018) proposed a data integration model that begins by asking whether there is evidence of an emotional, cognitive, behavioral, thought, interpersonal, or other psychological impairment. If not, the employee does not satisfy the first and foundational criterion necessary to be psychologically unfit for duty. If the officer does have a mental health condition, this fact alone is insufficient for finding the employee unfit for duty. Instead, the examiner next asks whether the condition limits the employee's *current* ability to perform the essential functions of the job, to perform them properly, or to perform them without posing a direct threat to the employee or others. If so, the

employee is unfit for duty; if not, the concerning behavior that may have prompted the evaluation is left to the employer for administrative disposition. However, if the examiner finds that the officer has a condition that is in remission at the time of the evaluation or is nonsymptomatic because of the ameliorative effects of treatment or environmental conditions,[8] the final step in the decision-making model is to assess the sustainability of fitness over time. Failure to consider this factor can have serious implications for the officer, the public, and fellow officers.

This approach underscores the importance of being knowledgeable about the job demands and working conditions of the position before making a fitness determination, and of not resting judgments about fitness for duty solely on the mere existence of a mental disorder. It also is consistent with Grisso's (2003) advice to consider the relationship between a person's clinical condition and functional capacities, and, in this respect, it is aligned with other kinds of forensic mental health assessments.

Other Preparations

A final set of preparations will help reduce the likelihood of conflicting expectations during and after the fitness evaluation. These include determining, in advance of the evaluation, whether

- the officer will be able to obtain a copy of the written report directly from the examiner or otherwise gain access to records in the examiner's possession, and
- a third-party observer will be permitted in the examination.

We discuss each of these in turn.

Examinee Access to the Report and Other Records

In contrast to suitability evaluations, examiners who perform fitness evaluations should expect that any employee determined to be unfit for duty will be permitted to obtain the report and underlying records. As we discussed in Chapter 1, US federal law provides public employees with the right to due process before removal from their position or the loss of other property rights. These due process rights were articulated by the US Supreme Court in *Cleveland Board of Education v. Loudermill* (1985). The Court held that, before dismissal, a public employee is entitled to "oral or written notice of the charges against him, an explanation of the employer's evidence, and an opportunity to present his side of the story" (p. 546). When a police chief relies on the findings from a psychological evaluation, even in part, for a decision that an officer is unfit for duty, those findings constitute part of the employer's evidence (e.g., *Bass v. City of Albany*, 1992; *Bauschard v. Martin*, 1993; *Nuss v. Township of Falls*, 1985). Consequently, although an officer may be required to obtain the report from the employer rather than from the examiner, it should be expected that the employee will receive a copy of the report at some point. Practitioners are well advised to keep this in mind when writing their reports.

Presence of Third-Party Observers

We can think of no circumstance in which a third-party observer is entitled to be present during a suitability evaluation of a police candidate. This is different in fitness evaluations. Provisions of a collective bargaining agreement may give an employee the right to be accompanied by an attorney or labor representative during a fitness evaluation. If not, such a right may be construed from the decision of the US Supreme Court in *NLRB v. Weingarten, Inc.* (1975). In the *Weingarten* ruling, the Court held that an employee from a collective-bargaining group who reasonably believes that an interview or evaluation may lead to discipline is entitled to the presence of a union representative, if requested. In turn, the representative may not impede the interview or evaluation.

An examiner's objections to the presence of third-party observers frequently center on the potential for either "invalidating" the evaluation or violating test security. Otto and Krauss (2009) contend that such validity concerns are ill-conceived with regard to the interview because the interview is rarely standardized and is seldom supported by validity evidence, and the potential for disruption can be managed by means of advance stipulations. Concerns about the presence of a third party invalidating standardized testing procedures, such as neuropsychological testing, have greater merit but may, at least in some circumstances, be addressed by recording the procedure or by the use of third-party observers who are obligated to protect test security (e.g., licensed psychologists).

Notes

1. 42 U.S.C. §12112(d)(4)(A); 29 C.F.R. §1630.14(c).
2. Law enforcement officers typically have to graduate from an accredited police academy to become certified. Some states allow enrollment of non–law enforcement officers in *self-sponsored* programs, in which the aspiring applicant pays the tuition out of pocket to complete the police academy curriculum. To some agencies, especially those without an in-house academy, such applicants are more attractive because the agency will not have to bear the cost (and salary) of putting a newly hired officer through the police academy.
3. Determining the trade-offs between establishing higher entrance requirements and the caliber of the hired employee is one aspect of *utility analysis*, an important topic in industrial and organizational psychology (e.g., Holling, 1998).
4. California Peace Officer Standards and Training (POST) Commission Regulation 1950(d) states that its requirements "serve as minimum standards. Departments retain the right and responsibility to adopt broader, more rigorous selection standards in accordance with their needs, including but not limited to conducting psychological evaluations on the officers listed above in 1950(c) who are exempted from POST selection requirements. It also supports the use of additional and/or more rigorous selection standards (including psychological standards) beyond those required by POST."
5. 11 C.C.R. § 1955.
6. This manual can be downloaded from https://post.ca.gov/peace-officer-psychological-screening-manual.
7. Legislative history refers to the documents, logs, and notes a legislative body used when writing a law or regulation. These items are researched when attorneys or a court attempt to discern the intent

of lawmakers when the law is vague or ambiguous in regard to the issue before the court.

8. Some conditions, such as bipolar disorder, may be controlled by medications but nevertheless tend to be chronically relapsing. Conditions that are "substantially limiting when active or have a high likelihood of recurrence in substantially limiting forms" (Equal Employment Opportunity Commission, 2009, Question 8) are covered conditions under the ADA Amendments Act of 2008 (ADAAA). Other conditions may be nonsymptomatic merely because the individual has been off work for a long period of time but is more likely than not to become symptomatic after returning to work and is once again exposed to stimuli that trigger the person's symptoms.

4
chapter

Data Collection 5

Three sources of assessment data are routinely used in suitability and fitness evaluations: psychological testing, a clinical interview, and personal history. Differences in the scope and purpose of the evaluations have implications for what and how data are considered. Nonetheless, for both suitability and fitness evaluations, it is an established standard of practice to

- select and rely on assessment tools that have been validated for use with a population appropriate to the evaluation (American Psychological Association [APA], 2018; Heilbrun, 2001);
- use multiple data sources of relevant and reliable information, collected according to established principles and methods (APA, 2018; Heilbrun, Grisso, & Goldstein, 2009; Otto, Goldstein, & Heilbrun, 2017); and
- recognize individual and group differences and the importance of practicing with cultural competence (APA, 2018).

How these inform practice in suitability and fitness evaluations differs somewhat for each data source. Before discussing these various data sources in detail, we present best practices related to both suitability and fitness evaluation procedures because data gathering in these evaluations often must be carefully timed to conform to legal, ethical, and institutional requirements. We must leave it to the reader to determine whether a specific practice is required in a given setting or jurisdiction. Keep in mind, however, that should a procedure be required by law or institutional policy, it must be consistently and thoroughly followed in order to maintain the integrity

Table 5.1	Procedural Steps Common to Suitability Evaluations

1. Administer written psychological testing and any personal history questionnaires.

2. Review findings from psychological testing and personal history questionnaires.

3. Conduct the psychological interview.

4. Determine if additional information is needed and take appropriate steps to acquire it.

5. Integrate the assessment data to make a suitability determination.

6. Prepare and submit the written report and declaration of candidate suitability.

and fairness of the assessment. In both types of evaluations, the examiner provides disclosure, obtains informed consent and waivers, and documents how they were obtained.

Common procedures in suitability and fitness evaluations are listed in Tables 5.1 and 5.2, respectively.

Best Practices When Conducting Occupationally Mandated Psychological Evaluations

Heilbrun, DeMatteo, Marczyk, and Goldstein (2008) ranked the preferred authoritative sources to be used when identifying best psychological practices. At the top of the hierarchy they placed ethical standards and pertinent regulations, laws, and case law applicable to all psychologists. This is followed by professional practice guidelines published by the APA, as well as regulatory enforcement guidance. Further down the ranking they placed professional practice guidelines prepared through consensus among practitioners in a particular practice area, followed by systematic reviews of what

Table 5.2 | Procedural Steps Common to Fitness Evaluations

1. Assess how the employer met the legal threshold for mandating a fitness evaluation.

2. Identify the relevant clinical and forensic questions.

3. Determine whether the referral falls within *your* area of expertise, boundaries of competence, and capacity for impartiality.

4. Identify the legal standard for determining fitness.

5. Provide appropriate disclosure to all stakeholders.

6. Gather clinical information using multiple methods, relying on relevance, reliability, and validity as guides.

7. Integrate the assessment data to make a fitness determination.

8. Prepare and submit the written report of findings and opinions.

recognized scholars and practitioners in the field have written, and ranking last a single study describing a survey, or offering an empirical description, of some aspect of practice.

We have taken a similar approach in this volume. We give greatest weight to professional standards and federal laws, then to APA-approved professional practice guidelines and regulatory guidance (e.g., Equal Employment Opportunity Commission [EEOC] guidance concerning its regulations), followed by professional practice guidelines developed from practitioner consensus. Borrowing a schema introduced by Heilbrun (2001), we identify a practice as *established* when these various sources agree concerning it. Where one or more sources is silent or in disagreement about a practice that another recommends, we identify it as *emerging*. As Heilbrun (2001) observed, established practices are likely to change little over time, but emerging ones "may appear considerably different in another decade" (p. 8).[1]

The Client

Identify ethical and professional responsibilities to each stakeholder. Throughout this volume we refer to the organization as the *organizational client* rather than the client. This is in keeping with the modern trend in professional psychology not to ask, "Who is the client?" or to identify a particular party as the sole client, but rather to ask, "What are my ethical responsibilities to each of the parties in this case?" (Fisher, 2009, p. 1). Also consistent with this trend, the Canadian Psychological Association Code of Ethics defines a "primary client," which includes the "individual or group (e.g., couples, families, organizations, communities, peoples) that has contracted for and/or is receiving services. . . . More than one individual or group can be primary clients in a single service contract" (Canadian Psychological Association, 2017).

Procedural Requirements

Understand and comply with procedural requirements invoked by jurisdictional or referral source requirements, or collective bargaining agreements. It is not enough that your assessment procedures are consistent with federal and state regulations or statutes. One must also consider organizational policies or collective bargaining agreements that apply to the assessment procedures. Such organizational or collective bargaining contingencies are most likely to affect the evaluation of incumbents whose employment has arguably conferred a property interest in their position. Besides collective bargaining agreements, a particular agency may add other requirements. For example, some agencies want the reported results condensed to a form they provide. Others may dictate the general procedures and even the specific type of psychological testing that must be used, although ethical standards (APA, 2017) and professional practice guidelines (APA, 2013, 2018) still require that the psychologist's use of an assessment instrument be consistent with its intended purpose and appropriate to the population and setting in which it is administered.

Individualized Examination

Provide an individualized examination, which assesses what the subject can and cannot do. The 19th century Canadian physician, William Osler, is said to have admonished his medical students that it is more important to know the patient who has the disease than the disease the patient has. This is also good advice for assessment professionals and is consistent with the Americans With Disabilities Act of 1990 (ADA) mandate requiring us to refrain from relying on stereotypes or preconceived notions about a candidate's or employee's abilities or limitations based solely on the knowledge that they have a given disease or condition.

Whether conducting a suitability or fitness evaluation, after it is determined that the person being evaluated has a mental health condition or a record of a condition (e.g., a military service–connected disability, a worker's compensation claim, historical or ongoing treatment for a diagnosed condition), any adverse action taken as a result of the evaluation will subject the evaluation to scrutiny under the ADA Amendments Act of 2008 (ADAAA). This highlights the importance of ensuring in such cases that a determination of unsuitability or unfitness is based on an individualized assessment that

(a) considers the person's particular symptoms (or, if in remission, the symptoms displayed when the condition was active);

(b) assesses the impact of those symptoms and any related functional deficits on the person's ability to perform the essential functions of the job, particularly those involving safety-sensitive work;

(c) evaluates the historical course of the person's condition, symptoms, and functioning over time;

(d) considers the quality and ameliorative effects of treatment, if any;

(e) evaluates the potential for the person posing a direct threat in the position; and

(f) assesses the likelihood that the person could perform safely and effectively in the position with reasonable accommodation.

5
chapter

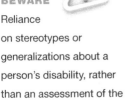

BEWARE
Reliance
on stereotypes or
generalizations about a
person's disability, rather
than an assessment of the
impact of the individual's
actual condition on their
ability to perform the job, is
precisely what the ADA is
intended to prohibit.

Reliance on stereotypes or generalizations about a person's disability, rather than an assessment of the impact of the individual's actual condition on their ability to perform the job, is precisely what the ADA is intended to prohibit. See *Holiday v. City of Chattanooga* (2000) for an illustration of this point from the Sixth Circuit Court of Appeals.

Standardized Procedures

Adhere to standardized procedures, including the review of as much assessment data as reasonably possible before the interview. We recommend that the practitioner, especially when conducting preemployment evaluations, defer the interview until they have an opportunity to review the findings from written testing and other collateral resources, such as the background investigation (International Association of Chiefs of Police [IACP], 2014; Spilberg & Corey, 2019). In fitness evaluations, in which there may be multiple interviews, it is important that, to the extent possible, all relevant materials be reviewed before the last interview. From a practical standpoint, this practice allows the practitioner to prepare and utilize the time allotted for the interview in the most efficient manner. From a legal standpoint, it allows the practitioner to tailor the individualized assessment that is required by the ADA. The practice of reviewing records before the examination also fostered comment in *Wurzel v. Whirlpool* (2012), in which the adverse administrative action toward Wurzel was supported because of the more in-depth analysis by Whirlpool's physicians, paired with the court's disdain for the "common practice to perform an IME without reviewing the medical records beforehand" (no pagination). For these reasons, we respectfully disagree with some of our colleagues who believe that the review of test data and other materials be deferred until after the interview, out of concern that an earlier review will provoke a confirmatory bias. Such a strategy may deprive the practitioner of developing a set of appropriate alternative hypotheses, which should be corroborated or ruled out in the course of the clinical interview.

Similarly, California law [11 C.C.R. § 1955(e)(4)] mandates that psychologists conducting a suitability evaluation of a police candidate conduct the interview "subsequent to a review and evaluation of the results of the written assessments." Doing so ensures both standardization across evaluations and, most important, that the psychologist is able to use the interview to clarify and refine the findings from psychological testing.

Failing to follow accepted professional practices and standards without reasonable justification may result in your report being disregarded by an adjudicative authority. For example, one arbitrator found that the credibility of a psychologist who conducted a fitness evaluation was undermined by holding one interview of the officer in a "public venue," making reference to statements from third parties in his report without citing his sources, and never giving the officer the opportunity to rebut or challenge the basis for the psychologist's conclusions. The arbitrator ordered that the terminated officer be reinstated and that the fitness-for-duty evaluation be expunged from the officer's personnel file (*City of Livingston v. Montana Public Employees Association*, 2014).

An unfortunately common lapse of standardization occurs when psychologists alter standardized test instructions. Although some psychologists (e.g., Butcher, Morfitt, Rouse, & Holden, 1997; Cigrang & Stall, 2001; Walfish, 2010) have advocated giving "specialized instructions" to persons being assessed in suitability and fitness evaluations in order to reduce the effect of defensiveness on test results, doing so only clouds the reliability of the findings and may even invalidate them. Writing about the impact of such altered instructions when administering the Minnesota Multiphasic Personality Inventory (MMPI) and its various versions, Corey and Ben-Porath (2018) advised against this practice, noting:

> Instructions altered in this manner deviate from the standard administration procedures used to develop, norm, and validate MMPI scales. Their use calls into question the validity and interpretability of the resulting test scores. In addition, this approach

5
chapter

may inadvertently "coach" evaluees on how to respond not only during the current evaluation but also in possible future assessments where the examiner would not know that a test taker had been subjected previously to nonstandard instructions. Moreover, the implications of the resulting scores, particularly if demonstrating significant psychopathology (as in the Butcher et al. 1997 study), are ambiguous. (p. 340)

Conducting the Evaluation

Conduct the evaluation in a manner consistent with evidentiary standards. The standard for the admissibility of expert testimony (or an expert's written report) generally follows the admissibility standards set forth under either *Frye v. United States* (1923) or *Daubert v. Merrell Dow Pharmaceuticals, Inc.* (1993), depending on the jurisdiction. Under the *Frye* standard, opinions of experts are admissible upon demonstrating that the procedure was generally accepted within the professional's field. Under the *Daubert* criteria, trial courts were given flexible guidelines by the Supreme Court to help them determine if the proposed evidence was "derived by the scientific method." Your work will usually survive a *Frye* or *Daubert* evidentiary test if you utilize well-accepted, standardized procedures and include measures that have been peer-reviewed and found to be valid in the context in which you use them.

BEST PRACTICE

Your work will usually survive a *Frye* or *Daubert* evidentiary test if you utilize well-accepted, standardized procedures and include measures that have been peer-reviewed and found to be valid in the context in which you use them.

There are occasions in which a psychologist may testify—but not in the role of expert. For example, if a psychologist who performed a suitability or fitness evaluation for an employer is sued and is later called to testify in court as a defendant or witness, that psychologist will testify, in whole or part, as a "fact witness." In such an instance, the psychologist will be asked to testify about what they did, why it was done, what findings they reached, and how the findings were integrated to reach the opinions contained in their report. Psychologists are sometimes chagrined and offended when they are subpoenaed in such matters and offered the token statutory fee authorized by the court for a fact witness,[2] believing, of course, that their expertise entitles them to be recognized—and paid—as an expert witness. But highly trained professionals can be fact witnesses, too, and when they are—such as when testifying about what they did and how they came to their expert opinions in a matter that is later litigated—attorneys are only obligated to recognize them as fact witnesses and pay them accordingly. Under these circumstances, their testimony is not subjected by the courts to tests of admissibility under the applicable rules governing expert testimony. Only the testimony of experts retained by the courts or legal counsel to aid a judge or jury in understanding a matter before the court (e.g., an expert witness retained to explain why a suitability or fitness evaluator's opinions were not supported by the methods they used) is subject to challenge under *Frye* or *Daubert* standards.[3] Still, it is prudent to perform all expert services as if they may someday be subjected to the rules of evidence admissibility.

Defining the Scope of the Evaluation

Strive to conduct evaluations no broader or more intrusive than necessary. The legal basis that permits an employer to order a fitness evaluation relies on the employer having demonstrated

that the privacy intrusion is warranted by business necessity. Although the threshold for proving business necessity varies with the job, the inquiry still should be no broader or more

BEST PRACTICE

Strive to conduct evaluations no broader or more intrusive than necessary.

intrusive on personal privacy than necessary. Striving toward this objective begins with obtaining a letter from the referring party, to include questions that define the concerns as specifically as possible. Furthermore, when the practitioner encounters information that is not relevant, this material should not be provided in the written report.

In both suitability and fitness evaluations, prudent examiners limit their questions to ones reasonably designed to yield clinically useful (and forensically relevant) information. Our own curiosity has certainly led us to ask questions that, in retrospect, had little or no relevance to the forensic question we were retained to address, but we also have come to recognize the risks of doing so. In most cases, it is better not to ask questions the answers to which have no bearing on the forensic question or are unlikely to yield information that can be defensibly interpreted. This becomes more important as the nature of the topic becomes more private and personal.

Scope of the Interview

Interview to clarify personal/social history questions, psychological test results, and other relevant information not otherwise available. By the time the interview is conducted, the examiner should have reviewed biographical questionnaires, test results, background investigations, and collateral documents. The interview time should be optimized to obtain information otherwise not provided, and *not* to follow a rigid outline in which one addresses issues that were asked and answered during the pre-interview assessment. The interview provides the opportunity to clarify what you do not yet know. It is also the time to administer any additional testing, which cannot be administered by clerical staff, such as various measures of executive functioning or memory, or other additional testing you deem appropriate. Approach the interview mindful of some hypotheses about the examinee that can be supported or dismissed with further exploration. This will be discussed further in Chapter 6.

Informed Consent

Fisher (2009) has made a convincing argument that "psychologists have ethical obligations toward every party in a case, no matter how many or how named" (Fisher, 2009, p. 1). Likewise, disclosure (and, oftentimes, informed consent) is owed not merely to one party but to all those with whom the examiner interacts. To the referring party, the examiner typically owes a duty to disclose costs, availability, expected timeline for report

> **INFO**
> Disclosure (and, oftentimes, informed consent) is owed not merely to one party, but to all those with whom the examiner interacts.

delivery, and factors that may lead to an interruption in services. For an examinee to provide informed consent, it is generally necessary to disclose

- the purpose and intended use(s) of the evaluation;
- limits of confidentiality;
- potential adverse consequences from participating, or from declining or prematurely ending participation, in the evaluation;
- any limitations in access to the written report and records of the evaluation; and
- the examiner's policies/procedures that pertain to requesting medical and other personal records.

Obtaining Informed Consent

Obtaining informed consent is an established standard of practice. In terms of practice relevant to psychologists who provide employment evaluations, one of the greatest gaps between the conduct required by the APA's Ethical Principles of Psychologists and Code of Conduct (EPPCC) and various practice standards is with informed consent. Section 9.03 of the current EPPCC does *not* require informed consent if "(1) testing is mandated by law or governmental regulations; (2) *informed consent is implied because testing is conducted as a routine educational, institutional, or organizational activity* (e.g., *when participants voluntarily agree to assessment when applying for a job*); or (3) one purpose of the testing is to evaluate decisional capacity" (APA, 2017, emphasis added). Thus, psychologists cannot be found to be in violation of the ethics code if they fail to obtain informed consent on the basis of one or

BEST PRACTICE

We recommend that you always obtain informed consent in suitability and fitness evaluations and that you decline to proceed if informed consent is withheld *regardless* of exceptions such as those enumerated in the EPPCC.

more of the exceptions listed in Section 9.[4] On the other hand, several sets of practice guidelines recommend obtaining informed consent or providing appropriate disclosure.[5] This is an area in which there are mixed opinions, with some important sources of authority (e.g., EPPCC) making an exception to the universal need for informed consent, and others (e.g., APA, 2018; IACP, 2014, 2018a) advocating that it be routinely obtained. We recommend that the examiner always obtain informed consent in suitability and fitness evaluations and that an evaluator decline to proceed if informed consent is withheld *regardless* of exceptions such as those enumerated in the EPPCC. As noted by Gold and Shuman (2009), "Failing to obtain a consent later determined to be required cannot be remedied" (p. 28).

There also are good practical reasons to use a thorough and plainly written informed consent document. Such a document helps the examinee make a decision regarding whether to participate. It also warns of the possible risks and notes the benefits of their participation. A comprehensive informed consent document may help shield a practitioner from having to respond to disputes before legal forums or their licensing boards, especially if the dispute can be resolved by referring to language within "the four corners" of the document. In addition, the use of an informed consent document structures the process and content of the evaluation. An informed consent document that anticipates common ethical issues is often the best prophylaxis against encountering ethical dilemmas and conflicts. It is well to remind ourselves that forensic practice is an area in which "the methods and procedures of forensic practitioners are complex and may not be accurately anticipated by the recipients of forensic services" (APA, 2013, preamble to Section 6, SPFG, p. 12). It is important that we dispel common myths about these procedures so that the organizational

BOX 5.1 INFORM EXAMINEES ABOUT THE NATURE AND PURPOSE
OF THE EXAMINATION

SGFP 6.03. "Forensic practitioners inform examinees about the nature
and purpose of the examination. . . . Such information may include
the purpose, nature, and anticipated use of the examination; who
will have access to the information; associated limitations on privacy,
confidentiality, and privilege including who is authorized to release or
access the information contained in the forensic practitioner's records;
the voluntary or involuntary nature of participation, including potential
consequences of participation or nonparticipation, if known; and, if the
cost of the service is the responsibility of the examinee, the anticipated
cost" (APA, 2013, pp. 12–13).

client and examinee are not alarmed when they encounter an unexpected procedure.

In some settings, particularly where the psychologist conducting
the evaluation is an employee of the referring agency or a related
entity, obtaining informed consent of the examinee may be inconsistent with institutional policies. In such cases, many or all of the
objectives of the informed consent process might still be achieved
through providing the examinee with an *advisement, disclosure,* or
notification of purpose. A key difference between informed consent
and these alternatives is that the latter simply documents that the
examinee was *told* about the upcoming examination and other related facts, but no explicit agreement is sought or documented.
Heilbrun, DeMatteo, Holliday, and LaDuke (2014) discuss four
elements of notification in forensic mental health evaluations,
which we have edited only slightly for application to suitability and
fitness evaluations. These include notice of

(a) the purpose of the evaluation,
(b) the potential uses of any disclosures made during the
evaluation,
(c) the conditions under which the employer will have
access to information obtained in the course of the
evaluation, and
(d) the potential consequences of the examinee's refusal to
cooperate in the evaluation (p. 220).

5
chapter

Such notice or disclosure is distinct from informed consent in that it does not characterize or construe the evaluation as voluntary, yet it overlaps with the concept of informed consent in that the examinee is, indeed, informed of key facts about the evaluation. But whether conceptualized as informed consent, assent, advisement, disclosure, or notification of purpose, the important thing is that the practitioner documents that the examinee was not in the dark about important elements of the assessment.

Although the focus of informed consent is on the examinee, we recommend that you also obtain informed consent from the organizational client (or, as just discussed, documentation of disclosure). Given the scope of our ethical responsibilities to various parties, we propose that practitioners in this area consider including the elements discussed below in their informed consent/disclosure document. This is not an exhaustive list, and readers may find that not all of these provisions apply to their practice, or that their informed consent documents may need additional components that we have not included.

BEST PRACTICE

Developing a thoughtful informed consent document is a golden opportunity to operationalize best practice guidelines into your practice setting and to structure the evaluative procedure so that unnecessary drama is avoided.

Informed Consent/Disclosure Provisions

Providing both the examinee and the organizational client or other referring party with pertinent facts about the suitability or fitness evaluation helps to achieve realistic expectations that, along with documentation of the consent and disclosure, can reduce the incidence of complaints and litigation. We focus next on several provisions that are key to this objective.

Informed Consent/Disclosure Provisions Applicable to the Examinee and Organizational Client

We start by discussing elements that we recommend be considered for inclusion in the documents given to *both* the examinee and the organizational client.

BOX 5.2 Communicate with those seeking to retain a forensic practitioner

SGFP Guideline 6.02. "As part of the initial process of being retained, or as soon thereafter as previously unknown information becomes available, forensic practitioners strive to disclose to the retaining party information that would reasonably be anticipated to affect a decision to retain or continue the services of the forensic practitioner. This disclosure may include, but is not limited to, the fee structure for anticipated services; prior and current personal or professional activities, obligations, and relationships that would reasonably lead to the fact or the appearance of a conflict of interest; the forensic practitioner's knowledge, skill, experience, and education relevant to the forensic services being considered, including any significant limitations; and the scientific bases and limitations of the methods and procedures which are expected to be employed" (APA, 2013, p. 12).

1. *Include the words "informed consent," "disclosure," "notification of purpose," or "advisement" in the title.* This simple convention may avoid a dispute between the practitioner and the various stakeholders regarding whether the document was understood to be what it was intended. Similarly, the document should be in plain language without professional jargon. While we recommend that practitioners periodically assess the reading level of the document, it is important to note that too much simplification may yield a diminishing return. Our colleagues in medical research have found that patients consenting to be involved in research clearly *prefer* a simplified form to a complex informed consent document, but patients who are given a consent written at the sixth or seventh grade level do not demonstrate better comprehension than groups who review documents composed at much higher reading levels (e.g., Davis, Holcombe, Berkel, Pramanik, & Divers, 1998).

2. *Describe the purpose of the evaluation* (i.e., to determine suitability for employment or a special assignment, to determine fitness for duty) and how those results will be reported.

3. *Include parameters that limit the use of the written report.* These provisions help ensure that the information is used

5
chapter

for its intended purpose and protected from inappropriate release. The informed consent/disclosure document is a good place to remind the organizational client that it is expected to safeguard the examinee's privacy in a manner consistent with the law, and that the evaluation should not be used for any purpose other than its explicitly intended use(s). In suitability and special assignment evaluations, we recommend that an expiration date be posted on the report. Although there is no consensus regarding the length of expiration, we note that Ontario's *Constable Selection System: Guidelines for Psychologists* (Ontario Chiefs of Police Association, 2018) recommends a 1-year expiration on preemployment reports, a recommendation that is consistent with conventional practice.[6]

4. *State explicitly that participation is voluntary.* If applicable, the examinee should be advised that, as far as the evaluator is concerned, the examinee's participation is voluntary. The fact that an examinee is ordered or required to participate does not change the examinee's right to discontinue an evaluation or refuse to answer a question. The examinee may assert that the employer (or prospective employer) is requiring the evaluation and, therefore, it is not truly voluntary, but this does not preclude the psychologist from respecting the individual's autonomy. Should an examinee object to participating in the evaluation or choose to discontinue participation in it, we recommend doing little or nothing to dissuade them. Similarly, if an examinee refuses to answer a question, efforts to persuade the individual to answer can create unintended consequences, although offering to clarify the purpose of your inquiry may yield positive results if not taken too far. Nevertheless, questions that are not answered, or evaluations that are discontinued, should be cited in the report, along with a discussion of any limitations this may have resulted in your ability to reach a conclusion and an acknowledgement of any limitations in the reliability of whatever conclusions were reached.

5. *Avoid conflicting roles.* The examinee should be advised that although the examiner is a licensed healthcare provider, the practitioner is neither providing nor offering to provide healthcare or personal counseling.

BEWARE Should an examinee object to participating in the evaluation or choose to discontinue participation in it, we recommend you do little or nothing to dissuade them.

6. *State the limits of confidentiality,* including the following:

- Whether you will furnish the examinee with a copy of the report.
- The scope and detail of the written report that is provided to the organization. Some jurisdictions have statutes restricting the types and scope of information that can be provided to an employer without the examinee's explicit (and written) authorization.
- Mandatory reporting. One should also remind the examinee and the referring entity that, as a licensed mental health professional, you are a mandated reporter of certain specific incidents (e.g., unreported sexual abuse of a child, elder abuse, threat to an identifiable target),[7] as required by law in the jurisdiction in which the evaluation is conducted.
- If you will require the examinee to sign releases in order for you to obtain medical records or other collateral documents, and the extent to which you will re-disclose any personal medical records to the organizational client.
- Your reliance (or possible reliance) on collateral informants.
- Whether you will use social media or data brokers to gather information about the examinee. (This topic is discussed further in this chapter.)
- The anticipated time that it will take the examinee to complete the assessment.

5
chapter

● Whether you plan to electronically record the evaluation and whether you will permit the examinee to record it. While we advise against allowing an examinee to record, other practitioners may not agree. In considering this issue, practitioners should consider whether they are conducting the evaluation in a "one-party jurisdiction," where the examinee would be allowed to legally record the meeting without disclosing the presence of a recording device to other people in the room, or a "two-party jurisdiction," where all of those being recorded must be notified.

● Your policy regarding the release of test materials and data,[8] which is advisably communicated to both the examinee and the organizational client.

● Whether either party will be permitted to have a legal representative or other third party present during the evaluation. Regardless of your personal preference regarding this topic, some jurisdictions are subject to collective bargaining agreements or organizational policies that grant an employee the right to have a representative present if the employee is at risk of discipline. (See discussion of *NLRB v. Weingarten* in Chapter 4.)

● The examinee should be advised of the anticipated intrusiveness of the evaluation. This is especially important with preemployment examinees, who should be forewarned if you intend, either directly or with your test materials and questionnaires, to ask them personal questions regarding their relationships with others, sexual behavior, medical history, and the use of legal and illicit substances. It is reasonable to advise candidates that the more safety-sensitive the job they are seeking, the more intrusive the evaluation will be.[9]

● The examinee's right to ask questions (and consult with one's attorney or union representative in the case of fitness evaluations) before executing the informed consent document. Indeed, we recommend that whenever possible, the examinee be provided the informed consent/ disclosure document in advance so that they can have a

BEST PRACTICE

We recommend that whenever possible, examinees be provided the informed consent/disclosure document in advance so that they can have a reasonable amount of time to seek counsel from a legal or labor representative.

reasonable amount of time to seek counsel from a legal or labor representative.

● Especially in matters involving fitness evaluations, the organizational client and the examinee should be reminded of the importance of providing the examiner with all relevant materials and that, if either side withholds such, they run the risk that the examiner may change their initial summary opinion upon subsequent disclosure of relevant materials.[10]

Informed Consent/Disclosure Provisions Applicable to the Organizational Client

These considerations also include the contractual relationship between the psychologist and the organizational client. This is not an exhaustive list, nor are all of the below components appropriate for all practitioners.

● *Explicit statement that the provider is offering services with the expectation that the organization will adhere to applicable federal and state civil rights or human rights legislation.* These legislative acts require that the summary report be maintained in a secure file and only released to those who have a legitimate need to review its contents. This would also include the referring agency's appropriate timing of conditional offers of employment, along with its obligation to refer all candidates for evaluation, not just those about whom they have concern.

5
chapter

● *Fees.* It is important that the practitioner and the organizational client have a shared understanding about fees and other expenses.

● *Indemnification.* Some practitioners believe that it is important to include an indemnity clause within the organizational informed consent or service contract. These clauses appear to be especially prevalent in jurisdictions where providers view themselves as being at heightened risk for malpractice complaints or other civil litigation filed by examinees or their labor groups. An indemnity clause generally contains language in which the organization agrees to shoulder the expenses involved in defending the practitioner as a result of any alleged improper acts or omissions of that practitioner. The construction of such a contractual provision is beyond the scope of this volume. The inclusion of an indemnity provision can be complicated, and there are instances in which an indemnity clause may result in unwanted consequences for the practitioner. Practitioners who believe they have a need for indemnification should consult with their attorney. The same holds true in instances where the organizational client includes an indemnity clause in its service contract with the practitioner. In agreeing to such language, we are always careful to only agree to indemnification language that obligates us to indemnify the organizational client *exclusively* for our actions that constitute professional negligence or malpractice, as opposed to any or all acts resulting in potential liability to the organization.

BEWARE

● For suitability evaluations, it is important that the examinee understand that the conditional offer of employment may be rescinded as a result of the evaluation.

● For fitness evaluations, the examinee should be told that a potential outcome is that the employee could be terminated or required to restore their psychological fitness, evidence for which may require the employee to seek treatment, perhaps at their own expense.

Informed Consent/Disclosure Provisions Applicable to the Examinee Only

There is at least one element of informed consent/disclosure that is essential for the examinee alone: disclosure of the potential outcomes and probable uses of the examination. In the context of suitability evaluations, it is important that the examinee understand that the conditional offer of employment may be rescinded as a result of the evaluation. With regard to fitness evaluations, the examinee should be explicitly told that a potential outcome is that the employee could be terminated or required to restore their psychological fitness, evidence for which may require the employee to seek treatment, perhaps at their own expense.

Informed Consent/Disclosure for Collateral Informants

If the examinee or organizational client authorizes speaking with a collateral informant, we recommend that you have the informant execute an informed consent/disclosure document as well, and that the signature be obtained either in your presence or in the presence of a suitable witness when feasible. It is important that informants know *why* you are seeking their input. They should be advised that it is reasonable to assume that all parties will learn of the information that they disclose, that nothing they reveal will be considered "off the record," and that it is possible that the information they provide will be released in a public forum, such as a court. See Otto, Goldstein, and Heilbrun (2017) for a thorough discussion of ethical issues involved in interviewing collateral informants.

Informed Consent/Disclosure as an Ongoing Process

Although we have emphasized the content of an informed consent/disclosure document (or at least what information is appropriately communicated to the parties if done orally), "it should be kept in mind that informed consent is a process, not simply an

5
chapter

event" (Corey, 2011, p. 276). Writing about this topic in the context of fitness evaluations, Corey noted:

> In the course of the examination, the examiner may need to revisit important aspects of the informed consent document in order to clarify, for example, the limits of confidentiality, the purpose of the examination, or the potential outcomes. Some clinicians request that examinees summarize key elements of the informed consent or disclosure in their own words both to ensure that consent is given knowingly and intelligently, even if not voluntarily, and to enable documentation of that fact in the event of subsequent litigation. (p. 276)

Data Collection in Suitability Evaluations

Mitchell (2017) and Serafino (2010) refer to the three primary data sources (testing, interview, and personal history) as the "basic model" of psychological screening of police candidates. A summary of the basic model is shown in Table 5.3.

Written Psychological Testing

Some jurisdictions or hiring agencies stipulate the tests or test battery that must be used in screening candidates, but most often this decision is left to the examiner with specific parameters. The most common requirement for written tests used in suitability evaluation is the "basic model," which is reflected in the regulations promulgated by the California Peace Officer Standards and Training (POST) Commission:

> Written assessments shall consist of a minimum of two written psychological instruments. One of these instruments shall be designed and validated to identify patterns of abnormal behavior; the other instrument shall be designed and validated to assess normal behavior. Both instruments shall have documented evidence of their relevance for evaluating peace officer suitability. Together, the instruments shall provide information about each

Table 5.3 | The "Basic Model" of Police Candidate Screening

- Written psychological testing with a minimum of two standardized assessment instruments:

  - A broadband written measure of abnormal personality functioning and psychopathology (i.e., one capable of assessing for emotional or mental conditions that might adversely affect the exercise of the powers of a police officer), normed and validated with the general adult population as well as with police officer candidates

  - A broadband written measure of normal-range personality functioning, also normed and validated with both a general adult population and police officer candidates

- Personal history information

  - Self-reported history

  - Agency-provided background investigation findings

  - Mental health treatment/assessment records from other healthcare professionals if relevant and available

- Clinical interview

  - Clarifying personal history information and findings from psychological testing

  - Gathering information about criterion-relevant constructs that are not adequately assessed by psychological testing and background information

---

candidate related to: (1) freedom from emotional and/or mental conditions that might adversely affect the exercise of the powers of a peace officer, and (2) psychological suitability per the POST Psychological Screening Dimensions. [11 C.C.R. § 1955(e)(2)]

Similar requirements have been adopted by many other jurisdictions, including Texas, which requires "at least two instruments, one which measures personality traits and one which measures psychopathology."[11]

Test Selection

The choice of which tests to use in suitability and fitness evaluations is a vitally important one. We offer the following considerations— adapted from guidance offered by Ackerman (2010); Melton, Petrila, Poythress, and Slobogin (2018); Otto, Edens, and Barcus (2000); and Spilberg and Corey (2019)—for making this decision in the context of suitability evaluations:

1. Are the constructs measured by the instrument directly relevant to the evaluation criteria?
2. How directly does the instrument assess the construct(s) of interest?
3. Are there alternative methods of assessment that assess the construct(s) of interest in more direct ways?
4. Does use of this instrument allow an acceptable degree of inference between the construct(s) it assesses and the psycholegal issue(s) of relevance?
5. Is the instrument commercially available?
6. Is a comprehensive technical manual or equivalent documentation available?
7. Have adequate levels of reliability been demonstrated?
8. Have adequate levels of validity been demonstrated?
9. Have the instrument and underlying validity evidence been subjected to peer review?
10. Is the instrument valid for the purpose for which it will be used?
11. Does the user have the qualifications and experience necessary to use the instrument?
12. Does the instrument include measures of test-taking approach or response style?
13. Are appropriate norms or comparison group (e.g., police candidate) data available?[12]

Starting this analysis with the first question ensures that the selection of instruments will measure, to the extent possible, the constructs linked to the appropriate criterion standard. For example, if the applicable standard in a suitability evaluation is the California POST Psychological Screening Dimensions (refer back to Table 4.1 in Chapter 4), then the evaluating psychologist will want to be certain to select tests with valid measures of constructs relevant to these 10 criteria. Naturally, most commercially available

tests will also contain scales unrelated to the criterion standard, and those scales should be ignored for purposes of your suitability or fitness determination. After the psychologist has identified a test as relevant to the criterion standard, consideration of the other factors will help guide the final selection.

Tests Commonly Used in Suitability Evaluations

Spilberg and Corey (2019) categorized the most commonly used assessment instruments in suitability evaluations as *omnibus tests* (multiconstruct measures of normal or abnormal adult personality functioning), *specialized tests* (tests developed solely for use in police suitability evaluations and not for use with the general adult population), and *adapted omnibus tests* (omnibus tests that are scored using specialized software that generates interpretive statements, compares the candidate's scale scores to both police candidate and general adult means and standard deviations, and/or includes scales or indices developed specifically for use in screening police candidates). In Table 5.4, we list the tests cited in the California POST *Psychological Screening Manual* (Spilberg & Corey, 2019) that also were reported to be used by 5% or more of the respondents ($N = 56$) in a recent national survey of police psychologists who conduct preemployment suitability evaluations of police officer candidates (Corey, 2016). In the remainder of this chapter, we provide brief descriptions of these tests, as well as an array of assessment tools for measuring executive functioning,

5
chapter

Table 5.4 | Written Assessment Instruments Commonly Used to Evaluate Police Candidate Suitability

Test	Category	Targets Abnormal or Normal Functioning
Sixteen Personality Factor Questionnaire, Fifth Edition (16PF-5)	Omnibus	Normal
16PF Protective Services Report (PSR)	Adapted Omnibus	Normal
16PF PSR Plus	Adapted Omnibus	Abnormal
California Psychological Inventory (CPI)	Omnibus	Normal
CPI Police and Public Safety Selection Report	Adapted Omnibus	Normal
Inwald Personality Inventory–2 (IPI-2)	Specialized	Abnormal
Minnesota Multiphasic Personality Inventory–2 (MMPI-2)	Omnibus	Abnormal
MMPI-2 *Revised Personnel System*, Third Edition	Adapted Omnibus	Abnormal
MMPI-2 Restructured Form (MMPI-2-RF)	Omnibus	Abnormal
MMPI-2-RF *Police Candidate Interpretive Report* (PCIR)	Adapted Omnibus	Abnormal
Personality Assessment Inventory (PAI)	Omnibus	Abnormal
PAI Police and Public Safety Selection Report	Adapted Omnibus	Abnormal

which, as we have noted throughout this volume, is a promising new target of assessment in suitability evaluations. In Chapter 3, we briefly summarized the validity evidence supporting the use of these tests.

Although specialized tests can provide useful collateral support in a suitability evaluation for assessing a police candidate's risk for counterproductive behavior, we contend that only the omnibus (and adapted omnibus) measures can form the foundation of a psychological evaluation. Specialized tests do not measure psychological/personality constructs applicable to the normative sample; rather, they are used to indicate whether a police candidate's responses correlate with an increased risk for counterproductive behavior.[13] Adapted omnibus measures like the California Psychological Inventory (CPI) *Police and Public Safety Selection Report* (CPI-PPSSR; Roberts & Johnson, 2001) and the Minnesota Multiphasic Personality Inventory–2 Restructured Form (MMPI-2-RF) *Police Candidate Interpretive Report* (PCIR; Corey & Ben-Porath, 2014) also are used to predict counterproductive behaviors, but they do so first by measuring psychological constructs relevant to the criterion standard, and second by reporting the counterproductive behaviors empirically associated with these constructs. This is a crucially important consideration when selecting written instruments for use in suitability screening. When using specialized instruments (e.g., Inwald Personality Inventory [IPI]), a score on a risk-related scale or index (e.g., IPI Driving Violations scale) indicating a high probability of future risk cannot be mitigated by other findings from the instrument unless the score is linked to an underlying psychological construct that can be better understood or explained by other assessment findings. This does not mean that the candidate is immediately excluded from further consideration, but rather that the examining psychologist must either explain away the prediction (without the traditional means of personality-based correlates) or accept it as a valid predictor of future counterproductive behavior as a police officer.

In contrast, when using an omnibus or adapted omnibus test, if the measure indicates that a candidate is at comparatively greater risk of future counterproductive behavior, one needs only to identify the construct (scale) triggering that prediction and, by considering other relevant assessment information (e.g., background, clinical interview, other test findings), determine whether convergent findings support the conclusion that the construct applies to that candidate. Alternatively, the test finding may be mitigated by other reliable and divergent findings. If the underlying construct does not apply to the candidate, then the behavioral correlates are inapplicable as well.

This is not to say that specialized instruments do not have a place in suitability assessment batteries. They can contribute incrementally to the validity of an evaluation and provide findings that help to refine an understanding of how a candidate's personality is likely to manifest behaviorally as a police officer. For example, a substantial body of literature has demonstrated the validity of the IPI in assessing police officer candidates, which we summarize later in this chapter. Indeed, one of the most important reasons for appreciating the differences between omnibus, adapted omnibus, and specialized tests is that one can compose a battery of tests that complement each other, yielding data that offer sources of divergent, convergent, and complementary information about the examinee.

Tests With Computer-Generated Narrative Reports

Many commercially available tests provide an option to print a narrative interpretation in addition to the test scores. Narratives designed for clinical populations are usually not appropriate for the generally healthy populations one encounters in the course of post-offer suitability evaluations. We caution against the use of computer-generated narrative interpretations unless the narrative cites the empirical basis for each given statement or hypothesis. Relying on narrative statements in a computerized interpretive report without knowing its source can be perilous when it comes time to defend the interpretation, inasmuch as "[p]sychologists retain responsibility for the appropriate application, interpretation, and use of assessment instruments, whether they score and interpret such tests themselves or use automated or other services" [APA, 2017; Standard 9.09(c)]. Accordingly, all of the narrative statements in the MMPI-2-RF interpretive reports (e.g., *Police Candidate Interpretive Report* and *Interpretive Report: Clinical Settings*) are annotated with the source(s) of the statement (e.g., empirical correlate, test response, authorial inference), along with the published research studies reporting the correlates. These annotations and references are periodically updated with the publication of new studies. Flens (2005) posed six questions to guide evaluators who may be considering the use of automated narrative reports in high-stakes evaluations. We believe these questions are also appropriate for clinicians conducting occupationally mandated psychological evaluations:

1. Is the program actuarial or automated?
2. Does the program consider response style when offering statements?
3. Is the level of significance used for cutoff scores known?
4. Are different statements used depending on the degree of elevation?
5. Does the program consider the profile configuration or combination of elevated scales or are statements based on single-scale elevations?
6. Does the program use context-specific normative data? (pp. 47–48)

As detailed in the *User's Guide for the MMPI-2-RF Police Candidate Interpretive Report* (Corey & Ben-Porath, 2014), the PCIR was purposefully developed to answer each of these questions in the affirmative. For other instruments, practitioners should consult the test manual or technical reports for answers to these questions. If an evaluator (i.e., test user) does not know the basis of the narrative interpretation or is unable to answer these six questions, considerable caution should be extended before using a narrative interpretation in any high-stakes evaluation.[14] It is impossible to mitigate narrative statements if

BEWARE

We caution against the use of computer-generated narrative interpretations unless the narrative cites the empirical basis for each given statement or hypothesis.

5
chapter

you do not know their origins, or to later defend your reliance on the statements in an adjudicative forum.

Tests Without Published Scoring Keys

There are some products, such as the IPI-2 and the CPI (both the 434-item and 260-item versions), for which the test manuals do not identify the items that make up the test's scales. Hand-scoring keys also are not available for these tests. Unfortunately, the publishers of these measures provide no information in their respective test manuals to enable a user to identify the scale items that the test taker answered in the keyed direction. Knowing the items that make up a scale is sometimes necessary for understanding an elevated (or an unexpectedly nonelevated) score. For example, if one encounters an elevation on the MMPI-2-RF Restructured Clinical (RC) Scale 4 (Antisocial Behavior), or the Antisocial Features Scale on the Personality Assessment Inventory (PAI; Morey, 1991)—both tests that disclose the item composition of their scales—the examiner can determine if those elevations were driven by items tapping adolescent rebelliousness that occurred many years before the date of the evaluation as opposed to more recent or long-standing behaviors or antisocial attitudes. Thus, a practitioner's ability to either substantiate or mitigate a test finding, or to conduct the individualized assessment mandated by the ADA, may be hampered when a test publisher denies access to the test scales' item content.

General Comments About Selecting Tests for Use in Suitability Evaluations

Several general considerations are important as part of this discussion:

- If you conduct pre-offer evaluations, do not use tests (or questionnaires) that tap the presence or absence of psychopathology or physical disease/disability. When considering a measure for which there is no consensus regarding its suitability for pre-hire evaluations, do not rely solely on the publisher's claims that the test is "ADA-compliant" or otherwise appropriate for pre-hire use. *Read the items yourself and make sure that no item asks about physical or mental health—topics that cannot be assessed lawfully until after a bona fide conditional offer of employment has been made.*

● According to the Civil Rights Act of 1991 (§ 106), only tests that have nongendered norms should be used for preemployment selection, although tests with gendered norms may be used for fitness evaluations. Keep in mind that some test publishers may label norms as nongendered that actually comprise an unequal number of male and female subjects, possibly rendering the norms biased in favor of the predominant group. Consult the test manual for details about the demographics of the normative or comparison sample.

● Conscientiousness has long been established as one of the most robust constructs related to success in many positions (Barrick & Mount, 1991). Although only a few tests of normal personality contain scales measuring this trait, it is highly correlated with historical behavior, thereby underscoring the importance of a careful review of a candidate's personal history, including past employment, when assessing this construct.

Tests of Normal-Range Personality

The following measures of normal personality are commonly used in conducting suitability evaluations. (In Chapter 3, we provide illustrative validity evidence supporting their use in suitability evaluations of police officer candidates.)

CALIFORNIA PSYCHOLOGICAL INVENTORY

The CPI (Gough & Bradley, 2002) was originally published as a 480-item test and later revised to its current 434-item and 260-item versions. This self-report, true–false inventory contains 20 "folk scales" measuring various aspects of interpersonal functioning including Dominance, Self-Control, Sociability, Social Presence, Independence, Empathy, Responsibility, Socialization, Tolerance, and Achievement via Conformance, as well as several "special purpose" scales, such as Managerial Potential, Work Orientation, Amicability, Anxiety, Narcissism, Leadership, and Law Enforcement Orientation. It also contains several scales and indices measuring response style. In the most recent national survey (Corey, 2016), the CPI-434 was reported to be the most frequently used (42.9%) measure of normal personality in police suitability evaluations. See Chapter 3 for a review of the empirical support for the CPI-434 in preemployment evaluations of police candidates.

CPI *POLICE AND PUBLIC SAFETY SELECTION REPORT*

Roberts and Johnson (2001) developed an adapted CPI-434 report, the CPI-PPSSR, which includes, in addition to the information provided in a standard CPI-434 report, the following three distinctive features:

- combined-gender comparison groups for multiple entry-level public safety positions (police officer, firefighter/emergency medical technician, correctional officer, and dispatcher, among others),
- comparison groups comprising a subsample of the entry-level subjects who were hired and successfully employed for at least 1 year, and
- eight Suitability Risk Statements (Johnson & Roberts, 1996) that are not included in the standard CPI-434 report.

These latter "suitability risk statements" are calculated from unpublished regression equations, six of which correlate with self-reported life history problems, one with a "poorly suited" rating from the post-offer psychological evaluation, and the other which correlates with "probability of involuntary departure." Among the CPI-434 users in the Corey (2016) national survey, 70.8% reported using the CPI-PPSSR in their suitability evaluations.

SIXTEEN PERSONALITY FACTOR QUESTIONNAIRE, FIFTH EDITION

The *Sixteen Personality Factor Questionnaire* (16PF) was first published in 1949. The fifth edition (16PF-5; Russell & Karol, 1994) is a 185-item self-report measure of normal personality and uses a multiple-choice response format. The 16PF-5 has three validity indices, 16 factor scales, and five scales measuring global personality traits. Scores at both ends of the test's 21 substantive scales are interpretable. The 16PF-5 is reported to be the second most commonly used (32.2%) measure of normal personality after the CPI-434 (Corey, 2016). The sixth edition of the 16PF was published in 2018, and, for the time being, the publisher supports both the 16PF-5 and 16PF-6. As discussed in Chapter 3, however, there are no published, peer-reviewed studies demonstrating either version's validity for use in assessing police candidate suitability.

16PF *PROTECTIVE SERVICES REPORT* AND 16PF *PROTECTIVE SERVICES REPORT PLUS*

The 16PF Protective Services Report (PSR) and Protective Services Report Plus (PSR+) are adapted reports that produce a score profile of the 16PF validity, factor, and global scales and a narrative interpretation based on unpublished proprietary research findings to assess a candidate's functioning relevant to four composite dimensions: emotional adjustment, intellectual efficiency, integrity/control, and interpersonal relations. Whereas the test publisher describes the 16PF-PSR as suitable for preconditional and postconditional offer suitability screening, the 16PF-PSR+ is derived from a 325-item questionnaire that incorporates the 185 items from 16PF-5 *plus* another 140 items intended to measure psychopathology and other abnormal functioning (e.g., Health Concerns, Suicidal Thinking, Paranoid Ideation, Anxious Depression) and, therefore, is only suitable in post-offer evaluations.

5
chapter

OTHER MEASURES OF NORMAL PERSONALITY

Several other relevant measures of normal personality functioning also are available commercially. We will describe these instruments briefly.

NEO Personality Inventory

Although only 1.8% of the respondents in the national survey (Corey, 2016) reported using the NEO Personality Inventory (NEO PI), a self-report measure associated with the Five Factor Model of personality (Barrick & Mount, 1991), a fair body of research indicates that the test has good utility in suitability evaluations, as we discussed in Chapter 3. Paul Detrick and John Chibnall have contributed much of the NEO PI literature relevant to police suitability assessment (e.g., Detrick & Chibnall, 2017), including police candidate normative data for the NEO PI-R (Detrick & Chibnall, 2013). The NEO PI instruments have been criticized for failing to include measures of response style (Widiger, 1995), a criticism that has prompted others to develop measures of response style for the test (e.g., Schinka, Kinder, & Kremer, 1997).

Matrix-Predictive Uniform Law Enforcement Selection
Evaluation Inventory

The Matrix-Predictive Uniform Law Enforcement Selection Evaluation (M-PULSE) Inventory is a 455-item self-report measure developed specifically for use in assessing an individual's actuarial risk for counterproductive behavior as a police officer and was "designed to have utility at both the pre-offer and post-conditional offer phases of the hiring or selection process" (Davis & Rostow, 2010, p. 145).[15] However, Spilberg and Corey (2019) questioned the appropriateness of using the M-PULSE as a measure of normal personality in light of the test's inclusion of scales assessing the risk for chemical abuse/dependency and substance abuse. In the national survey (Corey, 2016), 3.6% of respondents reported using the M-PULSE.

Tests of Psychopathology and Abnormal Personality Functioning

In addition to measures of normal personality functioning, other tests are designed to appraise psychopathology. We now turn to these measures.

MINNESOTA MULTIPHASIC PERSONALITY INVENTORY–2 RESTRUCTURED FORM

At the time of this writing, the MMPI-2-RF is the most current and up-to-date version of the MMPI, the most widely used self-report measure of psychopathology and personality problems (Ben-Porath, Corey, & Tarescavage, 2017). It was reported in the national survey (Corey, 2016) to be used by 42.6% of psychologists performing police candidate suitability evaluations, with nearly two-thirds (62.5%) of those psychologists using the MMPI-2-RF PCIR (Corey & Ben-Porath, 2014), thus rendering the MMPI-2-RF the most commonly used measure of abnormal functioning in this context. The MMPI-2-RF is a self-report measure comprising 338 true–false items (a subset of the 567 items of its predecessor, the MMPI-2). (See Chapter 3 for a summary of the validity studies supporting the use of the MMPI-2-RF in police candidate screening, and Corey and Ben-Porath [2018] for an in-depth treatment of this topic.)

MMPI-2-RF *POLICE CANDIDATE INTERPRETIVE REPORT*

The studies summarized in Chapter 3 identified more than 200 job-relevant correlates associated with 30 of the 42 MMPI-2-RF substantive scales at varying levels of score magnitude, with some findings supported at T-scores as low as 57, and others at T-scores as high as 65 and above. Reliably linking these scales and score elevations to the specific correlates would be challenging, if not impossible, for even the most knowledgeable test user. This raises the possibility of two errors when interpreting any protocol in a police candidate suitability evaluation: (a) failure to identify the behavioral risks of a scale score, as warranted by the empirical findings; and (b) erroneously drawing inferences from a score that are not supported by the research literature. Corey and Ben-Porath (2014) developed the PCIR to minimize the likelihood of these two errors.

Among other features, the PCIR's software logic limits interpretive statements to those that are supported by empirical research findings and transparently annotates each statement to show the test scale with which the finding is associated and the specific published, peer-reviewed research that reports the correlations. Computer-generated interpretative reports that link test scores to published validity evidence help to ensure consistent, evidence-based interpretations across candidates and test users. Other features of the PCIR, including its rationale and structure, are described by Corey and Ben-Porath (2014). By default, the PCIR displays a test taker's scores using both the normative sample and a comparison group of police officer candidates (n = 2,078) consisting of an equal number of male and female candidates from across the United States and Canada. Users of the MMPI-2-RF *Score Report* may also choose to display this comparison group, although without the evidence-based interpretive content contained in the PCIR. Updated PCIR scoring software will incorporate new empirical findings.[16]

MINNESOTA MULTIPHASIC PERSONALITY INVENTORY–2

Among the respondents to the Corey (2016) national survey, 37.5% reported using the 567-item MMPI-2 (Butcher, Dahlstrom, Graham, Tellegen, & Kaemmer, 1989) as a component of their assessment battery in post-offer suitability evaluations. Approximately three-fourths (76.2%) of these psychologists indicated that they obtain MMPI-2 results by use of the Extended Score Report, which includes both Clinical Scale scores and Restructured Clinical Scale scores (upon which the MMPI-2-RF and MMPI-3 are based). The remaining respondents reported either hand-scoring (4.8%) or using one of the Minnesota Reports: the Revised Personnel System Interpretive Report (14.3%), the Revised Personnel System Adjustment Rating Report (14.3%), or the Adult Clinical System Report (9.5%).

PERSONALITY ASSESSMENT INVENTORY

The PAI is a multiple-choice, self-report measure of psychopathology and personality. There is little peer-reviewed, published research regarding use of the PAI (Morey, 1991) in preemployment selection of law enforcement personnel, and only mixed support for it—a somewhat surprising outcome given evidence of the test's construct validity (Morey, 2014). Nevertheless, 37.5% of respondents in the national survey (Corey, 2016) reported using the PAI as part of their screening battery. The 344 items on the questionnaire make up 22 non-overlapping validity, clinical, treatment consideration, and interpersonal scales.

PAI *POLICE AND PUBLIC SAFETY SELECTION REPORT*

Roberts et al. (2004) developed an adapted PAI score report that includes the full set of scores normally provided by a standard PAI score report, as well as

- combined-gender comparison groups for multiple entry-level public safety positions (police officer, firefighter/ emergency medical technician, correctional officer, and dispatcher, among others),
- comparison groups comprising a subsample of the entry-level subjects who were hired and successfully employed for at least 1 year, and
- seven Suitability Risk Statements (Roberts et al., 2004) that are not included in the standard PAI score report.

As with the CPI-PPSSR previously discussed, the risk statements are calculated from unpublished regression equations, six of which correlate with self-reported life history problems, and one with a "poorly suited" rating from the post-offer psychological evaluation. (Unlike with the CPI-PPSSR, the PAI-PPSSR does not contain an index score indicating the "probability of involuntary departure.") Among the PAI users in the Corey (2016) national survey, 90.5% reported using the PAI-PPSSR in their suitability evaluations.

INWALD PERSONALITY INVENTORY AND INWALD PERSONALITY INVENTORY–2

As we discussed in Chapter 3, the IPI (the only version of the test for which peer-reviewed validity evidence has been published) has been discontinued and replaced by the substantially revised IPI-2. The IPI-2 comprises 202 true–false items, and the report contains one validity scale, 16 content scales, a listing of critical items for follow-up evaluation, predictions of psychologist rating ("likely to recommend" vs. "not likely to recommend"), and predictions of four field training officer ratings.

Tests Commonly Used in Fitness Evaluations

A pervasive theme throughout this volume is that the ADA requires, particularly in fitness evaluations, an "individualized assessment" of the ability of a person to perform a particular job, one that focuses on the impairment's actual effect on the candidate or employee. Even in preemployment evaluations, in which candidates generally receive the same battery, the examiner is given free rein to do additional testing when indicated.

There is no "standard battery" for fitness evaluations because test selection is driven by the individual nature of the specific referral question, the characteristics of the incumbent, and a decision regarding the best way to measure the relevant psychometric constructs. Because a variety of issues may arise that require additional specialized testing, it is invaluable for the psychologist to have a large tool chest, selecting the most appropriate instruments to conduct a complete and thorough individualized assessment.

Fitness evaluations are assessments in which the presence or absence of a mental health condition is a central focus; therefore, broadband measures of psychopathology and personality problems (e.g., MMPI-2-RF/MMPI-3, PAI) are most commonly used. Other instruments frequently used include symptom checklists and symptom-targeted measures (e.g., Beck Depression Inventory–2, Clinician-Administered Posttraumatic Stress Disorder [PTSD] Scale for the *Diagnostic and Statistical Manual of Mental Disorders,* Fifth Edition [DSM-5]).

When interpreting test protocols of police officers in fitness evaluations, standard adult norms are used for assessing a score's clinical significance. However, it can be useful to compare a test taker's scores to those of other law enforcement officers who took the test under like conditions. (See Corey & Ben-Porath, 2018, for MMPI-2-RF comparison group means and standard deviations of police and other public safety personnel who took the test in the context of a fitness evaluation.)

Neuropsychological Screening and Measures of Executive Functioning

If the evaluator suspects a neuropsychological impairment in a fitness evaluation, and they do not have sufficient training and experience in neuropsychological assessment, they either should refer the case to an appropriately trained specialist or work with one as a consultant. Neuropsychological *screening*, however, does not require this same level of expertise and can provide useful information about circumscribed cognitive functioning. One of the most underdeveloped areas in post-offer preemployment screening is neuropsychological screening, especially as it pertains to executive functioning. Accordingly, the discussion that follows pertains to screening and should not be read as a prescription for a full neuropsychological assessment.

Zelig, Sperbeck, and Craig (2017) discussed this topic as it pertains to preemployment screening of police officer candidates and defined executive functioning as:

> the capacity of a person to inhibit responses, shift plans in response to changing circumstances, maintain and update working memory (i.e., the chalkboard of the brain), resist interference from distractions, and simultaneously orchestrate an appropriate response to a specific situation. Although some executive functions are related to intelligence, people with high IQ can have impaired executive functioning, especially when encountering stressful situations. (no pagination)

Lezak, Howieson, Bigler, and Tranel (2012) remind us that measures of cognitive ability ask the examinee, "What do you know?" In contrast, measures of executive functioning ask the examinee, "What can you do?" and "How will you do it?" Obviously, the *way* someone carries out a task is a key variable that differentiates success from failure in law enforcement and other high-risk professions.

Although there is no definitive list of executive functions, the three most commonly described executive functions are also relevant to the ability of police officers to perform safely and effectively. These include:

1. *Inhibition*—the ability to stop, put the brakes on, and think before responding.
2. *Working memory and updating*—the ability to hold information in one's mind long enough to do something with it, such as solve a problem or complete a task, and to refresh it as needed. Sometimes working memory has been analogized as random-access memory (RAM) or the chalkboard of the brain. Effective and adaptive working memory requires that the function is stable (i.e., information is actively and robustly maintained) and flexible (i.e., when information needs to be replaced and updated). See Nyberg and Erickson (2015).
3. *Shifting/flexibility skills*, which include the ability to adapt, adjust, or shift when circumstances demand going to an alternative plan (Zelig et al., 2017).

There is ample research indicating the relevance of executive functioning to public safety populations. We will briefly review several illustrative studies.

RESISTANCE TO POSTTRAUMATIC STRESS DISORDER

Bardeen and Orcutt (2011) found that self-ratings of attentional control and the severity of PTSD are related—the lower one's attentional control, the more severe the condition. Although this study was correlational, Birk, Opitz, and Urry (2017) demonstrated that subjects who rated themselves low on attentional control subsequently became more stressed (in comparison to subjects who reported higher levels of attentional control) when asked to give an impromptu speech. Similar findings were reported by Hendrawan, Yamakawa, Kimura, Murakami, and Oshira (2012), who found that a variety of simple executive functioning tests predicted subjective and psychological levels of stress reactivity.

VULNERABILITY TO IMPLICIT BIAS

Another area in which executive functioning is relevant is in identifying people who are the most vulnerable to the effects of implicit racial bias. Ito et al. (2015) obtained baseline measures of inhibition, working memory, updating, and task-shifting in 485 students from three different universities, who took several implicit racial bias tests. One of these tests included a video in which subjects saw black and white actors, some of whom were handling a handgun and others who were handling a wallet. The subjects were instructed to shoot the gun-wielding subjects and to not injure the subjects who were carrying a wallet. These researchers found that those subjects who produced the lowest scores on shifting and working memory were most likely to exhibit racial bias in their shooting decisions. Other studies addressing the relationship between executive functioning and implicit racial bias include Klaur, Schmitz, Teige-Mocigemba, and Voss (2010), and Stewart, von Hippel, and Radvansky (2009).

ABILITY TO EXERCISE SOUND JUDGMENT IN STRESSFUL ENVIRONMENTS

Kleider, Parrott, and King (2010) explored these issues with 24 in-service police officers by obtaining two sets of measures. At the outset, measures of working memory were obtained. They also measured physiological reactivity while the officers watched a real-life video of an officer shot on a traffic stop. The second set of data was obtained when the officers performed on the same shoot/don't shoot measure as that used in the previously cited experiments. Kleider and colleagues found that the officers with the highest level of physiological reactivity to the video of the officer being shot, and who had the lowest scores on working memory, were the most likely to shoot unarmed suspects and more hesitant to shoot the armed suspects.

Combined measures of executive functioning are typically the best predictor of performance in stressful situations (e.g., Miyake & Friedman, 2012). For these reasons, we believe that it is important when appropriate to review various measures of executive functioning because they appear to offer valuable data not tapped by personality or intelligence tests. It should be noted, however, that all of the experiments just cited used experimenter-generated executive functioning tests, which appeared to be more difficult than the commercially available tests. We suspect that these more difficult tests were developed to obtain sufficient variation within samples of nonclinical subjects. Accordingly, we encourage our colleagues who use commercially available versions of these tasks to publish their data.

SUGGESTED MEASURES OF EXECUTIVE FUNCTIONING

We focus on measures of executive functioning that are best suited to the screening environment. These measures take relatively little time and are likely to fall within the boundaries of most clinicians' expertise, especially psychologists whose backgrounds include a solid core in clinical assessment.

Delis-Kaplan Executive Function System

The Delis-Kaplan Executive Function System (D-KEFS; Delis Kaplan, & Kramer, 2001) contains nine subtests, each with two different forms. Whereas the full D-KEFS battery takes a skilled clinician about 2 hours to administer, individual tests can be given as stand-alone measures. Most of the individual tests can be administered in 10 minutes. One of the appealing aspects of this battery is that it is like having a library of executive function tests. Indeed, most of the tests we suggest have a version available within this battery. There are, however, two specific drawbacks to this battery when used in occupationally mandated evaluations:

1. Some of the subtests are difficult to administer and interpret if one does not have a background or training in neuropsychology.
2. Scoring is complicated. This drawback can be overcome if the clinician purchases the computerized scoring program, which is available from the publisher.

Conners Continuous Performance Test

The Connors computer-administered test (Conners, 2004) was developed to diagnose attention-deficit disorders in adults and children. The administration takes 14 minutes. It taps concentration, vigilance, and the ability to resist distractions and maintain strong inhibition skills. This test must be interpreted by a psychologist.

Category Test

The Category Test (Choca et al., 2008) is commonly administered on a computer, which takes about 20 minutes. It arose from Halstead's original battery in 1943. Lezak et al. (2012) assert that the Category Test is the most sensitive test of neuropsychological impairment in the Halstead battery. It measures organizational skills, sustained attention, working memory, nonverbal problem-solving, and cognitive flexibility. Subsequent research has demonstrated that results obtained by computer administration are comparable to those using the earlier manual forms (Nici & Hom, 2013). Although the computerized version is easy to administer, and probably could be administered by most paraprofessional office staff, one needs sufficient training to interpret the test and to determine which follow-up tests are necessary if the examinee scores within the impaired range. Like all executive function tests, a poor score can be due to a number of factors.

Verbal and Semantic Fluency Tests

Tests of *verbal* fluency measure the subject's ability to name as many objects (or nouns) that begin with a specific *letter* within a defined time limit. So, for example, if the examiner states the letter "T," the subject will name words such as tooth, tomato, tornado, and so on, within a prescribed time limit (typically 60 seconds). There are various versions of verbal fluency tests found in the literature. The D-KEFS, mentioned earlier, also has a version of verbal fluency. Performance on verbal fluency tasks is influenced by education, with only slight effects for age (Tombaugh, Kozak, & Rees, 1999). As simple as this task is to administer, it is actually a sensitive measure of executive functioning.

Measures of *semantic* fluency ask the subject to name as many different items belonging to a defined category within a time limit. For example, the subject may be asked to name as many animals as they can think of within 60 seconds. There are different versions available, including the D-KEFS, from various test publishers. Measures of semantic fluency are positively correlated with level of education and do not show age decline until one is about 60 years of age (Tombaugh, Kozak, & Rees, 1999). Since most measures

5 chapter

of verbal or semantic fluency contain two or three trials, either one can typically be administered in less than 5 minutes.

Wechsler Adult Intelligence Scale, Fourth Edition

A well-recognized measure of working memory is obtained from the combined scale scores from the WAIS-IV Digit Span and the Arithmetic subtests. These two subtests can typically be administered in less than 12 minutes.

Trail-Making Test

The Trail-Making Test (Allen & Haderlie, 2010) is a measure of visual scanning, complex attention, psychomotor speed, and mental flexibility and is described as "one of the most popular neuropsychological tests and is included in most test batteries" (Tombaugh, 2004, p. 203). This test is incorporated in the Halstead-Reitan neuropsychological test battery. A version is also available within the D-KEFS battery. Two of the advantages of administering this simple test are that it usually can be completed in 7 to 8 minutes and that most clinicians with clinical training have had experience with it.

Stroop Tasks

After the initial version of this popular neuropsychological screening test was published by John Ridley Stroop in 1935, numerous versions of it have appeared, some of which are now in the public domain. In the typical Stroop task, the subject is initially asked to read the names of colors printed in black ink—such as red, green, blue, or brown. The subject then encounters a page with colored blocks or circles. They are told to name the colors. The most critical phase then follows. The subject is confronted with a list of words in which the word is printed in a nonmatching color, such as the word *red* printed in green ink. In this final phase, the task is to recite the *color* of the ink, not the word. The subject's score is the number of correct responses within a prescribed time limit. Responses to this last trial indicate processing speed, shifting, and inhibition (resisting the pull to recite the word and naming the color instead). Of the various versions, we most often use the test by Trenerry, Crosson, Deboe, and Leber (1988). It can be administered in less than 6 minutes.

LIMITATIONS AND SUMMARY

Like all tests, executive function measures also have limitations when used with post-offer candidates:

- There are very few studies that provide validation data or separate norms for law enforcement candidates or incumbents.

- All executive function tests are multifactorial. This means that if one obtains a score in the impaired range on a particular test, it is difficult and sometimes impossible to identify the specific deficit(s) that contributed to that score without other testing or corroborative biographical information. This is the reason that neuropsychologists, when investigating the extent of impairment in a clinically referred client, often administer lengthy batteries of tests.

- Many of these tests are very sensitive to practice effects, and some of the tests, in which the score represents the speed or efficiency in which the solution is learned, are often single-use tests. After the examinee knows the solution to the test, a retest is usually of little value. For this reason, while we appreciate the power of the *Wisconsin Card Sort* or *Iowa Gambling Task* to derive useful information about decision-making and shifting, these tests are not recommended because applicants often apply multiple times for law enforcement positions.

We have attempted in this chapter to list and describe tests commonly used in both suitability and fitness evaluations and to describe instruments with promising potential for measuring executive functioning, which may be the new frontier (along with assessing cultural competence, and in combination with personality measures) in police suitability evaluations. In order to evaluate and properly interpret these and other measures, well-designed, executed, and published peer-reviewed studies are needed. We encourage readers to collaborate with academic researchers who have needed analytical expertise but who often lack access to real-world data. It is this collaboration that has brought us to where we are today: an unprecedented time for evidence-based practice.

Personal History Information

There is a significant correlation between personality test scores and self-reported history (e.g., Corey, Sellbom, & Ben-Porath, 2018; Sarchione, Cuttler, Muchinsky, & Nelson-Gray, 1998). As such, test-based evidence of a personality construct, in combination with a behavioral history that is known to be correlated with that construct, strengthens confidence in the risks predicted by the test score. Furthermore, research consistently reveals an independent and robust relationship between past problems (e.g., job termination and disciplinary actions) and future work performance (Cohen & Chaiken, 1972; Corey, Sellbom, & Ben-Porath, 2018; Cuttler & Muchinsky, 2006; Malouff & Schutte, 1986; Poland, 1978). Thus, while test scales that focus on biographical history as predictors of future problems (e.g., IPI and M-PULSE) are devoid of psychological constructs that allow for mitigation, they do capitalize on relating self-reported life experience to occupational outcomes and thus can be considered as complementary measures.

Although self-reported history information is routinely gathered as part of a psychological suitability evaluation, some police candidates will attempt to conceal or misrepresent negative aspects of their history. To protect against erroneous suitability judgments resulting from such deceptive efforts, evaluators should review findings from the background investigation conducted by the hiring agency. In the two most populous states in the United States (California and Texas), regulations require that the psychological evaluation be based, in part, on a review of background investigation documents.[17] Because the candidate could conceal personal history information crucial for making a valid suitability determination, California regulations place primary emphasis on the psychologist's consideration of agency-provided background information and only secondary emphasis on information provided by the candidate: "Personal history information includes the candidate's relevant work, life, and developmental history based on information collected during the background investigation [Regulation 1953(g)(3)]. This information may be augmented by responses on a personal history questionnaire collected as part of the psychological evaluation" [11 C.C.R. § 1955(e)(3)].

A third category of personal history information important to consider in psychological suitability evaluations consists of mental health treatment/assessment records from other healthcare professionals, to the extent that they are relevant and available. Johnson and Roberts (2005) reported that approximately one-fourth of police candidates have consulted a professional for help with personal problems at some point in their lives, and 1% have been treated in an inpatient facility. Spilberg and Corey (2019) advise, "For those candidates who have sought help, psychologists should have an accurate understanding of the nature and extent of the psychological problem and whether it has relevance for the purposes of determining psychological suitability" (p. 129). Inasmuch as all states require, with limited exceptions, a patient's authorization before a healthcare provider can release medical records, it is necessary either to have the candidate sign an authorization form to obtain the relevant records or to instruct the candidate to obtain and provide them. The California POST *Psychological Screening Manual* contains two forms (Appendices K and M) that evaluators can use or adapt for purposes of seeking a limited range of information about a candidate's potentially relevant mental health problems.

When evaluating military veterans and reservists returning from combat deployment who report having been awarded a service-connected mental disability by the Department of Veterans Affairs (VA), frequently but not exclusively for PTSD, it is often useful to obtain a copy of the Compensation and Pension (C&P) evaluation report that supports the award or the VA "rating decision" letter that explains how the findings from the C&P evaluation justified the disability rating decision. Requesting these or other mental health records necessarily delays the suitability determination until the documents are received and reviewed, but

BEST PRACTICE

To protect against erroneous suitability judgments resulting from a police candidate's deceptive efforts, review findings from the background investigation conducted by the hiring agency.

5
chapter

failing to obtain them can result in serious error that cannot later be undone.

Finally, psychologists conducting suitability evaluations may also benefit from reviewing information obtained from a polygraph examination administered as part of the hiring agency's background investigation. The federal Employee Polygraph Protection Act of 1988 (29 U.S.C. Chapter 22) virtually banned the use of polygraph tests for purposes of preemployment evaluations or for incumbent employees. However, the law does not apply to federal, state, or local government employers, and exceptions are made for certain sensitive positions (e.g., security firms and pharmaceutical manufacturers, distributors, and dispensers). Most states permit police employers to conduct polygraph examinations, although not all agencies require them. When available, they can be useful sources of personal history information that may augment (or contradict) information provided by the candidate during the psychological evaluation.

Clinical Interview

Nearly every jurisdiction in the United States and Canada requires a clinical interview as a component of the psychological suitability evaluation. In at least one state (New Hampshire), a police officer can presumably be appointed based on a "psychological screening test" alone, but "[n]o person shall be denied employment as the result of such a testing process unless they have been given the opportunity for a personal interview with a licensed psychologist or psychiatrist employed by the agency."[18] As described in the California POST regulations, the purpose of the interview is "to address all issues arising from the reviewed [psychological testing and personal history] information and other issues that may arise during the interview" [11 C.C.R. § 1955(e)(4)]. This squarely places the interview at the end of the evaluation process in order to ensure that the evaluator is able to use the interview to clarify discrepancies, assess hypotheses, and give the candidate an opportunity to explain problematic aspects of their personal history. Spilberg and Corey (2019) caution that "[w]hether the interview adds more validity than error variance hinges on how it is constructed and conducted, and on how the resulting information is analyzed and used" (p. 133).

Viewing the interview as something that is *constructed*, rather than passively and unwaveringly carried out in the same way for all candidates, enables evaluators to harness its unique benefits and features. One of these is the opportunity it offers to investigate questions generated by a review of the psychological testing and personal history. Another is the ability to observe the candidate engaged in decision-making, judgment under stress, reasoning, self-reflection, and social interaction—each relevant to the criterion standards used to evaluate the suitability of a police candidate.

BEST PRACTICE

Viewing the interview as something that is *constructed*, rather than passively and unwaveringly carried out in the same way for all candidates, enables you to harness its unique benefits and features.

Texas regulations also require that the interview be "conducted after the instruments have been scored" [TAC Title 37, Part 7, Rule § 217.1(12)]. After reviewing the results of psychological testing, the evaluator has a set of findings that portray the candidate in a particular way—a person, for example, who is highly controlled, perhaps even rigid, who may have difficulty making decisions under pressure. Informed by these findings, the evaluator is now able to construct an interview designed to assess the accuracy of the test-based findings and their impact on the candidate's behavior. Some candidates with problematic tendencies (e.g., impulsiveness, anxiety, or shyness) may also have the ability to compensate for or modulate those tendencies. A well-constructed interview in which the evaluating professional creates opportunities for the candidate to display (or not) those compensating or modulating qualities provides a behaviorally anchored tool for evaluating risk-confirming and risk-mitigating factors.

The usefulness of a clinical interview in a suitability evaluation can be enhanced by relying on a structured or semi-structured format. Not only may sticking to an outline help the evaluator cover all of the relevant topics, but it also may be perceived by the

5
chapter

candidate as fairer. There have been some occasions in which we have encountered candidates who were comforted knowing that the sensitive questions they were being asked were part of a structured or routine outline.[19]

Cultural Considerations

Professional practice guidelines call on psychologists conducting occupationally mandated psychological evaluations to "recognize individual and group differences, and the importance of practicing with cultural competence" (APA, 2018). There are two ways to accomplish this in the context of a suitability evaluation. First, if a candidate's dominant identity (which may be related to race or another identity) falls "outside a psychologist's boundary of competence" (APA, 2018, p. 194), they are advised to seek education, training, consultation, or supervision before performing the evaluation, when possible. Psychologists conducting an evaluation of a transgender police candidate, for example, may wish to consult with a colleague experienced in conducting suitability evaluations with such candidates or, at the least, experienced in evaluating this population. Second, when reporting the findings from a suitability evaluation, "psychologists strive to consider whether an examinee's cultural background may affect evaluation findings. Psychologists also are encouraged to note any significant limitations of their interpretations based on a consideration of situational, personal, linguistic, socioeconomic, and cultural differences" (p. 194). This is especially important when evaluating candidates from a demographic group unlikely to have been included as subjects, at least in any substantial numbers, in the validity studies supporting the test's inferences.

Data Collection in Fitness Evaluations

There are a number of sources of data that are relevant in conducting fitness evaluations. We discuss these sources in this section.

Referral Letter

The IACP *Fitness-for-Duty Evaluation Guidelines* (IACP, 2018a) recommend obtaining a written referral letter from the employer or other referring entity, which should include "a description of the objective evidence giving rise to concerns about the employee's fitness for duty and any particular questions that the employer wishes the examiner to address" (Guideline 7.3). This referral letter is also important for understanding the legitimacy of the referral and to aid in assessing the scope of the evaluation and the examiner's professional competence in addressing the referral questions (see the *Professional Practice Guidelines for Occupationally Mandated Psychological Evaluations* [OMPE Guidelines]; APA, 2018). Data collection in fitness evaluations begins with this referral letter.

Collateral Documents

A fitness evaluation is a kind of forensic evaluation, wherein multimethod and multimodal assessments are important (Heilbrun, Grisso, & Goldstein, 2009; Otto, Goldstein, & Heilbrun, 2017).

INFO

Collateral documents lie at the heart of any forensic evaluation, and fitness evaluations are no exception.

Collateral documents lie at the heart of any forensic evaluation, and fitness evaluations are no exception. There are a number of specific reasons that occupationally mandated psychological evaluations rely on relevant collateral documents and that their inclusion is a form of best practice.

5
chapter

1. *Collateral documents increase the face validity of evaluation.* Grisso, Borum, Edens, Moye, and Otto (2003) noted that while face validity, from a statistical standpoint, may be the weakest form of test validity in research, it is often the most compelling in the legal arena.

2. *Examinees are not always accurate historians.* Collateral documents that are relevant for answering the fitness question may compensate for the reality that examinees sometimes lie, omit important information, misinterpret life events, or simply forget pertinent information.

Examinees may even understate or neglect to describe events that would otherwise provide a reasonable explanation for why they acted in a way that appears impaired. One should not assume that the subject or the referral source knows all of the pertinent data that would be favorable to their respective positions. Similarly, collateral material may unearth a cause for the examinee's impairments that was not suspected by either the examinee or the referring entity. Such has been the case in our own work when we discovered that, for example, a traumatic or other brain injury, which was believed to be benign or inconsequential at the time, was a major factor in causing a significant behavioral change in the employee.

3. *Humans are not good lie detectors.* Whatever our confidence in our own ability to detect deception, empirical studies—in which ground truth is known—indicate that our ability to detect deception and accurately identify truth tellers is modest. Indeed, Bond and De Paulo's (2006) meta-analysis, which analyzed 206 studies with more than 4,000 subjects, showed that those who were charged in detecting deception were correct only 54% of the time in studies of binary choices in which guessing at the base rate (or a coin flip) would have resulted in 50% accuracy.

4. *Examinees may be more forthcoming during the interview and testing when they know the examiner will review pertinent collateral documents.* Examinees who know that the examiner is aware of their vulnerabilities may be more likely to be forthright on psychological testing. So, for example, if an employee knows that you have or will obtain records that indicate they have a substance use problem, the examinee may be more likely to respond truthfully to questions on psychological testing that deal with that topic.

TYPES OF COLLATERAL DOCUMENTS AND PROTOCOL FOR PROCUREMENT

Consistent with the methodology commonly used in other forensic evaluations, if the psychologist desires collateral information that is held by the employer or other referring party, they should begin by turning to the referral source to request that material. The categories of collateral material include employment-related records, medical records—held both in and outside of the organization—and miscellaneous records, including military files and social media compilations (unless prohibited by state law, institutional policies, or collective bargaining agreements). Obtaining as complete a record as is reasonably possible is necessary to ensure a competent and objective appraisal of fitness (Corey & Borum, 2013).

Job/Position Description

For ADA purposes, employers are not required to have a job or position description (Rennert, 2004). However, if available, a job/position description that identifies essential job functions may be helpful and should be included with the referral. Unless the suspected impairment poses a direct threat, a fitness evaluation can only proceed if the employer believes the impairment limits an essential (as opposed to marginal) job function. When the job-limiting effects of an impairment are confined to marginal job functions, it is assumed that the employee can be relieved of those duties as part of reasonable accommodation [42 U.S.C. § 12112(d)(4)(A)].[20]

Social Media and Data Brokers

In a world in which personal (and sometimes relevant) information can be obtained from Internet or social media sources, it is surprising that professional psychology has not adopted any professional guidelines regarding the collection and use of such data as a potential source of information that may contribute to forensic findings (Pirelli, Otto, & Estoup, 2016), even after a number of studies or reviews have concluded that valid information about one's functional abilities can be acquired from online social media sources such as Facebook (e.g., Back et al., 2010; Zoufal, Webber,

& Parmegiaini, 2017). However, both in psychology and psychiatry, efforts are currently underway to develop professional practice guidelines addressing this topic.

A recent survey of forensic psychologists found that most respondents did not believe forensic evaluators are obligated to conduct Internet-based searches, but they also did not see it as contraindicated (Pirelli, Hartrigan, & Zapf, 2018). These authors also noted the proliferation of data or information brokers, who collect and sell information to their clients and who often have access to databases that are unavailable to the general public. If one chooses to use such material, we agree with the recommendation offered by Pirelli, Otto, and Estoup (2016) that the examinee be advised of the evaluator's reliance on such material and be given the opportunity to either challenge the data or further explain the context in which the data were generated. These authors also recommend that, if the clinician uses such data, their reliance on it be noted in the informed consent or disclosure documents.

Personnel Files

Personnel records fall into a variety of types. These may include disciplinary records, internal or administrative investigations, performance appraisals, commendations, complaints, and police reports authored by or referencing the examinee. There are generally no complications in requesting these materials because they are typically available in a general personnel file or otherwise available from

---

BOX 5.3 Applicable guideline: Internet searches to obtain collateral information about the examinee

Internet searches regarding the evaluee can also provide useful information. Social networking sites and other Internet social forums may contain information about the evaluee that conflicts with data provided by the evaluee or others, warranting further examination to contextualize this apparent conflict. An evaluee's online persona may constitute impression management or posturing because people often behave or present themselves differently online than in person. It is also possible that the online information is more accurate than what the evaluee is telling the police and experts (Guideline 5.32, Glancy et al. [2015], American Academy of Psychiatry and the Law, p. S10).

the referral source. Other records, such as medical files and prior psychological evaluations held by the employer, may not be available to the person who requested your services. Employers are usually *not* covered entities under the Health Insurance Portability and Accountability Act of 1996 (HIPAA), so obtaining these records may not be difficult. These records may be particularly useful if they include prior fitness evaluations or other baseline psychological testing.

It is possible that some of the relevant records will be delivered with portions of the information redacted. This is especially common if the records sought include internal affairs documents. In those cases, identifying information may be redacted to protect the identity of witnesses or confidential matters involving other officers. This is not unlike the situation that forensic psychologists may encounter when involved in child custody or termination of parental rights cases, in which the identities of various informants collected by the state's protective service agencies are redacted.

Personal Medical Records

As with employment records, the evaluator may seek medical records that are possessed or whose release must be authorized by the employee. In most cases, it is appropriate to request the examinee's medical records, as long as that request is restricted to records reasonably expected to be probative. When doing so, it is important to provide the healthcare provider or records custodian with the Genetic Information Nondiscrimination Act of 2008 (GINA) admonition we discussed in Chapter 1. Without this admonition, the receipt of records containing GINA-prohibited information (e.g., the employee's family medical history) cannot be deemed inadvertent.

Other information sources that sometimes yield valuable data are controlled substance databases. Such databases are available in all Canadian provinces and 45 US states (Furlan et al., 2014; National Association of Boards of Pharmacy, 2018). In most jurisdictions, database material may be provided to the psychologist if the examinee executes a release of information. Often these releases contain specific statutory language and are printed by the jurisdiction. They may require a notary signature, so it is unlikely that a standard authorization or release will suffice. The psychologist should note, however, that these state databases only report prescriptions that have been filed in a particular geographical jurisdiction. We have encountered cases in which the examinee is aware of this limitation and crosses state lines to have prescriptions filled for various controlled substances.

Employee-Nominated Documents or Collateral Informants

We advise the examinee of the materials that we have or intend to review (unless deemed confidential by the referral source). If the examinee believes this is an incomplete or biased data set, they are invited to provide or nominate any other important documents or information sources that may help us arrive at a more accurate and unbiased opinion. In addition to possibly providing important information about the examinee's fitness, this invitation also promotes fairness by leveling the playing field in the event that a referral source selectively withholds important information.

There also have been occasions in which an examinee's nominations produced material or collateral contacts that wound up providing far more evidence of job-relevant impairment beyond what the employer provided. For example, one of us had an occasion to evaluate a correctional officer who had made threatening remarks to his coworkers. He also was having marital problems. Believing that the administrator who made the referral was unfairly biased, this employee insisted that the evaluator speak with a former supervisor, who was also one of the SWAT team leaders. The employee believed that the observations of this former supervisor would expose what he asserted to be the unfounded and petty concerns of the administration. Instead, when the supervisor was contacted, he made two points that were considered significant. First, he chastised the administration for taking so long to refer an obviously impaired employee for evaluation. Second, and far more ominous, he reported that the employee had been asking him repeatedly in past weeks how the SWAT team would respond if it discovered that the barricaded subject in a domestic dispute was a law enforcement officer.

When the employee's personal medical records are requested, it is important to remind the employee and employer that only information that is relevant or potentially relevant will be contained in the clinician's summary report. Without this assurance, it is not unusual to obtain push-back from employees who are concerned that sensitive information (having no bearing on their job) will be provided to the employer. This is often the case when the medical records contain information on reproductive health issues or other sensitive topics that are irrelevant to the employee's ability to perform essential job functions. For example, one of us conducted a fitness evaluation of a police dispatcher who strongly resisted the request to review her medical records. Ultimately, she agreed to authorize their release when she received reassurance that the abortion she obtained a year prior was not relevant to the fitness question and would not be noted in the summary report.

We do not provide or "re-disclose" an employee's personal medical records to the employer, except for information we include in our report that is directly relevant to the evaluation's findings and conclusions (e.g., the impact of these findings on job performance and their associated risks). Similarly, while we inform the employee of any records the employer has provided for our review, we do not release those records to the employee. The specific policy regarding the dissemination of records should be described in the informed consent documents so that each side agrees to the ground rules regarding the release of records.

BEST PRACTICE

We do not provide or "re-disclose" an employee's personal medical records to the employer, except for information we include in our report that is directly relevant to the evaluation's findings and conclusions.

Clinical Interview

Although there is evidence that clinical interviews are not particularly helpful for assessing risk of violence or other important behaviors when used as a standalone assessment strategy (e.g., Grove, Zald, Lebow, Snitz, & Nelson, 2000), they are indispensable in fitness evaluations. Fischler, McElroy, Miller, Saxe-Clifford, and Zelig (2011) described three purposes of a clinical interview in the context of a fitness evaluation (p. 75):

1. It assesses the officer's perspective regarding the reason for the referral.
2. It explores the officer's personal and professional history for patterns of vulnerability or resiliency that are relevant to making predictions regarding the examinee's ability to cope with the demands of the job.
3. It evaluates the officer's mental status, symptoms of mental illness (e.g., major depression, psychosis, and PTSD), personality problems (e.g., impulsivity and rebelliousness), and other potential problems (e.g., family or financial problems and alcohol or drug abuse).

In addition, the clinical interview is useful for identifying potentially valuable collateral documents and collateral informants. It may also provide clinical information that may inform your decision regarding which psychological test(s) to use or the need to obtain consultation from a colleague if the condition affecting job performance lies outside of your expertise. Such may be the case, for example, if you learn that a sleep, neuropsychological, or primary medical issue lies at the heart of the matter but falls outside your scope of practice or boundaries of competence. Finally, information provided by the candidate in the clinical interview can sometimes lead to the discovery of third-party records (e.g., police reports, disability decision letters from the Department of Veterans Affairs, child protection agency reports) that should be reviewed before making a final determination of fitness for duty. Except for mental health and other medical records, examining psychologists should request third-party records from the referral source.

COLLATERAL INTERVIEWS

Collateral informants may provide information that is otherwise unavailable. Before speaking with a collateral informant, however, a couple of considerations should be noted. First, if the informant is also an employee of the same organization as the examinee, the request for contact should be made through the organizational client. Second, all collateral informants should be advised that the

information they provide is not confidential and that their participation is voluntary. It is our practice to have the informant sign
an informed consent or disclosure document that outlines the
parameters and use of information that is being sought. We do
not interview informants who refuse to allow information from the
interview to be used and disclosed, as appropriate, in the written
report. Although the majority of the fitness evaluations we conduct include information provided by collateral informants, most
often that information is obtained by the employer and is included
as part of the original referral records. In less than one-fourth of
the evaluations we conduct do we find it necessary to conduct
interviews with collateral informants. (See earlier in Chapter 5 for
a discussion of the need for disclosure/informed consent in collateral interviews.)

PSYCHOLOGICAL TESTING

The use of a standardized assessment battery is recommended when
conducting preemployment suitability evaluations, but that is not
typically the case for fitness evaluations. There is no standard psychological test battery to use when conducting a fitness evaluation,
although an omnibus or broadband test of psychopathology and
personality problems is commonly used. Indeed, it is the responsibility of the psychologist to perform an *individualized* assessment
that addresses the questions and issues in the referral letter, and this
is especially important when the psychologist anticipates that the
employer will have to address reasonable accommodation after the
evaluation is completed.[21]

Tests used in fitness evaluations, as with suitability evaluations,
should be selected in part because they have a scientific basis
for measuring the relevant construct(s) and conducting an
individualized assessment. In addition to the considerations already
listed in this chapter for choosing tests to be used in suitability
evaluations, we also suggest the following when evaluating tests for
use in fitness evaluations:

- Since the presence or absence of psychopathology is a
  primary question in every fitness evaluation, it is important
  that the test battery contain at least one omnibus,

broadband measure that taps related constructs. Corey and Ben-Porath (2018) provide means and standard deviations for all MMPI-2-RF scales for male and female comparison groups comprised of subjects who took the test in the context of fitness evaluations.[22]

- In some cases, it may be helpful for the examiner to include a measure that is generally sensitive to the presence of nonpathological personality traits. Such measures may provide information about the examinee's psychological resources and coping abilities. One should be careful, however, not to equate deviant scores on measures of normal personality as indicating unfitness, inasmuch as fitness is always a clinical construct.

- It also may be useful to consider narrowband measures to learn more about a suspected clinical problem that may interfere with the employee's functional abilities. For example, if the employee is compromised by a trauma-related disorder, the use of the Trauma Symptom Inventory–2 (Briere, 2010) or a similar measure may be appropriate. Another example may be an employee suspected of significant deficiencies in memory or executive functioning. In such a case, administration of selected neuropsychological tests may be appropriate either by the examiner or, if lacking the expertise, then by a consulting neuropsychologist.

- Either as a component of the broadband measure of psychopathology or as a separate assessment instrument, it is important to include standardized measures of response style to aid in the evaluation of overreporting or underreporting. Examinees in fitness evaluations may, depending on any anticipated secondary gains, be motivated to feign or malinger mental illness in order to, for example, qualify for a medical retirement or mitigate responsibility for past behavior

BEWARE
Do not equate deviant scores on measures of normal personality as indicating unfitness, inasmuch as fitness is always a clinical construct.

that is the subject of disciplinary investigation. Of course, many examinees are more apt to underreport problems.

Notes

1. At least two of the professional standards and professional practice guidelines referenced in this chapter are currently under review and revision, and others are scheduled for review in the next several years. Readers should confirm that they are familiar with the most recent edition of the standards and guidelines.

2. At the time of this writing, a fact witness is entitled to receive $30 for each day's attendance and testimony in an Oregon court, and mileage reimbursement at the rate of 25 cents per mile if the witness is required to travel from a place within or outside the state to give testimony (ORS § 44.415). In Utah, a witness fares worse: the one-day witness fee is $18.50 plus $1.00 for each 4 miles traveled over 50 miles in one direction ("Notice to Persons Served With a Subpoena," Utah Board of District Court Judges, revised December 21, 2018). If this is a concern to the evaluator, they should consider adding a provision to the referral source's informed consent document (or retainer agreement), indicating their expectations regarding compensation if they are required to appear at a deposition or before a tribunal.

3. In some cases, a person may testify as *both* a fact witness and expert witness. Under *Federal Rules of Civil Procedure* Rule 26(a)(2)(B), a *hybrid witness* is one whose opinion testimony arose "not from his enlistment as an expert, but, rather, from his ground-level involvement in the events giving rise to the litigation" (*Downey v. Bob's Discount Furniture Holdings, Inc.*, 2011). A hybrid witness is not required to provide a written report and may both testify as an expert *and* testify concerning facts unrelated to the expert opinions to be presented as an expert. See also *Indianapolis Airport Authority v. Travelers Property Casualty Co. of America* (2017).

4. Many jurisdictions define professional conduct in their licensing statute by reference to the EPPCC, thereby elevating it to a legal standard, not merely a professional one.

5. See the American Academy of Psychiatry and the Law, *Practice Guidelines for the Forensic Evaluation of Psychiatric Disability* (Gold et al., 2008); APA, *Specialty Guidelines for Forensic Psychology* (2013) and *Professional Practice Guidelines for Occupationally Mandated Psychological Evaluations* (2018); Ontario Chiefs of Police Association, *Constable Selection System: Guidelines for Psychologists* (2018); IACP, *Fitness-for-Duty Evaluation Guidelines* (2018a) and *Preemployment Psychological Evaluation Guidelines* (2014); and

5
chapter

Canadian Psychological Association, *Canadian Code of Ethics for Psychologists* (2017).

6. California POST regulations also stipulate that preemployment suitability evaluations of peace officer candidates are valid for a maximum of 1 year [11 C.C.R. § 1955(c)], but this time period varies across jurisdictions. Washington State, for example, specifies that evaluations must be completed within 6 months of a police officer's certification [Washington Administrative Code 139-07-030(1)(c)].

7. The only exception to mandatory reporting may be those instances in which the psychologist is retained by an attorney, and an attorney–client relationship exists in a jurisdiction in which attorneys are exempted from mandatory reporting requirements. (See Chapter 1 for further discussion on this topic.)

8. *The Ethical Principles of Psychologists and Code of Conduct* (APA, 2017) distinguishes between test *materials* (e.g., manuals, instruments, test questions) and test *data* (raw and scaled scores, client/patient responses to test questions or stimuli, and psychologists' notes and recordings concerning client/patient statements and behavior during an examination).

9. Spilberg and Corey (2019) note in the context of suitability screening that "[s]ome personally sensitive topics are worth the intrusiveness. In particular, inappropriate and illegal sexual behavior is one of the most frequent reasons that police officers are fired. Although this behavior is uncommon, it makes up about 25% of the causes for termination—much higher than termination for excessive force or other types of misconduct. But even questions regarding sexual behavior are best limited to those that focus on illegal acts—such as child molestation, viewing child pornography, prostitution, voyeurism, sexual assault, indecent exposure, sexual harassment, on-duty sexual behavior, and selling sexual favors—or on sexual behaviors with known or reasonably established links to adult sexual misconduct, such as sexual boundary violations, viewing pornography at work, and on-the-job sexual contact" (p. 141).

10. Indeed, sometimes we have encouraged the referring party and the examinee to provide materials that are *contrary* or *nonsupportive* of their respective position in hope of averting this possibility.

11. TAC Title 37, Part 7, Rule § 217.1(12).

12. Spilberg and Corey (2019) admonished that not only should information be available concerning the reference group used to develop the test and score interpretations but also "[p]referably the reference group should consist of job applicants in general and peace officer applicants in particular" (p. 104).

13. In some jurisdictions, specialized tests will not meet the legal requirements for inclusion in a suitability evaluation of a police officer candidate. For example, Washington State requires that a minimum

of two written psychological tests be used and that they "be objective, job-related psychological instruments validated for use in evaluating law enforcement officers. For the purpose of this section, a validated test is defined as a test that has a substantial research base for interpretation *with normal range populations in general and public safety applica[nts] in particular*" [Washington Administrative Code 139-07-030(5)(a)(i), emphasis added].

14. In an employment discrimination case, a federal district court prohibited the testimony of a psychologist who could not explain the empirical basis of a proprietary MMPI-2 narrative report. "Because of her rote reliance on a report whose basis she does not understand, its conclusions (that she incorporated almost wholesale into her report) cannot be tested on cross-examination, and it is not a proper basis for her testimony" (no pagination, *Lindsey v. Costco Wholesale Corporation*, 2016).

15. Of course, any measure that can be lawfully used during a pre-offer exam can also be used in post-conditional offer examinations.

16. The MMPI-3 (Ben-Porath & Tellegen, 2020) will be the next generation of the MMPI instruments for use with adults. The updated inventory has a new, nationally representative normative sample, which replaces the 30-plus-year-old MMPI-2/MMPI-2-RF norms. The MMPI-3 includes 335 items, approximately 80% of which are carried over from the MMPI-2-RF. It contains most of the MMPI-2-RF scales, with some modifications designed primarily to improve their efficiency. New scales target constructs not adequately covered by the MMPI-2/MMPI-2-RF item pool (e.g., compulsivity and impulsivity). Similar to the MMPI-2-RF, the MMPI-3 manuals and scoring software provide comparison groups, including a new sample of individuals assessed as part of their preemployment evaluation for law enforcement officer positions. An MMPI-3 version of the PCIR also will be released with the new test.

17. See 11 California Code of Regulations § 1955 and Texas Administrative Code, Title 37, Part 7, Rule § 217.1(12).

18. New Hampshire POST Organizational Rules, Chapter 100, Part 301.07(e).

19. The power of a structured interview in conveying fairness and impartiality cannot be overstated. When considering general job interviews, the use of unstructured interviews was deemed the most common factor in cases in which plaintiffs sought relief for discriminatory hiring practices (Terpstra, Mohamed, & Kethley, 1999).

20. One commentator has objected to the term marginal job function, noting, " 'Marginal' is an unfortunate choice of words in that even marginal functions or tasks under the ADA are important to us. For these purposes, marginal just means those functions that are not essential" (University of Idaho, undated).

5
chapter

21. In the 2002 case of *Chevron v. Echazabal,* the US Supreme Court dealt with a dispute in which Echazabal was fired from a Chevron plant because the company feared that chemicals scheduled to be brought onto the facility would pose a direct threat by exacerbating Echazabal's liver disease. The court sided with Chevron, but also ruled that if the direct threat defense arises, that the examiner is required to produce "a reasonable medical judgment that relies on the most current medical knowledge and/or the best available objective evidence, and upon an expressly individualized assessment of the individual's present ability to safely perform the essential functions of the job" (p. 85).

22. The Civil Rights Act of 1991 § 106, which prohibits an employer's use of gender- or race-based norms for tests used in making employment decisions, applies to selection and promotion, not to clinical assessment in fitness evaluations.

Data Interpretation 6

Avoiding reliance on a single data source is a well-established principle in forensic practice (American Psychological Association [APA], 2013, 2018). Indeed, as we discussed in Chapter 5, suitability evaluations of police officers frequently are regulated by statute or various Peace Officer Standards and Training (POST) commissions, most often requiring that the screening psychologist base a determination of suitability on the "basic model" (Mitchell, 2017; Serafino, 2010). The basic screening model involves findings from no fewer than two written tests (one measuring psychopathology and another measuring normal traits), personal history information, any relevant medical records, and a clinical interview. Fitness evaluations also routinely require consideration of data from similar sources.

BEST PRACTICE

Avoiding reliance on a single data source is a well-established principle in forensic practice.

Using a Model in Suitability and Fitness Evaluations

In evaluations we have conducted, the findings from all data sources have often converged neatly in support of a clear determination. Even in fitness evaluations, some officers come to the evaluation tearfully acknowledging that they have been privately struggling for months with depression, anxiety, a substance use disorder, or some other mental health challenge. Their performance evaluations document a decline in performance, collateral interviews confirm social isolation and mood changes, personal medical records attest to efforts to manage insomnia and other symptoms with medication, and psychological testing indicates credible reports of problems consistent with the other clinical evidence. Similarly, in suitability evaluations, many candidates present on testing and interview precisely how the hiring agency's background investigation shows them to be after extensive interviews with neighbors, employers, coworkers, family members, and associates: emotionally and behaviorally well-adjusted, socially competent, and prosocial, and possessing all of the other traits required by the criterion standard. In such cases, the data fit together neatly like pieces of a jigsaw puzzle, and the resulting suitability and fitness determinations are "no-brainers."

But the typical scenario is not so ideal. More often, there is some information that points to problems that are contradicted (or not reported) by other sources. These more typical cases reflect the reality that people can be complicated, and behavior is contextual. Even emotionally well-adjusted people sometimes have bad days, and persons with serious mental illness may continue to function well in some settings but not in others. In these more classic cases, the data are murky, messy, frustrating, and inconsistent, and result in a head-scratching challenge to combine or integrate these data to answer the referral question(s). This challenge is the focal subject of this chapter.

Heilbrun (2001; Heilbrun, Grisso, & Goldstein, 2009) has advocated for the use of a model to help guide the forensic examiner in data gathering, data interpretation, and the communication of findings and opinions. Gawande, in his 2009 best-seller, *The Checklist Manifesto: How to Get Things Right*, also demonstrated the utility of sequential checklists—another form of a model—to guide decision-making in business, medicine, and other pursuits. The California POST *Psychological Screening Manual* (Spilberg & Corey, 2019) devotes a full chapter to this topic and introduced a data integration model for use in police officer suitability assessments. Corey and Ben-Porath (2018) adapted this model in their *Practical Guide* for the use of the Minnesota Multiphasic Personality Inventory–2 Restructured Form (MMPI-2-RF) in suitability evaluations, along with a separate model specific to fitness evaluations, and they demonstrate their use of the model with multiple case studies that combine findings from other tests, personal history, and clinical interviews. We will discuss these and other models but refer the reader to Spilberg and Corey (2019) and Corey and Ben-Porath (2018) for more in-depth explanation of their respective approaches.

The principal utility of using a data integration model is to guide clinical decision-making or, as Grisso (2003) puts it, "to structure our thinking" (p. 19). Additional advantages include

(a) facilitating consistency across evaluations—and, when multiple psychologists are performing evaluations for a single agency, also promoting consistency across evaluators;

(b) guiding decisions about what data to gather and consider, and what weight to give the data;

(c) reducing the influence of clinical intuition by restricting data integration to relevant and reliable findings; and

(d) communicating findings and opinions in a manner that shows "how you got there" (Grisso, 2008, p. 33).

Two versions of forensic models also have been proposed by Battista (1988) and Grisso (2003), each with relevance to occupationally mandated psychological evaluations. We discuss each in turn.

Battista's Work Capacity Model

Battista (1988) proposed a three-component model for clinical decision-making in occupational evaluations. The first, *work demand,* is composed primarily of the work skills and other requirements needed to perform effectively in a given position. Information about the requisite work demands can be found in a job analysis or position description. The second component of the Battista model involves an analysis of *work supply,* comprising the employee's history performing interpersonal, repetitive, complex/varied, stressful, routine, and supervised/unsupervised tasks. The third and final element of Battista's model centers on *work capacity,* which refers to the interaction or balance/imbalance between work demand and work supply, with the preferred state being that the employee has enough work supply (demonstrated ability) to meet or exceed the work demands.

In Battista's model, a deficit in work capacity can result either from a change in the individual worker that leads to work supply falling below work demand, or from an environmental change in which demand rises to exceed supply. This model is a particularly useful framework for assessing the causes for observed deficits in work capacity. Experienced fitness evaluators can easily recall cases in which concerns about an employee's fitness resulted not from changes in work supply but from increases in work demands associated with a new supervisor or other organizational change. This does not absolve concerns about an employee's fitness, but the model helps to pinpoint causes of any observed deficits in fitness (i.e., work capacity) as stemming from environmental factors (e.g., heightened work demands) rather than from the individual's degrading work supply. Battista's model also serves to remind the clinician that decisions about an employee's fitness for duty inevitably require an assessment not only of the worker's psychological functioning (i.e., work supply) but also of its interaction with the demands of the particular job. Just as a very depressed single mother may still retain sufficient parental competency to meet the needs of a high-functioning and adaptive teen but not be competent to parent a high-needs toddler, a police officer with attention-deficit/hyperactivity disorder (ADHD) may have sufficient work supply to meet the demands of a busy patrol assignment owing to the high level of stimulation and structure. After the officer writes their initial report from a patrol assignment, they are usually done with the case and are not required to conduct follow-up investigation. However, placing that officer on a SWAT team or investigation assignment in which they must focus on the same (often monotonous) task may quickly overwhelm their self-regulatory capacity or work supply.[1]

Grisso's Competency Assessment Model

Grisso (2003) proposed a model for assessing competencies relevant to various legal competencies (e.g., to parent, stand trial, waive *Miranda* rights, enter into a contract, refuse treatment), which conceptualizes five analytic steps. The first consists of a *functional analysis*, centering on what the examinee can and cannot do that is relevant to the legal competency in question, which necessarily requires a consideration of situational demands as well. Thus, in suitability or fitness evaluations, this element may include an examinee's performance of essential and marginal job tasks as well as activities of daily living (e.g., sleep, preparing meals, hygiene) that have important implications for work. Because a functional analysis is concerned both with retained and impaired abilities, it "is related to, but distinct from, psychiatric diagnoses or conclusions about general intellectual abilities and personality traits" (p. 24).[2]

The second component in Grisso's model involves a *causal analysis* of the "hypothetical origins of any functional deficits, their relation to past or future events, and their stability, change, or remediation" (p. 40), which he cautions should be guided by reliable theories and empirical research findings rather than mere speculation. The third component, an *interactive analysis,* is similar to Battista's "work capacity," in that both involve an assessment "of the congruency or incongruency between a person's functional abilities [Battista's notion of 'work supply'] and the degree of performance demand [Battista's 'work demands'] that is made by the specific instance of the context in that case" (Grisso, 2003, p. 40). Grisso emphasizes that this component requires an analysis of both the person and the context relevant to the psycholegal question.

The fourth Grisso component is *judgmental analysis,* which involves a judgment as to whether a person–context incongruency is sufficient to impair the individual's competence-relevant capacities. Finally, the fifth component, *dispositional analysis,* is concerned with decisions necessitated by the judgment analysis. Whereas the interactive analysis focuses on the degree to which a person's functional abilities meet or fall short of the demands of the specific situation, the judgmental component calls for a determination as to whether any gap between abilities and demands is meaningful in relation to the psycholegal question. The importance of reaching a judgment derives from the fact that conclusions about an individual's legal competence lead to certain dispositions

6
chapter

or outcomes. Applied to police suitability and fitness evaluations, the judgmental analysis requires a determination that the examinee is suitable/unsuitable for hire or fit/unfit for duty, whereas the dispositional decision (i.e., to rescind a conditional offer of employment or to terminate an employee) always belongs to the employer. In Chapter 7, we discuss further the question of whether the judgmental analysis, as well, belongs to the evaluating practitioner or the employer.

A Model for Integrating Data in a Suitability Evaluation

Spilberg and Corey's (2019) model for integrating data in a suitability assessment begins with a review of findings from written testing (the data source with the highest known reliability and validity) and proceeds to an examination of findings from the personal history (which holds second place on the reliability/validity criterion), followed by an analysis of findings from the clinical interview (which, despite the affection mental health practitioners hold for it, has the lowest demonstrated reliability and validity). By means of an iterative set of questions, the Spilberg and Corey model then provides a strategy for combining these data to reach a suitability determination, and culminates in a reevaluation and refinement of the decision-making model through periodic analysis of the outcomes of hired candidates in the hopes of detecting risk factors that previously were given insufficient weight or, alternatively, revising prior risk indicators.

The Corey and Ben-Porath (2018) adaptation of the Spilberg and Corey model starts with a review of test findings (beginning with an assessment of protocol validity) and also progresses sequentially to personal history and clinical interview findings. As in the Spilberg and Corey version, after the clinician has identified all relevant risk-related findings from these three data sources, Corey and Ben-Porath propose a set of questions to "[d]etermine whether the weight of the findings (convergent, complementary, and divergent) supports the conclusion that the candidate meets the selection standards" (p. 179). This is reminiscent of Grisso's

BOX 6.1 COREY AND BEN-PORATH MODEL FOR INTEGRATING DATA IN A SUITABILITY EVALUATION

1. Considering all risk-related findings from all sources, what evidence-based inferences can be drawn from them?
2. What divergent findings mitigate these inferences?
3. Are any surviving risk-related inferences of sufficient relevance and quality to warrant the candidate's disqualification? (Corey & Ben-Porath, 2018, p. 179)

judgmental analysis, which involves consideration of the sufficiency or meaningfulness of any assessed gap between an individual's context-relevant functional abilities and the situational demands. The three sequential questions in this model are listed in Box 6.1.

Because post-offer suitability evaluations are designed to screen-out unsuitable candidates rather than select-in the best ones, these questions begin only after the evaluator has assembled all risk-related findings, starting with the data source with the highest known reliability and validity (i.e., psychological testing). In addressing the first question, clinicians are cautioned to eliminate any inferences drawn from test scores, personal history, and clinical interview that are insufficiently related to the criterion standard because these are irrelevant to the referral question. Indeed, many tests contain scales measuring constructs that do not fit well with a particular criterion standard, and these should not be given any consideration at all, no matter how deviant they may be from the normative sample or comparison group, because doing so necessarily introduces error that will diminish the validity of the examiner's final determination.

When evaluating how to weigh divergent findings, it is wise to adhere to Heilbrun et al.'s (2009) counsel to forensic clinicians: To optimize the validity of their forensic opinions, data from multiple sources should be weighed according to their *relevance* and *reliability*. Heilbrun et al.'s reference to "reliability" was meant in the legal sense of the term, which includes both reliability and *validity*. Paul Meehl (1954) persuasively wrote about the error of giving undeserved weight to impressionistic judgments, no matter how strong those impressions may be. This is not to say that behavioral observations always lack probative value, but we should be reluctant to dismiss risk-related findings from data sources with a high degree of relevance and validity when contradicted by a limited sample of behavior. On the other hand, it is an important function of assessment to determine whether test findings indicating that a test taker more likely than not has certain traits *actually has them*. Many validity studies (e.g., Sellbom, Fischler, & Ben-Porath, 2007; Tarescavage, Corey, & Ben-Porath, 2016) have demonstrated robust associations between scores on a large number of MMPI-2-RF scales, for example, and post-hire performance of police officers, thereby supporting inferences that a test taker whose scores on those scales meet or exceed the cutoff is at risk of exhibiting problems as an officer or trainee. But it is the role of the screening psychologist, armed with a more expansive set of collateral data, to judge whether the construct measured by a particular scale (along with its component risks) can justifiably be ascribed to the particular candidate.

BEST PRACTICE

To optimize the validity of your forensic opinions, data from multiple sources should be weighed according to their *relevance* and *reliability*.

BEWARE

Be reluctant to dismiss risk-related findings from data sources with a high degree of relevance and validity when contradicted by a limited sample of behavior.

For example, consider the validity evidence indicating that elevation on Restructured Clinical Scale 2 (RC2), as measured by either the MMPI-2 or MMPI-2-RF, is correlated with various negative outcomes with medium to large effect sizes (Tarescavage, Corey, Gupton, & Ben-Porath, 2015). To be sure, it is not the candidate's responses to the test items making up RC2 that produce the negative outcomes; rather, it is the *construct* (i.e., a deficit of positive emotional responsiveness) that arguably is linked *causally* to the observed performance problems. With this knowledge and faced with a candidate with an RC2 score at or above the cutoff (58T) triggering the negative inferences, the screening psychologist must assess what evidence corroborates or contradicts this presumed deficit in positive emotional responsiveness.

The MMPI-2-RF *Police Candidate Interpretive Report* (PCIR; Corey & Ben-Porath, 2014) facilitates this analysis by describing personality- and behavior-related correlates of elevated MMPI-2-RF scales (and transparently reporting which published peer-reviewed studies report those correlates). For example, the PCIR reports that a person with an RC2 scale score at or above 58T is, in comparison with other police officer candidates, more likely to "become easily discouraged," "have difficulty coping with stress," "worry about problems and be uncertain about how to deal with them," and "be ill at ease in dealing with others" (Corey & Ben-Porath, 2018, p. 478). A screening psychologist can make use of this information in deciding whether the broader features of a person with low positive emotions are present in the candidate. If so, this finding would give weight to the performance risks associated with hiring the person as a police officer; if not, that finding could well constitute the "divergent findings" contemplated by the integration model, which may justify mitigating (and eliminating) the risk-related findings associated with the RC2 scale elevation.

The final analytic step in this model is prompted by the third question, "Are any surviving risk-related inferences of sufficient relevance and quality to warrant the candidate's disqualification?" This step is similar to the judgmental component in Grisso's (2003) competency model in which the clinician decides how much discrepancy between a person's functional abilities and the demands of the forensically relevant situation warrants a finding that the person lacks sufficient capacities.

The evaluator who is guided by these three questions in reaching a suitability determination also is well-positioned to explain how it was reached.

6
chapter

A Model for Integrating Data in a Fitness Evaluation

Corey and Ben-Porath (2018) also proposed a three-step model for integrating data in fitness evaluations, as shown in Box 6.2.

As a clinical assessment, a fitness evaluation begins with an analysis of evidence of a mental condition. Recall from Chapter 1

BOX 6.2 COREY AND BEN-PORATH MODEL FOR INTEGRATING DATA IN FITNESS EVALUATIONS

1. Is there evidence of an emotional, cognitive, behavioral, thought, interpersonal, or other psychological condition?
2. Does the condition substantially limit the employee's *current* ability to properly perform the essential functions of the job, or to perform them without posing a direct threat to the employee or others?
3. If the employee has a mental health condition that is currently nonlimiting, is the employee's fitness sustainable? (Corey & Ben-Porath, 2018, p. 350)

that the ADA prohibits an employer from requiring a medical evaluation of an employee *except* when the employer has a reasonable belief, based on objective evidence, that the employee *may have* a medical condition that substantially limits their ability to perform essential job functions or poses a direct threat to the employee or others. Consequently, the first prong of the psycholegal question in any fitness evaluation is whether the employee does, in fact, have a mental condition. This is not to say that the examining psychologist must reach a formal diagnosis.[3] Diagnostic reliability is hampered by efforts to conceal symptoms that make up the diagnostic criteria, and many examinees in fitness evaluations fear (usually unnecessarily) that an honest acknowledgment of their symptoms will lead to job termination. Consequently, they sometimes work hard to keep the examiner from discovering their problems.

INFO

The first prong of the psycholegal question in any fitness evaluation is whether the employee does, in fact, have a mental condition.

Despite such efforts, a fitness evaluator may be able to conclude, for example, that the employee suffers from a detectible mood disorder, but still be unable to reach a more refined diagnosis that distinguishes between a major depressive disorder, persistent depressive disorder, manic episode with irritable mood, mood disorder due to another medical condition, substance/medication-induced depressive or bipolar disorder, or adjustment disorder with depressed mood. Of course, as with any mental health condition, it is not the symptoms alone that justify diagnosis of a disorder, but rather also evidence of "clinically significant distress or impairment in social, occupational, or other important areas of functioning" (American Psychiatric Association, 2013, p. 161).

As we have repeatedly observed throughout this volume, the presence of a mental or emotional condition is a necessary but insufficient basis for any determination that an employee is psychologically unfit for duty. As such, if the evaluation yields no persuasive evidence of such a condition, there is no need to move to the second step in the data integration process. Instead, the conclusion can only be that whatever problems may underlie the employer's concerns about the examinee, they are not due to a mental health condition. They may be attitudinal, motivational, intentional, or due to malice, retribution, or simply bad character, but not all employee misconduct and behavior problems are linked to mental health conditions.

> **INFO**
>
> The presence of a mental or emotional condition is a *necessary but insufficient* basis for any determination that an employee is psychologically unfit for duty. If the evaluation yields no persuasive evidence of such a condition, there is no need to move to the second step in the data integration process.

It also remains possible that the employer may still conclude, notwithstanding such a determination by the evaluating psychologist, that the employee is unfit for duty. As the California Court of Appeal held in *Sager v. County of Yuba* (2007), this ultimate question can be reached by the employer on the basis of its own observations about an employee and need not be supported by medical findings. In addition, *psychological fitness* is not the only type of fitness relevant to the continued certification of a police officer. In most states, *moral fitness* is also a requisite condition for ongoing certification, and mental health practitioners, including forensic specialists, have no greater knowledge or expertise for adjudging moral fitness than do lay persons.

On the other hand, if the fitness examiner determines that the aggregate evidence warrants the conclusion that the employee does have a mental health condition, then the examiner proceeds to step

6
chapter

two in the model, which assesses whether the condition substantially limits the employee's *current* ability to properly perform the essential functions of the job, or to perform them without posing a direct threat to the employee or others.[4] This step approximates Grisso's causal and interactive components by analyzing the nexus between the mental health condition and any observed or anticipated limits in performing essential job functions or posing a direct threat. As Grisso noted, "some individuals may manifest deficits in functional abilities at a particular time for reasons other than mental illness or mental disability (even in cases in which the individual in question does have a mental illness or disability)" (2003, p. 30). As such, it is possible that a police officer's mental health condition has no causal nexus to the observed deficits in performance or conduct. In such a case, the model would guide the practitioner to conclude that the officer is psychologically fit for duty because the condition is not job-limiting.

Step three in the Corey and Ben-Porath (2018) model stems from the recognition that fitness evaluations sometimes take place *after* an employee has received treatment and the symptoms are only temporarily ameliorated or in remission. This could be the case, for example, when an officer completes 30 days of residential treatment for an alcohol use disorder and immediately is referred for a fitness evaluation, or when an officer who exhibited a psychotic episode at work was subsequently diagnosed with bipolar disorder and was seen for a fitness evaluation 4 weeks after being prescribed a mood stabilizer or antipsychotic medication, with no other manic episodes since the incident at work. In each of these cases, the data integration model would result in an affirmative response to the question at step one (evidence of a mental disorder) but likely a negative response to the second question (no evidence of current job-limiting effects). Step three is designed to identify employees with a currently inactive condition for which there exists persuasive evidence to conclude that the remission is not sustainable. For example, when evaluating the fitness of a police officer diagnosed with bipolar disorder, a clinician should carefully consider the research showing that persons with bipolar disorder experience some degree of disability during the majority of long-term follow-up (54 to 59% of the time, including 19 to 23% of the time with moderate, and 7 to 9% with severe, overall impairment) (Judd et al., 2008).

Grisso (2003) observed that mental health practitioners have three broad categories of tools available to assist them in explaining and predicting behavior associated with mental health conditions. First, they have psychological tests and interviewing methods that "can be used to describe examinees reliably in terms of their emotional or motivational characteristics, their intellectual or cognitive conditions, neurological abnormalities, social histories, and everyday behaviors" (p. 31). Second, they have access to empirical research results "that describe relations between the above types of information and other past, present, or future behaviors and outcomes" (p. 31), as we just illustrated in the example of a police officer diagnosed with bipolar disorder. A third category of tools cited by Grisso (2003) as aiding mental health practitioners in explaining and predicting an examinee's behavior are theories of normal and abnormal behavior, with this important caveat:

> A psychological theory is a system of interrelated constructs and assumptions about human behavior and its causes. A theory by itself is a convenient fiction that is useful for generating hypotheses about how various events, behaviors, and human characteristics interrelate. When these hypotheses have been tested in empirical research, the theory serves as a logical system for organizing and describing what is known empirically. In this role, it provides causal explanations for what is known. Such causes are never proven true or false by either research or the elegance of a theory. Theoretical causal explanations merely seem more or less plausible or useful, given the strength or weakness of the empirical research results that the theory has generated. (p. 31)

Using this or a similar model for integrating data in a fitness evaluation may both facilitate the ultimate determination and, as with the use of a model for integrating data in a suitability evaluation, facilitate the crafting of clear and probative explanations. It is to this topic—report writing and testimony—that we turn next.

6
chapter

Notes

1. The reader interested in the executive functioning and self-regulatory challenges experienced by people with ADHD is referred to Barkley (2018).

2. Grisso's original conceptualization of his competency model included a separate *contextual analysis* that, much like Battista's *work demands* element, was concerned with identifying the requirements for competency in a particular context. Grisso later folded that component into the functional analysis component such that only functional abilities (e.g., what a person knows, understands, believes, can do) relevant to the competency in question are considered in this analysis—a modification that is closely aligned with the Americans With Disabilities Act of 1990 (ADA) model of impairment.

3. Even the publisher of the *Diagnostic and Statistical Manual of Mental Disorders*, Fifth Edition (DSM-5) warns practitioners of its limitations when applying diagnostic classifications to forensic contexts: "In most situations, the clinical diagnosis of a DSM-5 mental disorder . . . does not imply that an individual with such a condition meets legal criteria for the presence of a mental disorder or a specified legal standard (e.g., for competence, criminal responsibility, or disability). For the latter, additional information is usually required beyond that contained in the DSM-5 diagnosis, which might include information about the individual's functional impairments and how these impairments affect the particular abilities in question" (American Psychiatric Association, 2013, p. 25).

4. In many positions, there is good reason to distinguish between limitations that solely limit the employee's ability to perform essential job functions from the ability to perform them without posing a direct threat. This can sometimes be a distinction without a difference. "For a law enforcement officer, the failure to perform one's duties properly can result in dramatic repercussions, placing others in imminent peril" (Lassiter v. Reno, 1995). However, determinations that an employee poses a direct threat always requires "medical or other objective evidence" (Bragdon v. Abbott, 1998, p. 649). See also Stragapede v. City of Evanston, Illinois (2017).

Report Writing and Testimony

> The quality of our reports is often the most tangible and visible measure of our professionalism. At a basic level, misspellings, typographical errors, and poor grammar suggest carelessness, if not a lack of respect for the reader. Submitting a report that has these faults could be compared with submitting an amicus brief that has ketchup stains on it. (Appelbaum, 2010, p. 43)

In this chapter, we offer suggestions about how to craft a written response to the organizational client's referral questions in a logical and effective manner. In doing so, we draw on several sources of professional guidance to inform the process of writing a report and offering testimony when required. The guidelines referenced in this chapter include the *Professional Practice Guidelines for Occupationally Mandated Psychological Evaluations* (OMPE Guidelines; American Psychological Association [APA], 2018); *Specialty Guidelines for Forensic Psychology* (SGFP; APA, 2013); *Preemployment Psychological Evaluation Guidelines* (International Association of Chiefs of Police [IACP], 2014); and *Psychological Fitness-for-Duty Evaluation Guidelines* (IACP, 2018a). For an example of a redacted and annotated fitness evaluation report, see Otto, DeMier, and Boccaccini (2014, Appendix A).

The Written Report

Just as psychologists are best able to navigate their ethical responsibilities by asking what duties they owe to each party involved in the evaluation, rather than only to the identified "client" (Fisher, 2009), they also optimize the quality of their written reports when they anticipate all of the parties likely to scrutinize their written reports, both in the near– and long–term. In the following section, we consider the needs and interests of this broader audience when preparing written reports of suitability and fitness evaluations.

Describe How Informed Consent Was Obtained

Near the start of the report, it is useful to document how the examiner went about obtaining informed consent and disclosing important elements of the examination procedures to the examinee. Here is an example from one of our fitness reports:

> Upon Officer Smith's arrival, I provided him with a copy of a document titled, "Employee Disclosure and Informed Consent Statement Regarding Fitness-For-Duty Examination." This document informed him of the purpose, scope, and methods of the examination, as well as information about my professional background, limits of confidentiality, potential outcomes and uses of the evaluation, payment for services, complaint recourse, and the procedure for obtaining a copy of the report of findings and conclusions. Officer Smith read the document in what appeared to be a careful manner and, at the start of my interview with him, he was able to accurately restate key elements of the document in his own words, thereby indicating that he understood the terms outlined in it. He agreed to proceed with the examination as explained in the disclosure statement.

Use the Written Report as a Means of Memorializing One's Procedures and the Factual Basis of the Conclusions and Opinions

The written report should summarize the procedural steps taken to reach an impartial opinion regarding the relevant psycholegal and other referral questions in a logical and sequential manner. In contested cases, the well-organized report provides a testimonial guide to the attorneys. It should contain sections that describe

BOX 7.1 Knowledge of the Scientific Foundation for Opinions and Testimony

SGFP Guideline 2.05. "Forensic practitioners seek to provide opinions and testimony that are sufficiently based upon adequate scientific foundation, and reliable and valid principles and methods that have been applied appropriately to the facts of the case. When providing opinions and testimony that are based on novel or emerging principles and methods, forensic practitioners seek to make known the status and limitations of these principles and methods" (APA, 2013).

the sources of information, relevant background, observations, findings, and conclusions. As we describe shortly, even an evaluator constrained to writing a conclusory report should memorialize the all-important scientific foundation that is demanded in all adjudicative forums.

Support Conclusions About the Relevance of a Psychological Impairment With Established Scientific and Professional Knowledge

After learning of the issue that prompted the referral, the evaluator should determine if psychological science can assist in answering the referral or psycholegal question(s). The OMPE Guidelines urge psychologists "to refrain from conducting OMPEs in the absence of a sufficient scientific foundation of knowledge. In instances where there is limited scientific basis for an opinion or evaluation method, psychologists are encouraged to state clearly the limitations of their work" (APA, 2018, p. 191). If there is no psychological science that can be applied to a question posed by the referral source, the subject matter may not be an appropriate

BOX 7.2 Evaluations are based on scientific and professional knowledge

Preemployment Psychological Evaluation Guideline 4.4. "Examiners should base their work on established scientific and professional knowledge of the discipline. Examiners should be familiar with the research literature available on psychological testing for public safety positions" (IACP, 2014).

7
chapter

area of investigation for the practitioner. On the other hand, if the psychologist envisions an evaluative process in which they will be able to employ techniques that are generally accepted within the field, with testing procedures that have acceptable levels of validity, then participation may be appropriate (assuming no other barriers to accepting the referral). In such cases, the practitioner should also be able to cite research within the body of the report (or within their foundational materials) that is relevant to the subject matter or that supports the interpretation of the data used to form the expert's opinion. If the evaluator is unable to find scientific references relevant to the proposed evaluation, it is likely that there is insufficient scientific foundation to proceed.

Provide Opinions and Recommendations That Are Directly Relevant to One or More Well-Defined Referral Questions

Assuming that the referral question(s) can be addressed with psychological science, a psychologist in California, for example, who is asked to evaluate an individual to determine suitability as a police officer is answering the question, "Is this candidate 'free from any emotional or mental condition that might adversely affect the exercise of the powers of a peace officer and . . . capable of withstanding the psychological demands of the job?'" [citing 11 C.C.R. § 1955(a)]. With preconditional offer evaluations, where the psychologist is limited to using instruments that measure normal traits rather than psychopathology, the psychologist may be asked to identify which applicants are the most suitable or have the strongest likelihood of surviving the selection process, considering the number of vacancies and the anticipated attrition of applicants. Whether one is conducting a preconditional or postconditional offer evaluation, the written report focuses on answering the respective referral question(s).

Fitness-for-duty referrals are different. With fitness evaluations, the referral begins with an interactive process between the organizational client and the evaluator, with the possibility of concluding that a fitness evaluation is not indicated yet or at all. If the evaluation is appropriate, the evaluator may educate the referring party about the strengths and limitations of psychological science as it pertains to the particular situation. This discussion also may influence the framing of the referral question(s). It is likely that the specific referral questions will echo the general question asked in all fitness evaluations in the United States, one driven by the business necessity standard of the Americans With Disabilities Act of 1990 (ADA): *Does this employee have a mental or emotional impairment, and if so, is the employee nonetheless able to safely and effectively perform the essential functions of the position with or without accommodation?* The goal of the evaluation is to provide opinions and recommendations directly relevant to the referral question.

Document Findings and Conclusions Using Language Appropriate for the Intended Audience

Even though an evaluation typically begins with the assumption that the reader of the report will be the organizational client and, in some cases, also the examinee, events that unfold after the submission of the report may lead to an ever-expanding audience, which may include second-opinion experts, attorneys, civil service or merit boards, courts, juries, or professional licensing or credentialing boards. For this reason, the author should use a writing style that anticipates a wide audience. This reality underscores the importance of avoiding a forest of esoteric clinical jargon that runs the risk of losing the reader in the trees, or misleading other readers who seek an understanding of how the evaluator integrated various sources of data to arrive at their conclusions. The answer is *not* to "dumb-down" the report; oversimplification hosts its own collection of unintended consequences. We are reminded of an aphorism attributed to Albert Einstein: "Everything should be made as simple as possible, but not simpler" (Sessions, 1950, p. 89).

Melton et al. (2018) also caution against oversimplification, even suggesting that *some* clinical jargon is appropriate:

> It helps to establish that the clinician is dealing with a specialized body of knowledge. Psychological terms and constructs may also be useful in developing and explaining theoretical formulations

of the type that would not be obvious to the trier of fact, provided that they are explained. The obvious compromise is to explain these terms for legal consumers when they are first used; this approach conveys the message that the clinician is an expert in a specialized field, at the same time that it ensures more effective communication with the legal system. (p. 587)

So, even though superfluous or misleading jargon may obscure one's findings, an extreme effort to avoid common clinical jargon may render it more difficult to tie various sources of data together into a coherent, scientifically defensible conclusion.

Respect the Decision Maker's Responsibility to Decide the Ultimate Issue

Statutes and case law have consistently assigned responsibility for the ultimate decision in fitness evaluations to the employer. A goal of clinical guidance, however, does not preclude rendering a clearly articulated professional opinion. Neglecting the responsibility of providing a professional opinion creates its own problems. For example, consider an evaluation in which the evaluator completely defers any opinion by providing two columns of data and findings. One column supports the hypothesis that the employee is fit; the second contains contrary evidence. In this manner, the evaluator may believe they have assisted the employer in making an ultimate decision. However, this approach runs the risk that the decision maker may misunderstand the data and findings, resulting in an illogical conclusion or another conclusion that was completely unanticipated by the evaluator and contrary to their own opinion. It also ignores the fact that not all evidence is equally probative.

BOX 7.3 Defer the ultimate opinion to the employer when appropriate

Fitness-for-Duty Evaluation Guideline 10.3. "It is recognized that some examiners may be asked to provide opinions regarding necessary work restrictions, accommodations, interventions, or causation. However, whether a recommended restriction or accommodation is reasonable for the specific case and agency is a determination to be made by the employer, not the examiner" (IACP, 2018a).

The unintended consequences of not providing a professional opinion, when adequate data support doing so, are substantial. Moreover, finding someone fit/unfit for duty is not an ultimate decision—it is a *penultimate* opinion—which is appropriate to offer if the clinical evidence supports it. The ultimate decision—namely, the disposition of the employee—*belongs to the employer*. Even if the ultimate decision is conceived as fitness/unfitness, it remains in the hands of the employer, and the psychologist's opinion on the matter is simply that: an opinion, not a determination.

INFO

Statutes and case law have consistently assigned responsibility for the ultimate decision in fitness evaluations to the employer. Regarding reports of preemployment suitability evaluations, the ultimate decision as to whether the candidate meets the hiring standards also belongs to the employer.

The psychologist respects the employer's role as the ultimate decision maker, not by avoiding a penultimate opinion, but by *educating* the employer about the meaning and significance of the clinical findings. The evaluator also demonstrates this respect by discussing the alternative hypotheses that were considered and dismissed, the thinking process that led to the conclusion, and the limitations of one's procedures and findings. Indeed, as Buchanan (2006) noted, "much of the harm that courts identify as stemming from evidence going to the ultimate issue could be avoided if evidence were given with greater transparency" (p. 20). DeMier (2013) similarly

BEWARE

Neglecting the responsibility of providing a professional opinion creates its own problems.

argues that when psychologists adequately describe the basis for their opinions, the concern about the ultimate opinion issue diminishes because readers are able to draw their own conclusions. Such an approach not only avoids a situation in which the employer must completely rely on the evaluator's *ipse dixit* opinion,[1] which the US Supreme Court criticized with such disdain in *General Electric v. Joiner* (1997), but also arms the employer with more information to make the *ultimate* opinion to retain, reassign, terminate, provide reasonable accommodation, or even seek another professional opinion.

7
chapter

Regarding reports of preemployment suitability evaluations, the ultimate decision as to whether the candidate meets the hiring standards also belongs to the employer, even when, as in California and Texas, no peace officer can be certified by the state's law enforcement commission without a written declaration by a qualified psychologist or psychiatrist that the individual meets the qualifying standard.[2] In such jurisdictions, the qualified examiner's opinion is a necessary but insufficient component of the hiring decision. In other jurisdictions, the employer's continuing role in the hiring decision, even after a candidate has been determined to be psychologically qualified, is more explicitly defined. For example, in Washington State the results of the psychological evaluation "shall be used by the employer to determine the applicant's suitability for employment as a fully commissioned peace officer or a reserve officer" [RCW 43.101.070(19)], and in Connecticut, it is required only that a qualified examiner "provides the law enforcement unit with documentation of the examination and . . . provides a written opinion of the candidate's overall psychological stability to fill a position as a police officer" (Connecticut Administrative Code § 7-294e-16). Thus, practitioners who perform suitability evaluations should confirm with the hiring agency whether the evaluation report is to be prepared as a declaration of suitability or as a report to aid an ultimate decision maker in the employment or certification decision.

Functions of the Written Report

The written report has a number of important functions. We next describe each.

Help Organize Data and Document Procedures

The written report provides the mechanism by which the examiner compiles diverse sources of data into an organized presentation. As Melton et al. (2018) point out, a well-written and articulate forensic report may satisfy the different stakeholders in such a manner that the controversy, if any, can be resolved without further adjudication. These authors recommend that the circumstances for the referral, the date and nature of contacts with the examinee, the collateral data sources, and the relevant personal background be included in every type of forensic report. There should also be a section that addresses disclosure and informed consent, which also notes any questions that the examinee asked about informed consent and how their questions were answered.

Provide a Foundation for One's Findings and Conclusions

Black's Law Dictionary defines *foundation* as, "The basis on which something is supported; [especially], evidence or testimony that establishes the admissibility of other evidence" (Garner, 1999, p. 666). If an expert proffers a piece of evidence in court—such as a test score—without explaining where the evidence came from or what it represents, the opposing side may object because the evidence is being offered without foundation. The legal requirement to establish a foundation for the introduction of evidence is paralleled in a written report when the expert explains how the procedures and data led to the expert's opinion(s).

Some jurisdictions require the evaluator to provide only a conclusory opinion, and the evaluator is specifically instructed or prohibited from including additional data. This does not obviate the need for evaluators to provide a foundation for their findings. In such cases, the evaluator who complies with the requirement to provide only a "bottom line" report can also inform the reader of supplementary data held at the practitioner's office. Such supplementary information may include a full-length report, summaries of collateral documents and discussions with collateral informants, timeline/chronology, notes, and various medical or personnel records. While these documents are not given to the organizational client (at least not initially), they may still be referenced in the summary report and can provide the foundation for the evaluator's findings and opinions, if needed.

7
chapter

Describe Test Results so That They Are Easily Understood by Nonpsychologists

When describing test results, it may not be helpful to provide the name of a specific scale, given that the names of some scales in commonly used psychological tests have little relationship to the constructs they actually measure. For example, even a mild elevation on the Minnesota Multiphasic Personality Inventory–2 (MMPI-2) Schizophrenia Clinical Scale (Scale 8) is unusual for a police candidate and may reflect some idiosyncratic thought patterns and social navigation problems. However, if the evaluator reported that the candidate was "mildly elevated on the Schizophrenia Scale," instead of describing the possible functional limitations suggested by the score, the nonpsychologist reader might reasonably, but erroneously, conclude that the candidate is mildly psychotic. Also confusing to the lay reader are similarly named scales measuring psychological constructs with different meanings (e.g., Dominance scales on the Personality Assessment Inventory [PAI] and California Psychological Inventory [CPI]).

BEWARE

When describing test results, it may not be helpful to provide the name of a specific scale, given that the names of some scales in commonly used psychological tests have little relationship to the constructs they actually measure.

We generally refrain from listing specific critical test-item responses in a written report because the lay reader is unlikely to appreciate the lack of reliability that typifies single-item responses. Moreover, we see no need to educate the examinee about these atypical endorsements, which may better prepare them in the event they undergo another evaluation. Instead, we may discuss the *thematic content* of those critical items in the report, especially when the responses are unexpected in light of other information known about the examinee.

Some people think of psychological tests as invariably accurate and precise. But it is generally more helpful (and accurate) to describe test findings as hypotheses to be supported (or not) by other convergent or divergent findings (DeMier, 2013). Finally, every report should contain a statement regarding limits to the reliability of the test findings, along with reporting, at least broadly, results on scales designed to detect response inconsistency and response style. In some jurisdictions, this may be required when submitting reports of suitability evaluations.[3]

Document Consideration of Alternative Hypotheses and Acknowledge Limitations of Your Findings

As noted earlier, discussing alternative hypotheses and acknowledging limitations better equip the organizational client to render the ultimate opinion. Commonly encountered limitations include preemployment suitability evaluations for which some agencies will not provide their background reports to the evaluator because of local privacy provisions or organizational policy.[4] In fitness evaluations, one may encounter occasions in which not all of the records were produced or instances in which collateral informants refused to speak with the evaluator. There may be instances in which the examinee's scores on validity scales render a protocol invalid. These events should be clearly documented and the resulting limitations noted. Of course, if the limitations are significant and substantially undermine the reliability of the assessment, the evaluator should refrain from offering a penultimate or final opinion. Although rendering an opinion when the findings are inconclusive may be disquieting to an evaluator or organizational client, it is important to remember that every clinical science has occasions in which results are inconclusive.[5] In our own fitness evaluation reports, we have frequently included some variation of the following statement:

BOX 7.4 Guideline: Examinations with unavailable information

Fitness-for-Duty Evaluation Guideline 7.5. "When some portion of the information requested by an examiner is unavailable or is withheld, the examiner assesses the extent to which the absence of such information may limit the reliability or validity of his or her findings and conclusions before deciding to proceed. If the examiner proceeds with the examination, it is recommended that the subsequent report include a discussion of any such limitations *judged to exist*" (IACP, 2018a).

The reliability and validity of this assessment, like all psychological evaluations, depends in large part on the accuracy and completeness of the underlying information. As of the writing of this report, I have not been able to verify several of the examinee's statements about [his/her/their] treatment, participation in treatment, and amelioration of symptoms. Upon receipt of this information, I can, if requested, provide a follow-up report, which may include revisions to or clarification of the opinions and conclusions I have written in this report.

In cases in which our confidence in the assessment data from a suitability evaluation is undermined by excessive underreporting on psychological tests, we include a statement similar to this:

The level of underreporting indicated on personality testing was unusually high, even when compared with other police officer candidates. Consequently, the absence of elevated scores on substantive scales cannot be interpreted to indicate the absence of problems measured by them, and any elevations found may underestimate those problems. This necessitates greater reliance on findings from a thorough background investigation and clinical interview.

Be Mindful of Freedom of Information Rulings in Your Jurisdiction

As noted in Chapter 1, most petitions by candidates to have their preemployment psychological evaluations released to them have been denied under various Freedom of Information Act rulings, with the appellate body usually determining that the public interest in nondisclosure outweighed any interest in disclosing the test results. However, exceptions do occur. For example, in *Stamford v. Freedom of Information Commission* (1999), an appellate court held that a failed applicant was entitled to the report, with the test questions redacted. We raise this issue to remind the reader to be cognizant of applicable law and local policies regarding the release of a report, and to adjust content (and writing style) accordingly.

Grisso's Six Principles for Forensic Report Writing

We regard Grisso's six principles for forensic report writing (Grisso, 2008) as equally applicable to writing reports for occupationally mandated psychological evaluations. We review them briefly.

1. Let the Forensic Question Drive, Guide, and Limit the Content of the Report

This is the process by which the referral or psycholegal questions determine the relevant information that is provided in the summary report. As Otto, DeMier, and Boccaccini (2014) observed, "Forensic examiners who address psycholegal issues not referred for consideration expend effort unnecessarily, at best, and can compromise the rights of the persons they examine, at worst" (p. 19).

2. Report What Is Necessary, but Do Not Report What Is Not Necessary

Federal Rules of Evidence Rule 403 allows courts to exclude relevant evidence that, if admitted, would be so confusing, prejudicial, or distracting that the trier of fact (i.e., judge or jury) would be better off without it. Rule 403 states that the "court may exclude relevant evidence if its probative value is substantially outweighed by a danger of one or more of the following: unfair prejudice, confusing the issues, misleading the jury, undue delay, wasting time, or needlessly presenting cumulative evidence." Accordingly, a court may exclude evidence that is more prejudicial, confusing, or repetitive than probative.

DeMier (2013) suggests that forensic report writers should also consider a probative versus prejudicial analysis when they consider the inclusion of material. Adding material with only marginal relevance can just as easily confuse or prejudice the reader as it could a jury. Returning to the earlier example of the candidate who obtained an elevation on the MMPI-2 Schizophrenia Clinical Scale, referencing the name of a test scale may also be more prejudicial than probative, especially when the evaluator could simply (and more appropriately) describe the construct measured by the

BEWARE

● Adding material with only marginal relevance can confuse or prejudice the reader or jury.

● Prejudicial impact may exceed probative value when the author includes material that unnecessarily invades the employee's privacy.

scale and the functional limitation(s) that might accompany that finding.

Another context in which the prejudicial impact may exceed probative value are those cases in which the author includes material that unnecessarily invades the employee's privacy. Melton et al. (2018) remind us that a forensic evaluation "is not a license to inquire into any aspect of the client's life or behavior. . . . [E]xaminers should confine themselves to inquiries legitimately raised by the referral source and should restrict the substance of their report accordingly" (pp. 585–586). Similarly, Griffith, Stankovic, and Baranoski (2010) noted that "including in the report pejorative or embarrassing information that is irrelevant to the legal issue may demonstrate a completeness of the interview, but does so at the cost of the client's dignity" (p. 39). In light of these comments, we recommend that the evaluator carefully consider excluding material of marginal relevance, especially when its inclusion would unduly prejudice or confuse the reader. Examples might include reference to an examinee's religious beliefs or fidelity, sexual orientation, or gender identity.

3. Sequence and Describe Information in a Way That Makes Sense to the Reader

The examiner who has completed a thorough evaluation could probably make sense of a randomly assembled set of findings from that evaluation. Such is not the case when the report is in the hands of the reader who is naïve to the issues, or who does not know how the evaluator formulated their opinion. In such cases, a poorly sequenced report can cause confusion and misunderstanding. This raises the challenges of proofreading one's own writing, especially when the report is written to meet a tight deadline. Minor irregularities in sequence or omission of facts that link one event to the next may be difficult to detect when you are proofreading your own report. Try to edit the draft as if naïve to the content. This mindset helps in presenting key events in a logical sequence that will facilitate understanding. Closely monitor tense so that the reader can follow the development of thought and opinion. DeMier (2013) stated that a logically sequenced and developed report "is the opposite of a suspense novel; the reader should know how it is going to end before reading the ultimate conclusions" (p. 35). We agree, but with an important caveat. When reporting a well-conducted and well-reasoned evaluation, descriptions of the procedures, interactions with the examinee, the examinee's history, and interpretation of test results—in fact, anything that precedes the integrative analysis—need not (and should not attempt to) limit the available conclusions, much less make them inevitable. An evaluator's

BEST PRACTICE

Try to edit the draft as if naïve to the content. This mindset helps in presenting key events in a logical sequence that will facilitate understanding.

BEWARE

Your conclusions should logically derive from the data presented, but their credibility is undermined when they are presented from the start in a way that only one conclusion is possible.

conclusions should logically derive from the data presented, but their credibility is undermined when they are presented from the start in a way that only one conclusion is possible.

4. Separate Facts From Inferences and Opinions

Facts are objective and can be verified. On the other hand, inferences are derived from the relationships between facts, and opinions derive from inferences. Accordingly, it is important that the reader be able to understand these differences. In the same manner that a healthcare provider may use the SOAP format—Subjective, Objective, Assessment, and Plan—when writing treatment records, the evaluator should distinguish facts, inferences, and opinions by placing them in separate sections, clearly identified as such. The inferences and opinions logically appear at the end of the report and explain how the author used the preceding factual information and data to develop inferences and form their opinions. As Otto, DeMier, and Boccaccini (2014) recommended, "The most straightforward strategy is for the examiner to 'isolate' what is known or considered

INFO

- *Facts* are objective and can be verified.
- *Inferences* are derived from the relationships between facts.
- *Opinions* derive from inferences.

to be facts in a section or sections of the report, with inferences and opinions presented in a separate section (or a separate paragraph)" (p. 38). This latter section should not introduce new facts.

5. Explain Your Opinion by Showing *Why* You Think *What* You Think

This is the portion of our own reports where we connect the dots and help the reader understand how the facts have led us to our conclusions. As Grisso (2008) so aptly put it: "Explanations, not opinions, are the reason that one is an expert" (p. 33). Reports that are "entirely conclusory, devoid of any medical documentation or explanation in support of their conclusions" have "very little probative value" (*Slater v. Department of Homeland Security*, 2008, paragraph 8).

Our practice is to structure our written reports so that our opinions logically unfold from the facts presented. Early in the report, we list the sources of data (e.g., documents, interviews, assessment instruments) that we gathered or were provided to us, and as we later present the pertinent facts—both those that support and potentially contradict the opinions we will present later in the report—we use parenthetical citations or footnotes that link the fact to its source(s). Because we present the facts ahead of our opinions, our analysis section of the report tells the reader how we make sense of the facts. In doing so, we are careful to limit our opinions (and explanations of them) to ones that respond to the referral questions.

BEST PRACTICE

Our practice is to structure our written reports so that our opinions logically unfold from the facts presented.

6. Explain the Rejection of Other Possible Opinions and Conclusions

Even verifiable facts can be interpreted in broadly different ways. Where one psychologist might interpret an examinee's divorce, job termination, and bankruptcy as evidence of impaired functioning, another may see these facts as having no clinical significance at all. Evaluators can often forestall a challenge to their opinions by discussing the alternative hypotheses they considered and why they believe that the facts (and the inferences drawn from them) best support the opinion(s) offered in the report and not the alternatives. Writing reports with such transparency allows the decision maker not only to make an informed decision contrary to the evaluator but also to have greater confidence in a well-reasoned conclusion.

INFO

Even verifiable facts can be interpreted in broadly different ways.

Common Errors in Forensic Report Writing

Grisso (2010) published a study that considered 62 forensic reports that were submitted by 36 candidates seeking board certification in forensic psychology.[6] These reports failed the work sample review. That is, two judges with advanced expertise in forensic psychology believed that "the candidate's reports were so seriously flawed (contained 'many and diverse' problems) that the candidate was highly likely to fail the oral examination, or that the reports were too poor to serve as a basis for the oral examination" (p. 106). The 10 most common deficiencies found by the reviewers, which are errors also common in employment-based evaluations, are listed in their order of descending frequency in Table 7.1 and can provide readers with a useful checklist when preparing their own reports with the goal of identifying and resolving any of these deficiencies.

Litigation Contexts of Occupationally Mandated Psychological Examinations

7
chapter

Examiners may be asked to provide expert opinion(s) and testimony on issues related to occupationally mandated psychological

Table 7.1 | The 10 Most Common Deficiencies in Forensic Reports Submitted for Examination by the American Board of Forensic Psychology

Rank	Problem	Frequency	Description
1	Opinions without sufficient explanations	56%	Major interpretations or opinions were stated without sufficiently explaining their basis in data or logic (regardless of whether the report's data could have sustained the opinion).
2	Forensic purpose unclear	53%	The legal standard, legal question, or forensic purpose was not stated, not clear, inaccurate, or inappropriate.
3	Organizational problems	36%	Information was presented in a disorganized manner (usually without a reasonable logic for its sequence).
4	Irrelevant data or opinions	31%	Data and/or some opinions included in the report were not relevant for the forensic or clinical referral questions.
5	Failure to consider alternative hypotheses	30%	Data allowed for alternative interpretations, while the report did not offer explanations concerning why they were ruled out.
6	Inadequate data	28%	The referral question, case circumstances, or final opinion required additional types of data that were not obtained or were not reported, and for which absence was not explained in report.

Table 7.1 Continued

Rank	Problem	Frequency	Description
7	Data and interpretation mix	26%	Data and interpretations frequently appeared together in the section that reports data.
8	Overreliance on a single source of data	22%	An important interpretation/opinion relied wholly on one source of data when corroborating information from multiple sources was needed (often overreliance on examinee's self-report).
9	Language problems	19%	Multiple instances of jargon, biased phrases, pejorative terms, or gratuitous comments.
10.	Improper test uses	15%	Test data were used in inappropriate ways when interpreted and applied to the case, or tests were not appropriate for the case itself.

Grisso, T. (2010). Guidance for improving forensic reports: A review of common errors. *Open Access Journal of Forensic Psychology, 2,* 102–115. Retrieved from https://escholarship.umassmed.edu/psych_pp/282/

BOX 7.5 Federal Rules of Evidence Rule 702. Testimony by expert witnesses

"A witness who is qualified as an expert by knowledge, skill, experience, training, or education may testify in the form of an opinion or otherwise if:

(a) the expert's scientific, technical, or other specialized knowledge will help the trier of fact to understand the evidence or to determine a fact in issue;
(b) the testimony is based on sufficient facts or data;
(c) the testimony is the product of reliable principles and methods; and
(d) the expert has reliably applied the principles and methods to the facts of the case."

7 chapter

evaluations. At other times, they may be retained to offer second opinions following a disputed evaluation outcome.

Providing an Expert Opinion Regarding a Suitability or Fitness Evaluation and Rule 702 of the Federal Rules of Evidence

The general roles of an expert witness are (a) "to provide the jury with data beyond the common knowledge of jurors, such as scientific data, computations, tests, experiments, and the like" and (b) "in professional negligence cases, to establish the standard of care" (Kionka, 1999, p. 80). As we have emphasized, the evaluator should always conduct an occupationally mandated psychological evaluation in such a manner that the results and conclusion could be offered as expert evidence in an adjudicatory forum, whether or not the evaluator, employer, or examinee anticipates litigation. That said, it is worthwhile to discuss the definition of expert witness evidence and testimony and how such testimony is different from the testimony provided by a person not qualified to testify as an expert. In providing this discussion, we turn to the Federal Rules of Evidence, which provide the rules governing the admission and use of evidence in all federal courts. The rules in many state jurisdictions are similar and sometimes contain language identical to the federal rules, but there also can be important differences the expert should know.[7]

INFO

Expert witnesses are permitted to give an opinion based on their knowledge, experience, or training. An expert may also rely on most forms of hearsay evidence, if such evidence is typically used by experts in conducting their investigations and forming their opinions.

The main incentive for qualifying as an expert witness is that experts are permitted to give an opinion based on their knowledge, experience, or training. An expert may also rely on most forms of hearsay evidence, if such evidence is typically used by experts in conducting their investigations and forming their opinions.

An *expert* witness is contrasted with a *fact* witness, who is generally limited to testifying about events that they perceived through one of their senses. A fact witness can only opine on an issue that is "(a) rationally based on the witness's perception; (b) helpful to clearly understanding the witness's testimony or to determining a fact in issue; and (c) not based on scientific, technical, or other specialized knowledge within the scope of Rule 702" (Federal Rule 701). Take, for example, a psychologist who conducted a suitability evaluation of a police candidate who later sued the prospective employer in federal court for an alleged ADA violation. If the examining psychologist is subpoenaed to court and asked, "Did you administer a preemployment evaluation to George?" the witness will answer and be considered a fact witness as defined by Rule 701. On the other hand, if the same witness were to be asked to give an opinion on George's suitability for the position based on information not known at the time of the evaluation, the witness is then being asked to provide an expert opinion, as defined by Rule 702. An appropriate answer by the fact witness in that circumstance would be something like, "At the time I evaluated George, based on all the information available to me and that I generated, my opinion was that George didn't meet the psychological suitability criteria. If there is now new information, then I can't answer hypothetically how that would affect my opinion. I can say that it *could* be relevant, and that my standard practice is to consider new information that becomes available and possibly modify my opinion in a subsequent report."

An evaluation expert may be called on to offer testimony in matters such as grievance procedures, civil service appeals, discrimination suits, and in some instances, the policies and practices of an organization. Sometimes an evaluation expert may be asked by an attorney to author a petition or declaration that supports a *writ of mandamus*, which, if issued by the court, orders an agency or organization to properly execute its duties or correct an abuse of discretion.

An evaluator who has been retained as an expert for purposes of litigation in federal court is subject to the Federal Rules of Civil Procedure.[8] Although we limit this discussion to Federal Rule 26, it is always good practice to ask the retaining attorney if additional procedural rules are likely to apply to the case at hand.

7
chapter

Rule 26 of the Federal Rules of Civil Procedure

After an attorney decides to use an evaluator as an expert in federal court (or in a state court where the federal rules have been adopted), the evaluator and attorney must comply with Federal Rules of Civil Procedure Rule 26(2)(B), which specifies that notice will be given to the opposing side by providing an expert report containing the following:

(a) a complete statement of all opinions the expert will express and the basis and reasons for them;

(b) the facts or data considered by the expert in forming them;

(c) any exhibits that will be used to summarize or support them (which might include documents provided in connection with the evaluation, or research articles, books, chapters, tables, and other sources relied on by the expert);

(d) the expert's qualifications (usually satisfied by a curriculum vita), including a list of all publications authored in the previous 10 years;

(e) a list of all other cases in which, during the previous 4 years, the expert testified as an expert at trial or by deposition;[9] and

(f) a statement of the compensation to be paid for the report and testimony in the case.

Second and Tie-Breaking Opinions

It is not unusual for an aggrieved examinee to seek a second opinion. An employer also may reach out when it has two or more opinions in opposition to each other and seeks a third "tie-breaking" opinion. The Equal Employment Opportunity Commission (EEOC) offers enforcement guidance to aid employers in weighing the probative value of opposing opinions, which can also inform experts on how to strengthen their reports. The EEOC (2000) suggests weighing four considerations:

(a) the area of expertise of each medical professional who has provided information;
(b) the kind of information each person providing documentation has about the job's essential functions and the work environment in which they are performed;
(c) whether a particular opinion is based on speculation or on current, objectively verifiable information about the risks associated with a particular condition; and
(d) whether the medical opinion is contradicted by information known to or observed by the employer (e.g., information about the employee's actual experience in the job in question or in previous similar jobs).

We also have several suggestions of our own to help the evaluator negotiate requests for second or tie-breaking opinions:

- The customary bias check, in which the evaluator makes sure that no ethically prohibited multiple relationship or other conflict of interest with the examinee or organizational client exists (i.e., one that would foreclose impartiality or is exploitative), should also include consideration of one's relationship with the previous evaluator(s). It is not likely that one can conduct a second-opinion evaluation blind to the identity of the prior evaluator. Not only is the employee or candidate likely to provide the other evaluator's name, but you also may have to contact the previous evaluator to obtain copies of raw test data and other assessment materials.

- When aggrieved parties elect to appeal a judicial finding to a higher court, they file a pleading asserting the reasons they believe that the lower court abused its discretion and arrived at an erroneous decision. In the same way, a second-opinion examiner should begin by obtaining a thorough understanding of why the aggrieved party believes that the evaluator's methodology was improper or why the conclusions are believed to be erroneous. In all disputed cases the complainant is unhappy with the other evaluator's opinion or conclusion—that goes without saying—but disagreeing with the conclusion is not a basis for an appeal. Instead, the complainant must have a substantive concern about the evaluator's methods, behavior, reasoning, qualifications, and the like.

● After the prospective second-opinion examiner understands the reasons a stakeholder is requesting a second opinion, they should review the report(s) and the underlying data. The examiner should then consider if it is possible to resolve the discrepancies or concerns without further evaluation of the examinee. At this stage, one may find that the prior examiner's procedures were consistent with best practices and that the conclusions were reasonably based on the data obtained. In such a case, there may be little to nothing gained by conducting another evaluation. Providing this opinion to the retaining party may be adequate to resolve the issue.

● If a review of the first evaluator's data and findings demonstrates significant limitations or shortcomings in methodology, it may be proper to conduct a subsequent examination. In such a case, we recommend that, to the extent reasonable, the second-opinion examiner utilize the same criterion standard that was used in the initial evaluation, as long as it was proper to begin with.

● When asked to conduct a tie-breaking third evaluation, we also recommend that the evaluator determine if a resolution can be reached without conducting a *de novo* (i.e., "anew" or "starting from the beginning") evaluation. If not, a completely new evaluation is warranted. However, it is also possible that a limited evaluation, targeted to resolve a specific unresolved question, may be appropriate. Take, for example, a tie-breaking fitness evaluation in which the officer had significant impairment from repeated brain injuries incurred during military deployment, but neither of the prior two psychologists addressed this issue. Assuming that there were no other substantive deficiencies in their respective evaluations, it may be appropriate for the tie-breaking evaluation to be limited in scope to neuropsychological impairment.

Issues Distinctive to Examinee-Retained Evaluations

In second-opinion evaluations, the retaining party may be the employer, the examinee, or the examinee's attorney. In most jurisdictions, however, second-opinion evaluations are conducted at the candidate's or employee's expense. In these cases, ethical issues not present in the typical evaluation scenario—where the examiner is retained by the employer—may arise. We recommend that the evaluator have a separate informed consent document for these cases. Where the employee is represented by counsel, the evaluator should contract with the attorney so that the attorney is the client. When the employee does not have legal representation, the evaluator may consider these additional informed consent provisions:

- Requiring full payment for the anticipated cost before work commences. Such a practice may remove the possible perception—sometimes termed "bias due to deferred payment"—that a favorable outcome was influenced by the evaluator's desire to collect payment.

- Advising the examinee that the evaluation may sustain the results of the initial evaluation and may even discover adverse issues not previously detected (Khadivi, 2010).

- Clarifying that the evaluator cannot release the report to a third party without an appropriate authorization executed by the examinee. When not represented by an attorney, the examiner should anticipate that the examinee may request to review the report before making the decision to authorize its disclosure to a third party.

- We have encountered some self-funded candidates or employees who insist on providing an irrevocable release of information from the outset of the evaluation. While we understand that these examinees are motivated to assure the decision maker that they did not engage in

7
chapter

cherry-picking (i.e., allowing only the release of a favorable report), we know of no legal basis on which examinees can foreclose their right to revoke a release of information.

Conclusion to This Volume

Over the past four decades, police psychology has grown from an area of practice carried out by a few pioneering psychologists[10] to what is today a well-organized and recognized specialty in professional psychology, supported by a number of organizations that provide systems and structures to assure its ongoing development and vitality. In writing this volume, our intent was to provide further support and impetus to this growing specialty by publishing a comprehensive source of information about police suitability and fitness evaluations and the various issues that need to be considered when conducting them. We hope that our efforts will prove useful to readers (whatever their levels of expertise) by prompting them to consider new perspectives and ideas and by providing information that can support them in various challenges.

Each of the volumes in this series will eventually become outdated when changes in law, professional standards, and clinical practice make it so. Ours is no exception. When that occurs, it's our hope that this volume will provide a useful starting point for redefining best practices when conducting police suitability and fitness evaluations.

Notes

1. *Ipse dixit* means "it is so because I told you so." Courts are not fond of this pompous approach. In *General Electric v. Joiner* (1997), the Court held that a trial court reasonably excluded the testimony of an expert, stating: "[N]othing in either *Daubert* or the Federal Rules of Evidence requires a district court to admit opinion evidence which is connected to existing data only by the *ipse dixit* of the expert. A court may conclude that there is simply too great an analytical gap between the data and the opinion proffered" (p. 146).
2. For the requirements of the California Peace Officer Standards and Training [POST] Commission, see 11 C.C.R. § 1955(f)(2)(D); for the requirements of the Texas Commission on Law Enforcement,

see Texas Occupations Code, Title 10, Chapter 1701, Subchapter A, Section 1701.306.

3. For example, Washington law stipulates that examiners must report "[f]actors which could affect the reliability and validity of the assessment" [Washington Administrative Code 139-07-030(7)(3)].

4. Notably, California law *requires* that psychologists screening police candidates be provided with the background investigation [11 C.C.R. § 1953(a)(3)].

5. We find it interesting that psychologists and psychiatrists appear so unwilling to "conclude with a reasonable degree of scientific certainty that the results are inconclusive," even though such a conclusion is commonly elicited from other medical specialists, crime scene analysts, accident reconstruction experts, polygraphers, and a host of other professionals.

6. This article provides an excellent review of the literature regarding the general consensus of the elements that should be contained in a forensic report and provides other suggestions for effective forensic writing.

7. The *Daubert* guidelines are provided to allow a trial judge to determine if the proposed expert witness testimony satisfies the requirements contained in Rule 702. Most states use *Daubert*, or a variation thereof, to conduct a similar analysis when one side challenges the admissibility of the proposed testimony. At the time of this writing, the states that use the *Frye* general acceptance test include California, Florida, Illinois, Maryland, New Jersey, New York, Pennsylvania, and Washington. States using criteria other than *Frye* or *Daubert* include Nevada, North Dakota, and Virginia. This topic is discussed further in Chapter 4.

8. In Chapter 4, we cautioned against the common error of assuming that an expert psychologist or psychiatrist who conducted an evaluation that later becomes the subject of litigation will be subpoenaed as an expert witness. For reasons we explained there, this is far from certain.

9. There is no rule against providing more than 4 years of testimonial history. You can also include cases in which the other side received notice of your involvement but you did not testify in a deposition or court. However, you should never list cases in which the other side was not advised of your involvement because this would indicate that the retaining side did not waive the attorney–client privilege. These nondisclosed involvements have typically occurred when we rendered an opinion not helpful to the retaining side or when the case settled before expert disclosures were required.

10. See Trompetter (2017) for a comprehensive review of the history of police psychology.

References

Aamodt, M. G. (2004). Special issue on using MMPI-2 scale configurations in law enforcement selection: Introduction and meta-analysis. *Applied HRM Research, 9*(2), 41–52.

Ackerman, M. J. (2010). *Essentials of psychological assessment* (2nd ed.). Hoboken, NJ: John Wiley & Sons.

Allen, D. N., & Haderlie, M. M. (2010). Trail-making test. In I. B. Weiner & W. E. Craighead (Eds.), *The Corsini Encyclopedia of Psychology* (Vol. 1, pp. 1793–1794). Hoboken, NJ: Wiley.

Alpert, G. P., & Dunham, R. G. (2010). Police and training recommendations related to police use of CEDs: Overview of findings from a comprehensive national study. *Police Quarterly, 13*, 235–259.

American Psychiatric Association. (2013). *Diagnostic and statistical manual of mental disorders* (5th ed.). Washington, DC: Author

American Psychological Association. (2013). Specialty guidelines for forensic psychology. *American Psychologist, 68*, 7–19. doi:10.1037/a0029889

American Psychological Association. (2015). Professional practice guidelines: Guidance for developers and users. *American Psychologist, 70*, 823–831.

American Psychological Association. (2017). *Ethical principles of psychologists and code of conduct.* Retrieved from https://www.apa.org/ethics/code/ethics-code-2017.pdf

American Psychological Association. (2018). Professional practice guidelines for occupationally mandated psychological evaluations. *American Psychologist, 73*, 186–197.

Appelbaum, K. L. (2010). Commentary: The art of forensic report writing. *Journal of the American Academy of Psychiatry and the Law, 38*, 43–45.

Arbisi, P. A., Ben-Porath, Y. S., & McNulty, J. (2006). The ability of the MMPI-2 to detect feigned PTSD within the context of compensation seeking. *Psychological Services, 3*(4), 249.

Azen, S. P., Snibbe, H. M., & Montgomery, H. R. (1973). A longitudinal predictive study of success and performance of law enforcement officers. *Journal of Applied Psychology, 57*(2), 190–192.

Back, M. D., Stopfer, J. M., Vazire, S., Gaddis, S., Schmukle, S. C., Egloff, B., & Gosling, S. D. (2010). Facebook profiles reflect actual personality, not self-idealization. *Psychological Science, 21*, 372–374.

Bardeen, J. R., & Orcutt, H. K. (2011). Attentional control as a moderator of the relationship between posttraumatic stress symptoms and attentional threat bias. *Journal of Anxiety Disorders, 25*, 1008–1018.

Barkley, R. A. (2018). *Attention-deficit hyperactivity disorder: A handbook for diagnosis and treatment* (4th ed.). New York, NY: Guilford.

Barnett, J. E., Doll, B., Younggren, J. N., & Rubin, N. J. (2007). Clinical competence for practicing psychologists: Clearly a work in progress. *Professional Psychology: Research and Practice, 38,* 510–517.

Barrick, M. R., & Mount, M. K. (1991). The big five personality dimensions and job performance: A meta-analysis. *Personnel Psychology, 44,* 1–26.

Battista, M. E. (1988). Assessing work capacity. *Journal of Insurance Medicine, 20*(3), 16–22.

Ben-Porath, Y. S. (2012). *Interpreting the MMPI-2-RF.* Minneapolis, MN: University of Minnesota Press.

Ben-Porath, Y. S., Corey, D. M., & Tarescavage, A. M. (2017). Using the MMPI-2-RF in preemployment evaluations of police officer candidates. In C. L. Mitchell & E. Dorian (Eds.), *Police psychology and its growing impact on modern law enforcement* (pp. 51–78). Hershey, PA: IGI Global.

Ben-Porath, Y. S., & Tellegen, A. (2020). *The Minnesota Multiphasic Personality Inventory-3 (MMPI-3) Technical manual.* Minneapolis: University of Minnesota Press.

Bertrand, M., & Duflo, E. (2016). *Field experiments on* discrimination (working paper no. 22014). Cambridge, MA: National Bureau of Economic Research. Retrieved from http://www.nber.org/papers/w22014.

Beutler, L. E., Storm, A., Kirkish, P., Scogin, F., & Gaines, J. A. (1985). Parameters in the prediction of police officer performance. *Professional Psychology: Research and Practice, 16*(2), 324–335. doi:10.1037/0735-7028.16.2.324

Birk, J. L., Opitz, P. C., & Urry, H. L. (2017). Distractibility as a precursor to anxiety: Preexisting attentional control deficits predict subsequent autonomic arousal during anxiety. *Biological Psychology, 122,* 59–68.

Bittner, E. (1970). *The functions of the police in modern society* (Vol. 88). Chevy Chase, MD: National Institute of Mental Health.

Blair, I. V. (2002). The malleability of automatic stereotypes and prejudice. *Personality and Social Psychology Review, 6,* 242–261. doi:10.1207/S15327957PSPR0603_8

Blair, I. V., Ma, J. E., & Lenton, A. P. (2001). Imagining stereotypes away: The moderation of implicit stereotypes through mental imagery. *Journal of Personality and Social Psychology, 81*(5), 828–841.

Blau, T. (1994). *Psychological services for law enforcement.* New York, NY: Wiley.

Blum, R. H. (1964). *Police selection.* Springfield, IL: Charles C. Thomas.

Boes, J. O., Chandler, C. J., & Timm, H. W. (1997). *Police integrity: Use of personality measures to identify corruption-prone officers* (no. PERS-TR-97-003). Monterey, CA: Defense Personnel Security Research and Education Center.

Bond, C. F., & DePaulo, B. M. (2006). Accuracy of deception judgments. *Personality and Social Psychology Review, 10,* 214–234.

Bornstein, R. F. (2011). Toward a process-focused model of test score validity: Improving psychological assessment in science and practice. *Psychological Assessment, 23*(2), 532–544. doi: 10.1037/a0022402

Borum, R., Otto, R., & Golding, S. (1993). Improving clinical judgment and decision making in forensic evaluation. *Journal of Psychiatry and Law, 21,* 35–76.

Brewster, J., & Stoloff, M. L. (1999). Using the Good Cop/Bad Cop profile with the MMPI-2. *Journal of Police and Criminal Psychology, 14*(2), 29–34.

Briere, J. (2001). *DAPS—Detailed Assessment of Posttraumatic Stress professional manual.* Odessa, FL: Psychological Assessment Resources.

Briere, J. (2010). *Trauma Symptom Inventory–2 (TSI-2) professional manual.* Lutz, FL: Psychological Assessment Resources.

Brooks, J. (2018, September 7). Starved for recruits, Alaska police pin blame on retirement system. *Juneau Empire.* Retrieved from https://www.juneauempire.com/news/starved-for-recruits-alaska-police-pin-blame-on-retirement-system/

Buchanan, A. (2006). Psychiatric evidence on the ultimate issue. *Journal of the American Academy of Psychiatry and the Law, 34,* 14–21.

Butcher, J. N. (2000). Revising psychological tests: Lessons learned from the revision of the MMPI. *Psychological Assessment, 12*(3), 263–271.

Butcher, J. N., Dahlstrom, W. G., Graham, J. R., Tellegen, A., & Kaemmer, B. (1989). *Manual for the administration and scoring of the MMPI-2.* Minneapolis, MN: University of Minnesota Press.

Butcher, J. N., Morfitt, R. C., Rouse, S. V., & Holden, R. R. (1997). Reducing MMPI-2 defensiveness: The effect of specialized instructions on retest validity in a job applicant sample. *Journal of Personality Assessment, 68*(2), 385–401. doi:10.1207/s15327752jpa6802_9

Canadian Psychological Association. (2013). The pre-employment clinical assessment of police candidates: Principles and guidelines for Canadian psychologists. Ottawa, Ontario: Canadian Psychological Association. Retrieved from https://www.cpa.ca/docs/File/News/2013-07/Police%20assess%20guidelines%20April2013final.pdf

Canadian Psychological Association. (2017). *Canadian code of ethics for psychologists* (4th ed.). Ottawa, Ontario: Author.

Castelli, L., Zogmaister, C., & Tomelleri, S. (2009). The transmission of racial attitudes within the family. *Developmental Psychology, 45*(2), 586–591.

Castora, K., Brewster, J., & Stoloff, J. (2003). Predicting aggression in police officers using the MMPI-2. *Journal of Police and Criminal Psychology, 18*(1), 1–8.

Chibnall, J. T., & Detrick, P. (2003). The NEO PI-R, Inwald Personality Inventory, and MMPI-2 in the prediction of police academy performance: A case for incremental validity. *American Journal of Criminal Justice, 27*(2), 233–248.

Choca, J., Laatsch, L., Garside, D., Hupta, R., & Fenstermacher, J. (2008). *Category Test: Technical guide and software manual*. North Tonawanda, NY: Multi-Health Systems.

Cigrang, J. A., & Stall, M. A. (2001). Free administration of the MMPI-2 following defensive invalidation in a military job applicant sample. *Journal of Personality Assessment, 76*(3), 472–481.

Claussen-Rogers, N. L., & Arrigo, B. A. (2005). *Police corruption and psychological testing: A strategy for pre-employment screening*. Durham, NC: Carolina Academic Press.

Cohen, B., & Chaiken, J. M. (1972). *Police background characteristics and performance*. Lexington, MA: Lexington Books.

Colker, R. (1999). Americans With Disabilities Act: A windfall for defendants. *Harvard Civil Rights-Civil Liberties Law Review, 34*, 99–163.

Connell, M., & Koocher, G. P. (2003). HIPAA and forensic practice. *American Psychology Law Society News, 23*(2), 16–19.

Conners, C. K. (2004). *Conners' Continuous Performance Test II* (CPT II V. 5). North Tonawanda, NY: Multi-Health Systems.

Corey, D. M. (2008, October). *Bifurcation implications*. Paper presented at the annual conference of the Society of Police and Criminal Psychology, Walnut Creek, CA.

Corey, D. M. (2011). Principles of fitness-for-duty evaluations for police psychologists. In J. Kitaeff (Ed.), *Handbook of police psychology* (pp. 263–293). New York, NY: Routledge Psychology Press.

Corey, D. M. (2016, October). *Assessment protocols, procedures and pass rates for psychological evaluations of police candidates: A contemporary national survey*. Paper presented at the annual meeting of the International Association of Chiefs of Police, Police Psychological Services Section, San Diego, CA.

Corey, D. M. (2018, April). *Assessing for malleability of implicit bias in police officer candidates: Evidence and methods*. Presented at the American Academy of Forensic Psychology Workshops, New Orleans, LA.

Corey, D. M., & Ben-Porath, Y. S. (2014). *User's guide for the MMPI-2-RF police candidate interpretive report*. Minneapolis, MN: University of Minnesota Press.

Corey, D. M., & Ben-Porath, Y. S. (2018). *Assessing police and other public safety personnel using the MMPI-2-RF: A practical guide*. Minneapolis, MN: University of Minnesota Press.

Corey, D. M., & Borum, R. (2013). Forensic assessment for high-risk occupations. In R. K. Otto & I. B. Weiner (Vol. eds.), *Forensic psychology* (2nd ed., Vol. 11, pp. 246–270). Hoboken, NJ: John Wiley and Sons.

Corey, D. M., Sellbom, M., & Ben-Porath, Y. S. (2018). Risks associated with overcontrolled behavior in police officer recruits. *Psychological Assessment, 30*(12), 1691–1702.

Corey, D. M., & Stewart, C. O. (2015). Under the color of authority: Police officers as violent offenders. In C. A. Pietz & C. Mattson (Eds.), *Violent offenders: Understanding and assessment* (pp. 249–268). New York, NY: Oxford Press.

Corey, D. M., Trompetter, P. S., & Ben-Porath, Y. S. (2013). Establishing a peer review group. *California Psychologist, 46*(5), 25–27.

Costa, P. T., & McCrae, R. R. (1992). *Revised NEO Personality Inventory (NEO PI-R) and NEO Five-Factor Inventory (NEO-FFI): Professional manual.* Lutz, FL: Psychological Assessment Resources.

Cronbach, L. J. (1988). Five perspectives on validity argument. In H. Wainer & H. I. Braun (Eds.), *Test validity* (pp. 1–17). New York, NY: Routledge.

Curran, S. F., Holt, E. O., & Afanador, J. H. (2017). Transition and reintegration of military personnel to law enforcement careers. In C. L. Mitchell & E. H. Dorian (Eds.), *Police psychology and its growing impact on modern law enforcement* (pp. 158–175). Hershey, PA: IGI Global.

Cuttler, M. J., & Muchinsky, P. M. (2006). Prediction of law enforcement training performance and dysfunctional job performance with general mental ability, personality and life history variables. *Criminal Justice and Behavior, 33*(1), 3–25.

Dantzker, M. L. (2011). Psychological preemployment screening for police candidates: Seeking consistency if not standardization. *Professional Psychology: Research and Practice, 42*(3), 276–283. doi:10.1037/a0023736

Dasgupta, N. (2013). Implicit attitudes and beliefs adapt to situations: A decade of research on the malleability of implicit prejudice, stereotypes, and the self-concept. In *Advances in experimental social psychology* (Vol. 47, pp. 233–279). Cambridge, MA: Academic Press.

Davis, T. C., Holcombe, R. F., Berkel, H. J., Pramanik, S., & Divers, S. G. (1998). Informed consent for clinical trials: A comparative study of standard versus simplified forms. *Journal of the National Cancer Institute, 90,* 668–674.

Davis, R. D., & Rostow, C. D. (2010). The use of the M-PULSE inventory in law enforcement selection. In P. A. Weiss (Ed.), *Personality assessment in police psychology: A 21st century perspective* (pp. 132–158). Springfield, IL: Charles C Thomas Publisher.

Delis, D. C., Kaplan, E., & Kramer, J. H. (2001). *Delis-Kaplan executive function system: Technical manual.* Minneapolis, MN: Pearson.

DeMier, R. L. (2013, September 22). *Forensic report writing.* Workshop presented for the American Academy of Forensic Psychology, Alexandria, VA.

Detrick, P. (2012). Police officer preemployment evaluations: Seeking consistency if not standardization? *Professional Psychology: Research and Practice, 43*(2), 162. doi:10.1037/a0026874

Detrick, P., Ben-Porath, Y. S., & Sellbom, M. (2016). Associations between MMPI-2-RF (Restructured Form) and Inwald Personality Inventory (IPI) scale scores in a law enforcement personality screening sample. *Journal of Police and Criminal Psychology, 31*(2), 81–95.

Detrick, P., & Chibnall, J. T. (2002). Prediction of police officer performance with the Inwald Personality Inventory. *Journal of Police and Criminal Psychology, 17*(2), 9–17.

Detrick, P., & Chibnall, J. T. (2006). NEO PI-R personality characteristics of high performing entry-level police officers. *Psychological Services, 3*, 274–285.

Detrick, P., & Chibnall, J. T. (2013). Revised NEO Personality Inventory normative data for police officer selection. *Psychological Services, 10*, 372–277.

Detrick, P., & Chibnall, J. T. (2014). Underreporting on the MMPI-2-RF in a high-demand police officer selection context: An illustration. *Psychological Assessment, 26*(3), 1044–1049. doi:10.1037/pas0000013

Detrick, P., & Chibnall, J. T. (2017). A Five-Factor Model inventory for use in screening police officer applicants: The Revised NEO Personality Inventory (NEO PI-R). In C. L. Mitchell & E. H. Dorian (Eds.), *Police psychology and its growing impact on modern law enforcement* (pp. 79–92). Hershey, PA: IGI Global.

Detrick, P., & Chibnall, J. T. (2019, January 19). Frame-of-reference effects on police officer applicant responses to the Revised NEO Personality Inventory. *Journal of Police and Criminal Psychology.* Published online. https://link.springer.com/article/10.1007/s11896-019-9313-5

Detrick P., Chibnall, J. T., & Call, C. (2010). Demand effects on positive response distortion by police officer applicants on the revised NEO personality inventory. *Journal of Personality Assessment, 92*(5), 1–7.

Detrick, P., Chibnall, J. T., & Luebbert, M. C. (2004). The revised NEO Personality Inventory as predictor of police academy performance. *Criminal Justice and Behavior, 31*, 676–694.

Detrick, P., Chibnall, J. T., Rosso, M. (2001). MMPI-2 in police officer selection: Normative data and relation to the Inwald Personality Inventory. *Professional Psychology: Research and Practice, 32*(5), 484–490.

Drew, J., Carless, S. A., & Thompson, B. M. (2008). Predicting turnover of police officers using the Sixteen Personality Factor Questionnaire. *Journal of Criminal Justice, 36*(4), 326–331. doi:10.1016/j.jcrimjus.2008.06.003

Dubin, S. S. (1972). Obsolescence or lifelong education: A choice for the professional. *American Psychologist, 27*(5), 486.

Ellingwood, H., Williams, K. M., Sitarenios, G., & Solomon, J. (2018, December 14). Psychometric properties of a contextualized, actuarially informed assessment for law enforcement personnel selection: The

M-PULSE Inventory. *Journal of Police and Criminal Psychology.* doi:10.1007/s11896-018-9290-0

Epstein, R. M., & Hundert, E. M. (2002). Defining and assessing professional competence. *Journal of the American Medical Association, 287,* 226–235.

Equal Employment Opportunity Commission. (1995). *ADA enforcement guidance: Preemployment disability-related questions and medical examinations.* Retrieved from https://www.eeoc.gov/policy/docs/preemp.html

Equal Employment Opportunity Commission. (1996). *EEOC enforcement guidance: Workers' compensation and the ADA.* Retrieved from https://www.eeoc.gov/policy/docs/workcomp.html

Equal Employment Opportunity Commission. (1997). *EEOC Enforcement Guidance on the ADA and Psychiatric Disabilities.* Retrieved from https://www.eeoc.gov/policy/docs/psych.html

Equal Employment Opportunity Commission. (2000). *Enforcement guidance on disability-related inquiries and medical examinations of employees under the Americans With Disabilities Act: Compliance manual* (Vol. II, Sect. 902, No. 915.002). Washington, DC: Author.

Equal Employment Opportunity Commission. (2002, October 29). *ADA technical assistance manual: January 1992.* (Publication EEOC-M-1A, Addendum).

Equal Employment Opportunity Commission. (2011, May 31). *ADA and GINA: Confidentiality Requirements.* Retrieved from https://www.eeoc.gov/eeoc/foia/letters/2011/ada_gina_confidentrequre.html

Fabricatore, J. M., Azen, S., Schoentgen, S., & Snibbe, H. (1978). Predicting performance of police officers using the 16 Personality Factor Questionnaire. *American Journal of Community Psychology, 1*(6), 63–70.

Faigman, D. L., Kang, J., Bennett, M. W., Carbado, D. W., Casey, P., . . . Mnookin, J. (2012). Implicit bias in the courtroom. *UCLA Law Review, 59,* 1124–1186. Retrieved from http://repository.uchastings.edu/faculty_scholarship/1312

Fischler, G. L. (2004). Identifying psychological predictors of police officer integrity problems (CFDA No. 16.710, "Creating a Culture of Integrity"). Washington, DC: US Department of Justice.

Fischler, G. L., McElroy, H. K., Miller, L., Saxe-Clifford, S., Stewart, C. O., & Zelig, M. (2011, August). The role of psychological fitness-for-duty evaluations in law enforcement. *Police Chief, 78*(8), 72–78.

Fisher, M. A. (2009). Replacing "Who is the client?" with a different ethical question. *Professional Psychology: Research and Practice, 40,* 1–7.

Flens, J. R. (2005). The responsible use of psychological testing in child custody evaluations: Selection of tests. *Journal of Child Custody, 2,* 3–29.

Furlan, A. D., MacDougall, P., Pellerin, D., Shaw, K., Spitzig, D., Wilson, G., & Wright, J. (2014). Overview of four prescription monitoring/

review programs in Canada. *Pain Research and Management*, *19*, 102–106.

Garner, B. A. (1999). *Black's law dictionary* (7th ed.). St. Paul, MN: West Group.

Gawande, A. (2009). *The checklist manifesto*. New York, NY: Henry Holt.

Glancy, G. D., Ash, P., Bath, E. P., Buchanan, A., Fedoroff, P., Frierson, R. L., . . . Norko, M. (2015). AAPL practice guideline for the forensic assessment. *Journal of the American Academy of Psychiatry and the Law*, *43*(2 Suppl.), S3–S53.

Gold, L. H., Anfang, S. A., Drukteinis, A. M., Metzner, J. L., Price, M., Wall, B. W., . . . Zonana, H. V. (2008). AAPL practice guidelines for the forensic evaluation of psychiatric disability. *Journal of the American Academy of Psychiatry and the Law Online*, *36*(Suppl. 4), S3–S50.

Gold, L. H., & Shuman, D. W. (2009). *Evaluating mental health disability in the workplace*. New York: Springer Science & Business Media.

Gough, H. G., & Bradley, P. (2002). *CPI manual*. Mountain View, CA: Consulting Psychologists Press.

Graham, J. R. (2012). *MMPI-2: Assessing personality and psychopathology* (5th ed.). New York, NY: Oxford University Press.

Green, R. L. (2011). *MMPI-2/MMPI-2-RF: An interpretive manual* (3rd ed.). New York, NY: Allyn and Bacon.

Greenwald, A. G., Banaji, M. R., Rudman, L. A., Farnham, S. D., Nosek, B. A., & Mellott, D. S. (2002). A unified theory of implicit attitudes, stereotypes, self-esteem, and self-concept. *Psychological Review*, *109*(1), 3–25.

Greenwald, A. G., McGhee, D. E., & Schwartz, J. L. (1998). Measuring individual differences in implicit cognition: The implicit association test. *Journal of Personality and Social Psychology*, *74*(6), 1464–1480.

Griffith, E. E. H., Stankovic, A., & Baranoski, M. (2010). Conceptualizing the forensic psychiatry report as performative narrative. *Journal of the American Academy of Psychiatry and the Law*, *38*, 32–42.

Grisso, T. (2008, May 17). *Writing forensic reports*. Paper presented at the American Academy of Forensic Psychology workshop, San Francisco, CA.

Grisso, T. (2010). Guidance for improving forensic reports: A review of common errors. Retrieved from https://escholarship.umassmed.edu/cgi/viewcontent.cgi?article=1281&context=ps ych_pp

Grisso, T., Borum, R., Edens, J. F., Moye, J., & Otto, R. K. (2003). *Evaluating competencies: Forensic assessments and instruments* (2nd ed.). New York, NY: Kluwer Academic.

Grove, W. M., Zald, D. H., Lebow, B. S., Snitz, B. E., & Nelson, C. (2000). Clinical versus mechanical prediction: A meta-analysis. *Psychological Assessment*, *12*, 19–30.

Guion, R. M. (1991). Personnel assessment, selection, and placement. In M. D. Dunnette & L. M. Hough (Eds.), *Handbook of industrial and organizational psychology* (Vol. 2, 2nd ed., pp. 327–397). Palo Alto, CA: Consulting Psychologists Press.

Hales, G., & Higgins, A. (2016, September). *Prioritisation in a changing world: Seven challenges for policing.* The Police Effectiveness Project in a Changing World, Paper 2. London: Police Foundation. Retrieved from http://www.police-foundation.org.uk/uploads/catalogerfiles/prioritisation-in-a-changing-world/changing_world_paper_2.pdf

Hargrave, G. E., & Hiatt, D. (1989). Use of the California Psychological Inventory in law enforcement officer selection. *Journal of Personality Assessment, 53*(2), 267–277.

Hargrave, G. E., Hiatt, D., Ogard, E., & Karr, C. (1994). Comparison of the MMPI and the MMPI-2 for sample of peace officers. *Psychological Assessment, 6,* 27–32.

Harris, C. J. (2010). Problem officers? Analyzing problem behavior patterns from a large cohort. *Journal of Criminal Justice, 38,* 216–225.

Heilbrun, K. (2001). *Principles of forensic mental health assessment.* New York, NY: Kluwer Academic/Plenum Publishers.

Heilbrun, K., DeMatteo, D., Holliday, S. B., & LaDuke, C. (Eds.). (2014). *Forensic mental health assessment: A casebook.* New York, NY: Oxford University Press.

Heilbrun, K., DeMatteo, D., Marczyk, G., & Goldstein, A. M. (2008). Standards of practice and care in forensic mental health assessment: Legal, professional, and principles-based consideration. *Psychology, Public Policy, and Law, 14,* 1–26.

Heilbrun, K., Grisso, T., & Goldstein, A. M. (2009). *Foundations of forensic mental health assessment.* New York, NY: Oxford University Press.

Hendrawan, D., Yamakawa, K., Kimura, M., Murakami, H., & Ohira, H. (2012). Executive functioning performance predicts subjective and physiological acute stress reactivity: Preliminary results. *International Journal of Psychophysiology, 84,* 277–283.

Hickman, M. J., & Reaves, B. A. (2006). Local police departments, 2003. Publication NCJ 210118. Washington, DC: Bureau of Justice Statistics. Retrieved from https://www.bjs.gov/content/pub/pdf/lpd03.pdf

Hogan, R., Hogan, J., & Roberts, B. W. (1996). Personality measurement and employment decisions: Questions and answers. *American Psychologist, 51*(5), 469–477.

Holling, H. (1998). Utility analysis of personnel selection: An overview and empirical study based on objective performance measures. *Methods of Psychological Research, 3*(1), 5–24.

Hunter, J. E., & Schmidt, F. L. (1990). *Methods of meta-analysis: Correcting error and bias in research findings.* Newbury, CA: Sage Publications.

International Association of Chiefs of Police. (2001). *Police use of force in America.* Retrieved from https://www.theiacp.org/sites/default/files/2018-08/2001useofforce.pdf

International Association of Chiefs of Police. (2014). Police Psychological Services Section. *Guidelines for preemployment psychological evaluations.* Arlington, VA: Author.

International Association of Chiefs of Police. (2018a). Police Psychological Services Section. *Psychological fitness-for-duty evaluation guidelines.* Arlington, VA: Author.

International Association of Chiefs of Police. (2018b). *Officer-involved shooting guidelines.* Arlington, VA: Author.

Inwald, R., Knatz, H., & Shusman, E. (1982). *Inwald Personality Inventory manual.* Kew Gardens, NY: Hilson Research.

Inwald, R., & Shusman, E. (1984). The IPI and MMPI as predictors of academy performance for police recruits. *Journal of Police Science and Administration, 12*(1), 1–11.

Ito, T. A., Friedman, N. P., Bartholow, B. D., Correll, J., Loersch, C., Altamirano, L. J., & Miyake, A. (2015). Toward a comprehensive understanding of executive cognitive function in implicit racial bias. *Journal of Personality and Social Psychology, 108,* 187–218.

Johnson, M., & Roberts, M. (2005). Adding problem scores to the PsyQ Report. JR&A training program presentation, Miami, FL.

Johnson, W. B., Barnett, J. E., Elman, N. S., Forrest, L., & Kaslow, N. J. (2013). The competence constellation model: A communitarian approach to support professional competence. *Professional Psychology: Research and Practice, 44,* 343–345.

Jones, J. W., Cunningham, M. R., & Dages, K. D. (2010). Pre-offer police integrity testing: Scientific foundation and professional issues. In P. A. Weiss (Ed.), *Personality assessment in police psychology: A 21st century perspective* (pp. 159–187). Springfield, IL: Charles C. Thomas.

Judd, L. L., Schettler, P. J., Solomon, D. A., Maser, J. D., Coryell, W., Endicott, J., & Akiskal, H. S. (2008). Psychosocial disability and work role function compared across the long-term course of bipolar I, bipolar II and unipolar major depressive disorders. *Journal of Affective Disorders, 73,* 123–131.

Kane, M. T. (1992). An argument-based approach to validity. *Psychological Bulletin, 112*(3), 527–535. doi:10.1037/0033-2909.112.3.527

Kang, J. (2005). Trojan horses of race, 118. *Harvard Law Review, 1489,* 1494.

Kang, J. (2012). *Bits of bias.* UCLA School of Law Research Paper No. 11-40. Retrieved from https://ssrn.com/abstract=1968277

Kang, J., & Lane, K. (2010). Seeing through colorblindness: Implicit bias and the law. *UCLA Law Review, 58,* 465–520.

Khadivi, A. (2010). Conditional second opinion psychological evaluation of law enforcement candidates. In P. A. Weiss (Ed.), *Personality assessment in police psychology: A 21st century perspective* (pp. 333–346). Springfield, IL: Charles C. Thomas.

Kionka, E. J. (1999). *Torts in a nutshell* (3rd ed.). St. Paul, MN: West.

Klauer, K. C., Schmitz, F., Teige-Mocigemba, S., & Voss, A. (2010). Understanding the role of executive control in the Implicit Association Test: Why flexible people have small IAT effects. *Quarterly Journal of Experimental Psychology, 63,* 595–619.

Kleider, H. M., Parrott, D. J., & King, T. Z. (2010). Shooting behaviour: How working memory and negative emotionality influence police officer shoot decisions. *Applied Cognitive Psychology, 24,* 707–717.

Knatz, H. F., Inwald, R. E., Brockwell, A. L., & Tran, L. N. (1992). IPI and MMPI predictions of counterproductive job behaviors by racial group. *Journal of Business and Psychology, 7*(2), 189–201. doi:10.1007/BF01013928

Krause, M. (2009). History and evolution of the FBI's undercover safeguard program. *Consulting Psychology Journal: Practice and Research, 61,* 5–13.

Lezak, M., Howieson, D., Bigler, E., & Tranel, D. (2012). *Neuropsychological assessment* (5th ed.). New York, NY: Oxford University Press.

Lorr, M., & Strack, S. (1994). Personality profiles of police candidates. *Journal of Clinical Psychology, 50,* 200–207.

Lowmaster, S. E., & Morey, L. D. (2012). Predicting law enforcement officer job performance with the Personality Assessment Inventory. *Journal of Personality Assessment, 94*(3), 254–261.

Malouff, J. M., & Schutte, N. S. (1986). Development and validation of a measure of irrational belief. *Journal of Consulting and Clinical Psychology, 54*(6), 860–862.

Marsh, S. H. (1962). Validating the selection of deputy sheriffs. *Public Personnel Review, 23,* 41–44.

Mayer, M. J., & Corey, D. M. (2017). Current issues in psychological fitness-for-duty evaluations for law enforcement officers: Legal and practice implications. In C. L. Mitchell & E. Dorian (Eds.), *Police psychology and its growing impact on modern law enforcement* (pp. 93–117). Hershey, PA: IGI Global.

McCrae, R. R., & Costa, P. T., Jr., (2010). *NEO Inventories: Professional manual.* Lutz, FL: Psychological Assessment Resources.

Meehl, P. E. (1954). *Clinical vs. statistical prediction: A theoretical analysis and a review of the evidence.* Minneapolis, MN: University of Minnesota Press.

Melton, G. B., Petrila, J., Poythress, N. G., Slobogin, C., Otto, R. K., Mossman, D., & Condie, L. O. (2018). *Psychological evaluations for the courts: A handbook for mental health professionals and lawyers* (4th ed.). New York, NY: Guilford Press.

Milne, B. J., Caspi, A., Harrington, H., Poulton, R., Rutter, M., & Moffitt, T. E. (2009). Predictive value of family history on severity of illness: The case for depression, anxiety, alcohol dependence, and drug dependence. *Archives of General Psychiatry, 66,* 738–747.

Mitchell, C. L. (2017). Preemployment psychological screening of police officer applicants: Basic considerations and recent advances. In C. L. Mitchell & E. H. Dorian (Eds.), *Police psychology and its growing impact on modern law enforcement* (pp. 28–49). Hershey, PA: IGI Global.

Miyake, A., & Friedman, N. P. (2012). The nature and organization of individual differences in executive functions: Four general conclusions. *Current Directions in Psychological Science, 21,* 8–14.

Morey, L. C. (1991). *The Personality Assessment Inventory: Professional manual.* Lutz, FL: Psychological Assessment Resources.

Morey, L. C. (2014). The Personality Assessment Inventory. In R. R. Archer & S. R. Smith (Eds.), *Personality assessment* (2nd ed., pp. 193–240). New York, NY: Routledge.

Murrie, D. C., Boccaccini, M. T., Guarnera, L. A., & Rufino, K. A. (2013). Are forensic experts biased by the side that retained them? *Psychological Science, 24,* 1889–1897.

National Association of Boards of Pharmacy. (2018). New states added to national network of prescription drug monitoring programs. Retrieved from https://nabp.pharmacy/new-states-added-national-network-prescription-drug-monitoring-programs/

National Conference of State Legislatures. (2017). Retrieved from http://www.ncsl.org/research/telecommunications-and-information-technology/privacy-protections-in-state-constitutions.aspx

Neimeyer, G. J., Taylor, J. M., Rozensky, R. H., & Cox, D. R. (2014). The diminishing durability of knowledge in professional psychology: A second look at specializations. *Professional Psychology: Research and Practice, 45*(2), 92–98.

Nici, J., & Hom, J. (2013). Comparability of the computerized Halstead Category Test with the original version. *Archives of Clinical Neuropsychology, 28*(8), 824–828.

Nisbett, R. E., & Wilson, T. D. (1977). Telling more than we can know: Verbal reports on mental processes. *Psychological Review, 84*(3), 231–259.

Nosek, B. A., Banaji, M. R., & Greenwald, A. G. (2002). Harvesting implicit group attitudes and beliefs from a demonstration web site. *Group Dynamics: Theory, Research, and Practice, 6,* 101–115.

Nosek, B. A., Hawkins, C. B., & Frazier, R. S. (2011). Implicit social cognition: From measures to mechanisms. *Trends in Cognitive Sciences, 15,* 152–159.

Nosek, B. A., & Riskind, R. G. (2012). Policy implications of implicit social cognition. *Social Issues and Policy Review, 6*(1), 113–147.

Nosek, B. A., Smyth, F. L., Hansen, J. J., Devos, T., Lindner, N. M., Ranganath, K. A., . . . Banaji, M. R. (2007). Pervasiveness and correlates of implicit attitudes and stereotypes. *European Review of Social Psychology, 18*(1), 36–88.

Nyberg, L., & Eriksson, J. (2015). Working memory: Maintenance, updating, and the realization of Intentions. *Cold Spring Harbor Perspectives in Biology*, *8*(2), a021816. doi:10.1101/cshperspect.a021816

Ontario Chiefs of Police Association. (2018). *Constable selection system: Guidelines for Psychologists*. Retrieved from http://www.oacp.on.ca/programs-courses/constable-selection-system

Otto, R. K., DeMier, R. L., & Boccaccini, M. T. (2014). *Forensic reports and testimony: A guide to effective communication for psychologists and psychiatrists*. Hoboken, NJ: John Wiley and Sons.

Otto, R. K., Edens, J. F., & Barcus, E. H. (2000). The use of psychological testing in child custody evaluations. *Family and Conciliation Courts Review*, *38*(3), 312–340.

Otto, R. K., Goldstein, A. M., & Heilbrun, K. (2017). *Ethics in forensic psychology practice*. Hoboken, NJ: John Wiley and Sons.

Otto, R. K., & Krauss, D. A. (2009). Contemplating the presence of third-party observers and facilitators in psychological evaluations. *Assessment*, *16*(4), 362–372.

Pinker, S. (2018). *Enlightenment now: The case for reason, science, humanism, and progress*. New York, NY: Viking.

Pirelli, G., Hartigan, S., & Zapf, P. A. (2018). Using the Internet for collateral information in forensic mental health evaluations. *Behavioral Sciences and the Law*, *36*, 157–169.

Pirelli, G., Otto, R. K., & Estoup, A. (2016). Using Internet and social media data as collateral sources of information in forensic evaluations. *Professional Psychology: Research and Practice*, *47*, 12–17.

Powell, M., Cassematis, P., Benson, M., Smallbone, S., & Wortley, R. (2014). Police officers' strategies for coping with the stress of investigating Internet child exploitation. *Traumatology: An International Journal*, *20*, 32–42.

President's Commission on Law Enforcement and Administration of Justice. (1967a). *The challenge of crime in a free society*. Washington, DC: US Government Printing Office.

President's Commission on Law Enforcement and Administration of Justice. (1967b). *Task for report: The police*. Washington, DC: US Government Printing Office.

President's Task Force on 21st Century Policing. (2015). Final report of the President's Task Force on 21st Century Policing. Washington, DC: Office of Community Oriented Policing Services.

Reaves, B. A. (2010). Local police departments, 2007. Publication NCJ 231174. Washington, DC: Bureau of Justice Statistics. Retrieved from https://www.bjs.gov/content/pub/pdf/lpd07.pdf

Reaves, B. A. (2015). Local police departments, 2013: Personnel, policies, and practices. Publication NCJ 248677, Washington, DC: Bureau of Justice Statistics. Retrieved from https://www.bjs.gov/content/pub/pdf/lpd13ppp.pdf

Rennert, S. (2004, June 3). ADA: Essential functions/disability-related inquiries and medical examinations of applicants. Informal discussion letter. Washington, DC: Equal Employment Opportunity Commission.

Roberts, M. D., & Johnson, M. (2001). *CPI: Police and public safety selection report technical manual.* Los Gatos, CA: Law Enforcement Psychological Services. Retrieved from file:///H:/Downloads/JR&A.2001.CPI%20Manual.MJ28.edited.pdf

Roberts, M. D., Thompson, J. A., & Johnson, M. (2004). PAI law enforcement, corrections, and public safety selection report: Manual. Odessa, FL: Psychological Assessment Resources.

Roberts, R. M., Tarescavage, A. M., Ben-Porath, Y. S., & Roberts, M. D. (2018). Predicting postprobationary job performance of police officers using CPI and MMPI-2-RF test data obtained during preemployment psychological screening. *Journal of Personality Assessment,* 1–12.

Roos, L. E., Lebrecht, S., Tanaka, J. W., & Tarr, M. J. (2013). Can singular examples change implicit attitudes in the real-world? *Frontiers in Psychology, 4*(594), 1–14.

Rostow, C. D., & Davis, R. D. (2004). *A handbook of psychological fitness-for-duty evaluations in law enforcement.* New York, NY: Haworth Press.

Rothstein, M. A., Roberts, J., & Guidotti, T. L. (2015). Limiting occupational medical evaluations under the Americans With Disabilities Act and the Genetic Information Nondiscrimination Act. *American Journal of Law and Medicine, 41*, 523–567.

Rudman, L. A. (2004). Social justice in our minds, homes, and society: The nature, causes, and consequences of implicit bias. *Social Justice Research, 17*(2), 129–142.

Russell, M., & Karol, D. (1994). *16PF fifth edition administrator's manual.* Champaign, IL: Institute for Personality and Ability Testing.

Sarchione, C. D., Cuttler, M. J., Muchinsky, P. M., & Nelson-Gray, R. (1998). Prediction of dysfunctional job behaviors among law enforcement officers. *Journal of Applied Psychology, 83*, 904–912.

Saxe, S. J., & Reiser, M. (1976). A comparison of three police applicant groups using the MMPI. *Journal of Police Science and Administration, 4*(4), 419–425.

Schinka, J. A., Kinder, B. N., & Kremer, T. (1997). Research validity scales for the NEO-PI-R: Development and initial validation. *Journal of Personality Assessment, 68*, 127–138.

Schmidt, F. L., & Hunter, J. E. (1977). Development of a general solution to the problem of validity generalization. *Journal of Applied Psychology, 62*(5), 529.

Sellbom, M., Fischler, G. L., & Ben-Porath, Y. S. (2007). Identifying MMPI-2 predictors of police officer integrity and misconduct. *Criminal Justice and Behavior, 34*(8), 985–1004. doi:10.1177/0093854807301224

Serafino, G. F. (2010). Fundamental issues in police psychological assessment. In P. A. Weiss (Ed.), *Personality assessment in police psychology: A 21st century perspective* (pp. 29–55). Springfield, IL: Charles C. Thomas.

Sessions, R. (1950, January 8). How a "difficult" composer gets his way. *The New York Times*, p. 89.

Sheldon, O. J., Dunning, D., & Ames, D. R. (2014). Emotionally unskilled, unaware, and uninterested in learning more: Reactions to feedback about deficits in emotional intelligence. *Journal of Applied Psychology, 99*, 125–137.

Sherman, L. (1978). *Scandal and reform: Controlling police corruption.* Berkeley, CA: University of California Press.

Smith, C. P., & Freyd, J. J. (2014). Institutional betrayal. *American Psychologist, 69*(6), 575–587.

Son, I. S., Davis, M. S., & Rome, D. M. (1998). Race and its effect on police officers' perceptions of misconduct. *Journal of Criminal Justice, 26*(1), 21–28.

Spilberg, S. W., & Corey, D. M. (2019). Peace officer psychological screening manual. Sacramento, CA: California Commission on Peace Officer Standards and Training (POST). Retrieved from http://lib.post.ca.gov/Publications/Peace_Officer_Psychological_Screening_Manual.pdf

Stapleton, S. M., Bababekov, Y. J., Perez, N. P., Fong, Z. V., Hashimoto, D. A., Lillemoe, K. D., . . . Chang, D. C. (2018). Variation in amputation risk for black patients: Uncovering potential sources of bias and opportunities for intervention. *Journal of the American College of Surgeons, 226*, 641–649.

Stewart, B. D., von Hippel, W., & Radvansky, G. A. (2009). Age, race, and implicit prejudice. *Psychological Science, 20*, 164–168.

Strindberg, E., & Chamness, R. E. (1999, January 12). *Employment and labor law in Utah.* Eau Claire, WI: Lorman Education Services.

Stroop, J. R. (1935). Studies of interference in serial verbal reactions. *Journal of Experimental Psychology, 18*, 643–662.

Stubenrauch, S., & Young, J. (2015). *Interpreting the Inwald Personality Inventory-2 (IPI-2).* Retrieved from https://www.16pf.com/wp-content/uploads/Interpreting-the-IPI-2-WHITE-PAPER.pdf

Tarescavage, A. M., Brewster, J. A., Corey, D. M., & Ben-Porath, Y. S. (2015). Use of pre-hire MMPI-2-RF police candidate scores to predict supervisor ratings of post-hire performance. *Assessment, 22*(4), 411–428. doi:10.1177/1073191114548445

Tarescavage, A. M., Corey, D. M., & Ben-Porath, Y. S. (2015). Minnesota Multiphasic Personality Inventory–2–Restructured Form (MMPI-2-RF) predictors of police officer problem behavior. *Assessment, 22*(1), 116–132. doi:10.1177/1073191114534885

Tarescavage, A. M., Corey, D. M., & Ben-Porath, Y. S. (2016). A prorating method for estimating MMPI-2-RF scores from MMPI responses: Examination of score fidelity and illustration of empirical utility in the PERSEREC police integrity study sample. *Assessment*, 23(2), 173–190. doi:10.1177/1073191115575070

Tarescavage, A. M., Corey, D. M., Gupton, H. M., & Ben-Porath Y. S. (2015). Criterion validity and practical utility of the Minnesota Multiphasic Personality Inventory–2–Restructured Form (MMPI-2-RF) in assessments of police officer candidates. *Journal of Personality Assessment*, 97(4), 382–394. doi:10.1080/00223891.2014.995800

Tarescavage, A. M., Fischler, G., Cappo, B., Hill, D., Corey, D. M., & Ben-Porath, Y. S. (2015). Minnesota Multiphasic Personality Inventory–2–Restructured Form (MMPI-2-RF) predictors of police officer problem behavior and collateral self-report test scores. *Psychological Assessment*, 27(1), 125–137.

Tellegen, A., Ben-Porath, Y. S., McNulty, J. L., Arbisi, P. A., Graham, J. R., & Kaemmer, B. (2003). *The MMPI-2 restructured clinical scales: Development, validation, and interpretation.* Minneapolis, MN: University of Minnesota Press.

Terman, L. M., Otis, A. S., Dickson, V., Hubbard, O. S., Norton, J. K., Howard, L., . . . Cassingham, C. C. (1917). A trial of mental and pedagogical tests in a civil service examination for policemen and firemen. *Journal of Applied Psychology*, 1(1), 17–29.

Terpstra, D. A., Mohamed, A. A., Kethley, R. B. (1999). An analysis of federal court cases involving nine selection devices. *International Journal of Selection and Assessment*, 7(1), 26–34.

Tombaugh, T. N. (2004). Trail Making Test A and B: Normative data stratified by age and education. *Archives of Clinical Neuropsychology*, 19, 203–214.

Tombaugh, T. N., Kozak, J., & Rees, L. (1999). Normative data stratified by age and education for two measures of verbal fluency: FAS and animal naming. *Archives of Clinical Neuropsychology*, 14, 167–177.

Trenerry, M. R., Crosson, B., Deboe, J., & Leber, W. R. (1988). *Stroop neuropsychological screening test.* Lutz, FL: Psychological Assessment Resources.

Trompetter, P. S. (2017). A history of police psychology In C. L. Mitchell & E. Dorian (Eds.), *Police psychology and its growing impact on modern law enforcement* (pp. 1–27). Hershey, PA: IGI Global.

University of Idaho. (undated). Determining essential and marginal job functions. Retrieved from https://www.uidaho.edu/-/media/UIdaho-Responsive/Files/human-resources/employees/Classification/Essential-Marginal-Job-Functions.pdf

Varela, J. G., Boccaccini, M. T., Scogin, F., Stump, J., & Caputo, A. (2004). Personality testing in law enforcement employment settings: A meta-analytic review. *Criminal Justice and Behavior*, 31, 649–675.

Violanti, J. M. (2018). Effects of shift work on officer safety and wellness. *Police Chief*, 85(5), 32–34.

Walfish, S. (2010). Reducing MMPI-defensiveness in professionals presenting for evaluation. *Journal of Addictive Diseases*, *30*(1), 75–80.

Weathers, F. W., Bovin, M. J., Lee, D. J., Sloan, D. M., Schnurr, P. P., Kaloupek, D. G., . . . Marx, B. P. (2018). The Clinician-Administered PTSD Scale for DSM-5 (CAPS-5): Development and initial psychometric evaluation in military veterans. *Psychological Assessment*, *30*(3), 383–395. doi:10.1037/pas0000486

Weiss, P. A., Hitchcock, J. H., Weiss, W. U., Rostow, C., & Davis, R. (2008). The Personality Assessment Inventory Borderline, Drug, and Alcohol Scales as predictors of overall performance in police officers: A series of exploratory analyses. *Policing and Society*, *18*(3), 301–310.

Weiss, P. A., & Inwald, R. (2018). A brief history of personality assessment in police psychology: 1916–2008. *Journal of Police and Criminal Psychology*, *33*, 189–200. doi:10.1007/s11896-018-9272-2

Weiss, W. U., Rostow, C., Davis, R., & DeCoster-Martin, E. (2004). The Personality Assessment Inventory as a selection device for law enforcement personnel. *Journal of Police and Criminal Psychology*, *19*, 23–29.

Widiger, T. A. (1995). Review of the Revised NEO Personality Inventory. In J. C. Conoley & J. C. Impara (Eds.), *The twelfth mental measurements yearbook*. Lincoln, NE: Buros Institute of Mental Measurements.

Wilson, T. D., & Dunn, E. W. (2004). Self-knowledge: Its limits, value, and potential for improvement. *Annual Review of Psychology*, *55*, 17.1–17.26.

Wing, N. (2015, May 29). We pay a shocking amount for police misconduct, and cops want us just to accept it. We shouldn't. *HuffPost*. Retrieved from https://www.huffpost.com/entry/police-misconduct-settlements_n_7423386

Wong, J. G., & Lieh-Mak, F. (2001). Genetic discrimination and mental illness: A case report. *Journal of Medical Ethics*, *27*, 393–397.

Zelig, M. (1998, October). Families as victims in post incident trauma. *Police Chief*, *65*(10), 124–126.

Zelig, M., Sperbeck, D., & Craig, P. (2017, October 21). The importance of assessing executive functioning in police and fire applicants. Paper presented at the annual meeting of the International Chiefs of Police, Philadelphia, PA.

Zelig, M., & Trompetter, P. S. (2016, October 16). The Dunning Effect: Are you competent to assess your professional competencies? Paper presented at the annual meeting of the International Association of Chiefs of Police, San Diego, CA.

Zoufal, D., Webber, B., Parmegiani, J. (2017, October 22). Wolves in sheep's clothing: Tools for ascertaining fraudulent police disability claims. Paper presented at the annual meeting of the Annual Convention of the International Association of Chiefs of Police, Philadelphia, PA.

Cases and Statutes

42 U.S.C. § 1983 (2006).

ADA Amendments Act of 2008, Pub. L. 110–325 (2009).

Albert v. Runyon, 6 F.Supp. 2d 57 (D. Mass. 1998).

Americans With Disabilities Act of 1990, Pub. L. No. 101-336, §2, 104 Stat. 328 (1991).

Bahm v. Department of the Air Force, 1988.

Barnes v. Cochran, 944 F.Supp. 897 (S.D. Fla. 1996).

Bass v. City of Albany, 968 F.2d 1067 (11th Cir. 1992).

Baustain v. State of Louisiana, 910 F.Supp. 274 (E.D. La. 1996).

Bauschard v. Martin, 1993 WL 79259 (N.D. Ill. 1993) (not reported).

Board of Comm'rs of Bryan Cty. v. Brown, 520 U.S. 397, 117 S. Ct. 1382, 137 L. Ed. 2d 626 (1997).

Bonsignore v. City of New York, 521 F.Supp. 394 (S.D.N.Y. 1981).

Bragdon v. Abbott, 524 U.S. 624, 118 S.Ct. 2196, 141 L.Ed.2d 540 (1998).

Brown v. Sandy City Appeal Board, 2014.

Brownfield v. City of Yakima, 612 F.3d 1140 (9th Cir. 2010).

Buchanan v. City of San Antonio, 85 F.3d 196 (5th Cir. 1996).

California Fair Employment and Housing Act of 1959 (Government Code §§12900–12996).

Caver v. City of Trenton, 192 F.R.D. 154 (D.N.J. 2000).

Chevron USA Inc. v. Echazabal, 536 U.S. 73, 122 S. Ct. 2045, 153 L. Ed.2d 82 (2002).

City of Livingston v. Montana Public Employees Association, 339 P.3d 41, 2014 M.T. 314 Mont. 184 (2014).

Cleghorn v. Hess, 853 P.2d 1260, 109 Nev. 544 (1993).

Cleveland Bd. of Ed. v. Loudermill, 470 U.S. 532, 105 S. Ct. 1487, 84 L. Ed. 2d 494 (1985).

Colon v. City of Newark, 909 A.2d 725, 188 N.J. 489 (2006).

Conte v. Horcher (1977).

Daubert v. Merrell Dow Pharmaceuticals, Inc., 509 U.S. 579, 113 S. Ct. 2786, 125 L. Ed. 2d 469 (1993).

Daugherty v. City of El Paso, 1995.

Denhof v. City of Grand Rapids, 494 F.3d 534 (6th Cir. 2007).

Downey v. Bob's Discount Furniture Holdings, Inc., 633 F.3d 1, 6 (1st Cir. 2011).

EEOC v. Amego, Inc., 110 F.3d 135 (1st Cir. 1997).

EEOC v. BNSF Railway Company, No. C14-1488 MJP (9th Cir. 2018).

EEOC v. Hussey Copper Ltd., 22 A.D. Cases (BNA) 1821 (W.D. Pa. Mar. 10, 2010).

EEOC v. United States Steel Corporation, 2013 WL 625315 (W.D. Pennsylvania, February 20, 2013).

Elijah W. v. Superior Court, 216 Cal. App. 4th 140, 156 Cal. Rptr. 3d 592 (Ct. App. 2013).

Franklin v. City of Slidell, 936 F. Supp. 2d 691 (E.D. La. 2013).

Frye v. United States, 293 F. 1013 (D.C. Court of Appeals, 1923).

Garrity v. New Jersey, 385 U.S. 493, 87 S. Ct. 616, 17 L. Ed. 2d 562 (1967).

Gavins v. Rezaie, No. 16-24845-Civ-COOKE/TORRES (S.D. Fla. July 28, 2017).

General Electric Co. v. Joiner, 522 U.S. 136, 118 S. Ct. 512, 139 L. Ed. 2d 508 (1997).

Genetic Information Nondiscrimination Act of 2008 (P.L. 110-233, 122 Stat. 881).

Graham v. Connor, 490 U.S. 386, 109 S. Ct. 1865, 104 L. Ed. 2d 443 (1989).

Griggs v. Duke Power Co., 401 U.S. 424 (1971).

Health Insurance Portability and Accountability Act (HIPAA) Privacy Rule. (2000b). Title 45, Subtitle A, Subchapter C, Part 164, Subpart E, Privacy of Individually Identifiable Health Information.

Hild v. Bruner, 496 F. Supp. 93 (D.N.Y. 1980).

Holiday v. City of Chattanooga, 206 F.3d 637 (6th Cir. 2000).

In re Williams, 129 A.3d 393, 443 N.J. Super. 532 (Super. Ct. App. Div. 2016).

Indianapolis Airport Authority v. Travelers Property Casualty Co. of America, No. 16-2675 (7th Cir. Feb. 17, 2017).

Jaffee v. Redmond, 518 U.S. 1, 116 S. Ct. 1923, 135 L. Ed. 2d 337 (1996).

Jimenez v. DynCorp Intern., LLC, 635 F. Supp. 2d 592 (W.D. Tex. 2009).

Karraker v. Rent-A-Center, 411 F.3d 831 (7th Cir.2005).

Lassiter v. Reno, 86 F.3d 1151 (4th Cir. 1996), cert. denied, 519 U.S. 1091 (1997).

Leonel v. American Airlines, Inc., 400 F.3d 702 (9th Cir. 2005).

Lindsey v. Costco Wholesale Corporation, No. 15-cv-03006-WHO (N.D. Cal. Oct. 5, 2016).

Lowe v. Atlas Logistics Group Retail Services, 102 F.Supp.3d 1360 (N.D. Ga. 2015).

Maplewood and Law Enf. Labor Services, 108 LA (BNA) 572 (Daly, 1996).

McGreal v. Ostrov, 368 F.3d 657 (7th Cir. 2004).

Merillat v. MSU, 207 Mich. App. 240, 523 N.W.2d 802 (Ct. App. 1994).

Metropolitan School District of Martinsville v. Mason, 451 N.E.2d 349 (Ind. App. 1983).

Minton v. Guyer, Civil Action No. 12-6162 (E.D. Pa. May 7, 2014).

Monell v. New York City Dept. of Social Servs., 436 U.S. 658, 98 S. Ct. 2018, 56 L. Ed. 2d 611 (1978).

Monroe v. Pape, 365 U.S. 167 (1961).

Myers v. Hose, 50 F.3d 278 (4th Cir. 1995).

National Treasury Employees Union v. Von Raab, 1987.

National Treasury Employees Union v. Von Raab, 816 F.2d 170 (5th Cir. 1987).

NLRB v. Weingarten, Inc., 420 U.S.

Nuss v. Township of Falls, et al., 89 Pa. Commw. 97; 491 A.2d 971, 1985 Pa. Commw. LEXIS 1029.

O'Neal v. City of New Albany, 293 F.3d 998 (7th Cir. 2002).

Patton v. Federal Bur. of Investigation, 626 F. Supp. 445 (M.D. Pa. 1985).

Pettus v. Cole (1996).

Petty v. Metro. Gov't of Nashville-Davidson County, 538 F.3d 431 (6th Cir. 2008).

Policemen's Benevolent Association of New Jersey v. Township of Washington, 1988.

Policemen's Benev. Ass'n of NJ v. Washington Tp., 850 F.2d 133 (3d Cir. 1988).

Rehabilitation Act of 1973, (Pub.L. 93–112, 87 Stat. 355, 29 U.S.C. § 701 et seq.

Sager v. County of Yuba, 156 Cal.App.4th 1049 (Cal. Ct. App. 2007).

Schaefer v. Wilcock, 676 F.Supp. 1092 (D.Utah 1987).

Schroeder v. City of Detroit, 1997.

Schroeder v. City of Detroit, 561 N.W.2d 497, 221 Mich. App. 364 (Ct. App. 1997).

Shafer v. Preston Memorial Hospital Corporation, 107 F.3d 274 (1997).

Slater v. Department of Homeland Security, Docket No. SF-0752-06-0805-1-2, March 28, 2008

Stamford v. FOIC, WL 1212439 (Conn.Super., 1999).

Stewart v. Pearce, 484 F.2d 1031 (9th Cir. 1973).

Stragapede v. City of Evanston, Illinois, 865 F.3d 861 (7th Cir. 2017).

Sutton v. United Air Lines, Inc., 527 U.S. 471 (1999).

Thomas v. Corwin, 483 F.3d 516 (8th Cir. 2007).

Thompson v. City of Arlington, 838 F. Supp. 1137 (N.D. Tex. 1993).

Toyota Motor Manufacturing, Kentucky, Inc. v. Williams, 534 U.S. 184 (2002).

Transport Workers Union of America v. New York City Transit Authority, 02 Civ. 7659 (S.D.N.Y. Apr. 12, 2004).

Wards Cove Packing Co. v. Atonio, 490 U.S. 642, 109 S. Ct. 2115, 104 L. Ed. 2d 733 (1989).

Watson v. City of Miami Beach, 177 F.3d 932 (11th Cir. 1999).

White v. County of Los Angeles, 225 Cal.App.4th 690, 170 Cal. Rptr. 3d 472 (Ct. App. 2014).

Woods v. Town of Danville, WV, 712 F. Supp. 2d 502 (S.D.W. Va. 2010).

Wurzel v. Whirlpool Corp., No. 10-3629 (6th Cir. Apr. 27, 2012).

Yin v. State of California, 95 F.3d 864 (9th Cir. 1996).

About the Authors

David M. Corey, PhD is a licensed psychologist with more than 40 years of experience performing suitability and fitness evaluations for police and other safety-sensitive positions. He is the founding president of the American Board of Police & Public Safety Psychology, and a Fellow of the American Psychological Association (APA, Division 18). He is licensed to practice psychology in Oregon, Hawaii, Washington, California, Utah, and Arizona, and he is the examining psychologist for more than 200 local, state, and federal law enforcement agencies. His professional activities consist mainly of conducting, teaching, and researching about suitability, fitness, and other civil forensic evaluations, as well as providing expert testimony in related matters. Dr. Corey has authored or coauthored more than 30 books, chapters, and journal articles on these topics.

Mark Zelig, PhD is a licensed psychologist in private practice in Salt Lake City and Anchorage. He retired from the Salt Lake City Police Department as a lieutenant after 25 years of service. He has testified in more than 1,000 civil and criminal cases, and he conducts suitability and fitness evaluations for multiple police and other local, state, and federal government agencies. He is licensed to practice in Utah, Alaska, Colorado, Hawaii, Nevada, and Wyoming. Combining his experience as a police officer and forensic psychologist, he also consults on homicide and sex crime cases, and he conducts risk assessments of potentially violent or sexually aggressive persons. He regularly conducts workshops for the APA and was appointed by US Attorney General Janet Reno to a committee tasked with identifying best practices in police recruitment and selection.

Both Dr. Corey and Dr. Zelig served on the APA Committee on Legal Issues, in addition to other elected and appointed positions, are regular workshop presenters for the American Academy of Forensic Psychology, and are board-certified by the American Board of Professional Psychology in forensic psychology and in police and public safety psychology. Dr. Zelig is also board-certified in clinical psychology.

Index

Tables and boxes are indicated by *t* and *b* following the page number

Made in the USA
Coppell, TX
31 January 2025